Barbara M N

LET THIS LIFE SPEAK

LET THIS LIFE SPEAK

The Legacy of Henry Joel Cadbury

MARGARET HOPE BACON

 UNIVERSITY OF PENNSYLVANIA PRESS
Philadelphia · 1987

Permission is acknowledged to reprint material from the following sources.

The *Christian Century* (copyright Christian Century Foundation) for "The Conscientious Objector of Patmos" (June 1, 1922), "An Inadequate Pacifism (Jan. 1, 1924), "The Validity of Religious Pacifism" (Dec. 29, 1943), "Have Mercy Upon Me" (April 16, 1947), all by Henry Joel Cadbury.

The *Boston Herald* for "War Slaughter, Says Cadbury" (April 22, 1940).

Harvard Magazine (copyright 1975 Harvard Magazine) for "A Grammarian with a Difference" (May 1975, pp. 46–52) by Amos N. Wilder.

The jacket and frontispiece photographs are courtesy of the American Friends Service Committee.

Assistance in the production of this volume was provided by the Friends Historical Association, the Bequest Committee of Philadelphia Yearly Meeting, and the Shoemaker Fund.

Library of Congress Cataloging-in-Publication Data

Bacon, Margaret Hope.
  Let this life speak.

  Bibliography: p.
  Includes index.
  1. Cadbury, Henry Joel, 1883–   . 2. Quakers—United States—Biography.   3. New Testament scholars—United States—Biography.   4. Pacifists—United States—Biography.   I. Title.
BX7795.C18B33   1987   289.6'3 [B]   86-14669
ISBN 0-8122-8045-8 (alk. paper)

Designed by Adrianne Onderdonk Dudden

Contents

To my husband
S. Allen Bacon

Acknowledgments

Henry Cadbury was a beloved and central figure in three major communities: New Testament scholarship, Quaker history, and social activism. Men and women from each of these communities, and on both sides of the Atlantic, have contributed with heartwarming eagerness to my task of assembling the telling episodes in his life. In many ways I think of myself less as the author of the book than the channel through which Henry Cadbury's many friends have pooled their memories to bring his story to life.

To thank everyone who wrote me a letter, granted me an interview, found a picture or a pamphlet, or told me yet another wonderful Henry or Lydia Cadbury story is impossible in the space I have. In the bibliography I have listed many persons who contributed to this book, whether or not their words are quoted. There are doubtless others I should have mentioned.

I would have been both unable and unwilling to write the book without the cooperation, encouragement and assistance of Henry Cadbury's relatives. Mary Hoxie Jones, his niece, and Elizabeth Musgrave, his oldest daughter, were with me on every step of the journey. Another daughter, Winifred Beer, helped to furnish pictures, and to read a draft of the manuscript with a careful eye. His sons, Christopher and Warder, and their wives, Mary and Julia, were also very helpful and supportive. His nephews Bartram and John Cadbury, and John's wife, Elizabeth; and his cousin Leah Cadbury Furtmuller, added much.

I must thank Edwin Bronner of the Haverford College Library for reading and criticizing an early draft of the manuscript, and his entire staff for their endless and courteous responses to my needs. I did most of the work on this manuscript in the Quaker Collection, for one year under a T. Wistar Brown Fellowship, and I am grateful for all the assistance rendered me in collecting information as well as in searching it out, not only from the Henry J. Cadbury Papers, but from other collections.

J. William Frost of the Friends Historical Library also read the manuscript and provided helpful criticism. For allowing me to use the resources of the Swarthmore College Peace Collection, I am grateful to him and his staff. Other archivists who helped me include Lucy Fisher West of Bryn Mawr College, Damon Hickey of Guilford College, J. Arthur Funston of Earlham College, Harley P. Holden of the Harvard University Archives, and Jack Sutters of the American Friends Service Committee Archives. For permission to quote materials from these archives I thank the institutions listed.

Amos Wilder of the Harvard Divinity School was willing to take time from his busy life to talk with me at length about my project and subsequently to correspond with me, answering my many questions as I tried to understand a field new to me: biblical scholarship. William Beardslee and John Knox were others to whom I turned with questions and problems and from whom I met unceasing courtesy. Fredrick Kempner read all of Henry Cadbury's correspondence in German, translated many of the letters verbatim, and gave me notes on all the rest. I owe him a great debt of gratitude.

The idea for this book was born at the American Friends Service Committee. To my colleague James Lenhart I want to express my appreciation for encouraging me to undertake the project and to keep at it despite some initial discouragements. As editor of the *Friends Journal*, Jim had been Henry Cadbury's editor during his last years, and he knew just how unusual and just how beloved a man Henry Cadbury was.

Finally, I must thank my husband, S. Allen Bacon, for his role in reading text, accompanying me on interviews, encouraging me, and making my path smooth in many ways.

Introduction

On August 1, 1973, a group of lawyers, witnesses, and interested onlookers gathered in Room 3054 of the United States Courthouse in Philadelphia, presided over by Judge Clarence C. Newcomer of the U.S. District Court for Eastern Pennsylvania, to hear the third day of testimony in a unique civil action. The American Friends Service Committee (AFSC), a fifty-six-year-old Quaker service organization, was suing the United States government for relief from the requirement that it collect income taxes from those of its employees who were conscientiously opposed to the payment of that portion of their taxes which supported the war. This requirement, the AFSC was arguing, violated First Amendment rights and threatened the organization with serious loss, were such employees to leave for reasons of conscience. Let the government deal directly with the individuals in question, lawyers for the AFSC suggested, rather than ask the organization to violate its very reason for existence.

To describe that reason Marvin Karpatkin, chief attorney for the plaintiffs, had invited to the witness stand the man who had presided at the first meeting of the AFSC, on April 30, 1917. Henry Joel Cadbury had always been a man of slight build. Now at the age of eighty-nine and a half, he appeared frail and wizened, his rumpled suit hanging loosely, his manner occasionally hesitant, as though a little confused. He wore a hearing aid, but although it was turned up to full volume he still had to ask a speaker to repeat himself. Those in the courtroom who did not know him might have wondered what value his testimony could have.

Speaking slowly and clearly, Marvin Karpatkin led Henry Cadbury through a recitation of his educational background including his Ph.D. from Harvard University—a teaching career that included twenty years as Hollis Professor of Divinity at Harvard—his many published books and essays, his role in preparing the Revised Standard Version New Testament, his six honorary degrees. Henry Cadbury answered each question with careful modesty, but the on-lookers were impressed, and when he acknowledged, in response to further probing, that he had met with Presidents Woodrow Wilson, Herbert Hoover, Franklin Roosevelt, and John Kennedy, the lawyer for the defense rather plaintively objected to this line of questioning. The judge, however, appeared interested and denied the motion. In response to the next query, Henry Cadbury admitted that he had spoken with the king and crown prince of Norway when he was in Oslo in 1947 to receive the Nobel Peace Prize for the American Friends Service Committee. Switching to the subject of peace, the lawyer asked Henry Cadbury to describe the peace testimony.

"It is a belief that on account of our view of man's relation to God and God's relation to every man, that to engage in activities which we think God would disapprove of is a violation of our duty, and furthermore that killing other people is ignoring the potential in other people to be children of God," Henry Cadbury answered.

"And what is the meaning of the concept as used among Friends of 'bearing witness'?" the lawyer asked.

"Bearing witness means primarily, I suppose, a vocal expression of your belief in certain ideals, but beyond that in the consistent expression in your actions of those ideas."

"Could you say in a nutshell that it means practicing what you preach?" the lawyer pressed.

Henry Cadbury's eyes danced and his face lit up with a delightful, mischievous twinkle. Those who knew him well realized he was about to say something amusing. "Yes, or only preaching what you practice," he quipped.[1]

The delivery, as much as the bon mot, was funny. The onlookers chuckled, and even Judge Newcomer looked amused. Only the young lawyer for the U.S. government was uncomfortable. Well he might be. Bronson Clark, the executive secretary of the AFSC, thought that at that moment the balance had swung in favor of the AFSC's case. Months later, Judge Newcomer ruled in favor of the Quaker organization in a precedent-setting decision based on First Amendment rights, only to be overturned by the U.S. Supreme Court.

This was Henry Cadbury's last courtroom appearance, but it was not his first. Following World War I he had been ordered to appear before the U.S. district attorney to clear himself of charges of disloyalty stemming from his pacifism. During World War II, the Korean War, and the Vietnam War, he testified before draft boards and talked to FBI agents and other government officials in support of the appeals for conscientious objector status for hundreds of young men. Following World War II he made courtroom appearances for those refusing to register for the peacetime draft. For men and women who felt that they could not pay that portion of their income tax that went for war purposes, he combed Quaker history for precedent and made numerous statements prior to the AFSC tax case.

Nor was he himself uninvolved in action. A lifelong concern for academic freedom led him twice to put his own distinguished career in jeopardy for the sake of his beliefs. His concern about the requirement of a loyalty oath for teachers caused him to write articles, make speeches, and offer encouragement to individuals who chose to take a stand on that issue. In 1940 he provided the historical background to the Civil Liberties Committee of the American Bar Association in its defense of Jehovah's Witnesses and their objection to flying the American flag. In 1955 he was active in the struggle for the rights of a Plymouth Meeting, Pennsylvania, librarian to retain her position after refusing to testify against her former associates in one of the more celebrated cases of the Joseph McCarthy period.

A biblical scholar of world renown, Henry Cadbury believed that there were varieties of religious experience documented in the Bible as well as the history of Christianity and of the Society of Friends, and for him and others like him, religion had little meaning unless it was expressed in direct action. Indeed, direct action in response to religious impulse could be a path to a deeper religious experience. He spoke of it in Toronto in 1964: "I am impressed how much inner religion is fostered by social concern. If social work can be an escape from inner religion . . . is not the opposite true? Action, often incoherent and inarticulate, leads to thought and can also lead to spiritual growth."[2]

Men and women sometimes acted on deep religious impulse and then found reasons and rationalizations afterward for having taken that action, he believed. Quakers had written the first protest against slavery, in Germantown in 1688. They did not argue from overarching political and philosophic principles, he said, such as the statement that "there is a Divine spark in every human being no matter what the color of his skin." Rather, they presented a series of objections to slavery in the Quaker colony. Slavery violated the Golden Rule; Friends had spoken much about liberty of conscience; Friends as pacifists could not deal with slaves who were captured as spoils of war; slavery increased the practice of adultery: and slavery in the Quaker colony would give Quakers a bad reputation in Europe. "You see how unsatisfactory to one of these neat, logical minds this approach to Quaker concern is," Henry Cadbury argued. Yet the American Declaration of Independence, for all its ringing phrases of egalitarianism, made no mention of freeing the slaves.[3]

Several times in his own life he felt he had followed the path of action into belief, and in his ministry he often reached out to those who hesitated to make a religious commitment until they had completely worked out their theology. Yet he believed that service was only one of many paths. There was room within the religious community for mystics and for evangelicals as well as for those committed to social action. It need never be either/or, he insisted. Cannot we try both/and?

His own life was indeed both/and—as a scholar devoted almost equally to the study of the New Testament and the history of the Religious Society of Friends and as an activist in peace and social issues. A friend of Norman Thomas, A. J. Muste, Harry Emerson Fosdick, Roland Bainton, and others, he was one of the pioneers of the peace movement in the early decades of the twentieth century. Devoted to civil liberties, academic freedom, and racial equality, he helped to move the Society of Friends forward on these issues as well as to challenge the Christian church to a more prophetic stand. He not only influenced many Christians to a more active commitment; he also taught many social reformers and pacifists to understand that their motives were religious and that they need not stand apart from the church because of questions about creed. And he taught and preached and acted with such a charming wit and such sweetness of spirit that he was loved everywhere. People said of him that whether in words or in action, his whole life was spent translating the New Testament.

Surrounded by a loving circle of family and friends, Henry Cadbury sometimes experienced a certain bleak loneliness that can afflict the gifted. A Harvard colleague said of him that he "thought effortlessly" and he expressed himself simply and lucidly. Nevertheless, students and colleagues sometimes could not follow the adventures of his mind, especially when he questioned deeply held assumptions. And there was surprise and pain when members of the Society of Friends and former colleagues turned against him in the midst of war fever or anticommunist hysteria. Twice he battled deep private depression, while continuing to twinkle in public. Throughout his life he was so humble and quiet about his many lines of endeavor that even his immediate family never knew the whole story.

Several books could be written about the life of Henry Cadbury. A biblical scholar might write of his pioneering work in Luke-Acts; his introduction of form, linguistic, and motive criticism; and the stringent standards he set for biblical translation. A Quaker historian could look at his seminal work in cataloging the papers of George Fox and reconstructing a lost *Book of Miracles,* as well as countless other contributions to Quaker scholarship. And an author in the field of peace studies might want to address the story of his achievements for peace, from before World War I to his death in 1974, as well as his influence in moving the American Friends Service Committee from a provincial, Philadelphia-oriented organization to one of nationwide scope and worldwide renown.

I knew Henry Cadbury as a source of both inspiration and practical help in my work for the American Friends Service Committee, my patient teacher in the art of writing Quaker history and biography, and an influence on my own religious development. Rather than trying to present any single strand in his life, I have tried instead to write about the whole man, as he pursued his kaleidoscopic interests from day to day and as his thought developed and matured. Wherever possible, I have tried to find his own words, so that he may speak to the reader for himself. This has seemed to me to be the approach most in line with his own methods; working always from the particular to the general and understanding that it is not the enunciation of fine principles but their practical application that matters. Through the aid of a number of archival libraries, I have had access to his professional papers, and his family has generously aided me in finding what few personal papers he left behind him. Of great importance in my efforts to reconstruct his life have been a series of interviews with and letters from persons who knew him in all the various aspects of his life and whose memories are still fresh and vivid. Indeed, I first decided that I ought to attempt this biography when I realized how important it was that these memories not be lost. As a senior staff member of the American Friends Service Committee, I was in a favored position to interview many of his former colleagues and friends. I was able to spend time in Cambridge with his Harvard colleagues, as well as visiting members of his family, and places, such as Back Log Camp, that played an important role in his life.

Henry Cadbury believed that one can understand the religious basis of life best when it is exemplified in the lives of men and women, from Jesus of Nazareth to George Fox, from Margaret Fell to Lucretia Mott, to the peacemakers of today. Lives can thus preach or speak to us, as words cannot. The life of Henry Cadbury spoke to everyone who knew him. It is my hope that through the channel of this book, others will come to know him, and his life will speak to their condition for years to come.

CHAPTER 1
Quaker Roots

Henry Joel Cadbury was born on December 1, 1883, at 1125 Mount Vernon Street, Philadelphia, the youngest child and fourth son of Joel Cadbury, Jr., and Anna Kaighn Lowry Cadbury. His parents were both birthright members of the Religious Society of Friends (Quakers) with roots stretching back to the establishment of the Society in mid-seventeenth-century England and its early transmittal to American soil. An ancestor of Anna Cadbury's, John Bartram (1699–1777), was the pioneer American botanist, whose *Observations,* based on his travels in the Alleghenies, Catskills, Carolinas, and Florida earned him appointment as botanist to the king and are still studied today. John's son William Bartram, a naturalist as well as botanist, is best known for the excellent quality of his writings and illustrations in the journals of his travels. Though John Bartram was disowned by his monthly meeting when some members suspected him of deism, the Bartrams as a family have remained deeply entrenched in American Quakerism.

The Cadburys were an English Quaker family until one ancestor, Joel Cadbury, came to Philadelphia in 1815 and married his first cousin Caroline Warder in 1822, thus establishing an American branch. The English Cadburys developed Cadbury chocolate, known throughout the world, and were noted social reformers. Joel Cadbury's nephew George Cadbury (1839–1922) laid out a model garden village for his chocolate factory employees which influenced subsequent town planning in many countries. His wife, Elizabeth Cadbury, was named Dame Commander of the Order of the British Empire in recognition of her work in education, housing, and peace.

A tradition for social concern and of noblesse oblige was strong in the Cadbury family. Henry Cadbury was much impressed with a story told in the family about his great-grandfather, John Warder, who was at the time of the Napoleonic Wars a merchant and shared ownership in a merchant ship. When he received the Nobel Peace Prize in 1947 for the American Friends Service Committee, Henry told the story as part of his lecture:

> That ship turned privateer, without his knowledge, and captured a Dutch East Indiaman. His share of the prize was about £2,000. Now what would a Quaker do with £2,000 captured in war? He was a wise man, and the first thing he did was to insure his share of the ship with Lloyds of London. As a matter of fact, the ship was destroyed by a storm on its next trip—but he still had £2,000 which did not belong to him. Up to 1823 he and the Friends were still trying to find the owners of the Dutch ship because, as a Quaker, he could not keep those £2,000. In the end he found enough owners to pay them £3,345 principal and interest on that ship, and there were still over £2,000 that he could not dispose of. Although he advertised in the newspapers in Holland and tried to find the owners by the records and in every possible way, he was not able to do so. If you go to Amsterdam today, you will find a free school in Beerenstraat, with a picture on the top gable of the ship that was taken and my great grandfather's initials on a stone over the door. As final payment to the unknown enemies in that city the English Quakers gave the school.[1]

Henry Cadbury's father, Joel Cadbury, Jr., was of draft age during the Civil War and had to decide between paying a $300 bounty or going to war. Joel Cadbury paid the bounty and turned his energies to helping to create and support an organization called the Friends Freedmen Association, which sent supplies south for the newly freed slaves and later supported schools for the freedmen. This activity led him to take a lifelong interest in black education. Both he and Anna Cadbury were on the board of the Institute for Colored Youth (now Cheyney University) and often entertained in their home a noted black educator, Fanny Jackson Coppin, the institute's director. In later years Henry Cadbury was to trace his interest in race relations in part to the impact of these visits.[2]

The Quaker world into which Henry Cadbury was born was a congenial but constricted one. In 1827 the Philadelphia Yearly Meeting had been rent in two by a separation between a smaller group called the Orthodox, who had been influenced by the evangelical enthusiasm then sweeping through much of Protestantism and prevalent among the English Friends, and a larger, more old-fashioned group, who felt the new ideas were out of step with the

Quakerism they had inherited. This group was derisively called Hicksites after the preaching of a Long Island farmer, Elias Hicks. The separation later spread to encompass the Baltimore, New York, Ohio, and Indiana Yearly Meetings. In Philadelphia in particular the separation ran along class lines, the wealthier city Quakers, many of them merchants and bankers, adhering to the Orthodox position and the country Quakers, under the leadership of a Bucks County farmer, John Comly, becoming Hicksites. There were bitter quarrels and even lawsuits over meeting property and schools. The separation was so complete that Hicksite and Orthodox branches of the same family lost touch with one another, and many young Orthodox Quakers in the twentieth century grew up believing that the claims of the Hicksites to be true Quakers were spurious.

As prosperous city merchants with English connections, the Cadburys were a part of the smaller Orthodox group. But even this fellowship was threatened with schism in 1845, when a dispute arose among Orthodox Quakers throughout the country between the teachings of Joseph John Gurney, an evangelical English Friend, who toured the United States in 1837 preaching Bible study, the vicarious atonement, and an increased emphasis on education; and old-time quietists who found their champion in John Wilbur of Kingston, Rhode Island. A split in New England Yearly Meeting led to bitter controversy and schism in Ohio and North Carolina Yearly Meetings. Each of two yearly meetings in New England, Ohio, and North Carolina, claiming to be the true expression of the Society of Friends, invited Philadelphia to recognize its validity by exchanges of yearly epistles. To prevent the agony of further separation within its own ranks, Philadelphia finally decided to give up such exchanges with all other yearly meetings. Even so there were strong feelings. The Arch Street Monthly Meeting was Wilburite, or quietist, but the Philadelphia Monthly Meeting for the Western District, or Twelfth Street Meeting, to which the Cadburys belonged, was Gurneyite. Many of its members were well-to-do and active in affairs of the city.

The Cadbury family was large enough to form a society within a society. Since Friends of that time did not permit the marriage of first cousins, Joel and Caroline Warder Cadbury were disowned for their marriage in 1822 but reinstated ten years and five children later. In all they had eleven children, of whom two died as infants and three as young adults. Four married and produced large families of children and grandchildren. The spread between the oldest and the youngest in these families was so wide that the generations overlapped. Cadbury family parties at Thanksgiving or New Year's often numbered forty or fifty relatives, with adults dining in one room and children in another. It was never necessary to move beyond the family to find congenial companions. Although there were some elements of the born rebel in Henry Cadbury, he was nourished by a strong sense of family and of being rooted by family traditions. He spoke of this feeling in 1972:

> We were a united family and were a large family. Not only were there eight of us but we had lots of cousins, and then we had a group of cousins in England, and were in very close touch with the English Cadburys. They were also a largely Quaker family so that between us there was constant coming and going, so up to the present time the American Cadburys and the English Cadburys exchange visits across the ocean. . . . I meet people occasionally that have no relatives and no friends, and I feel a great sympathy with them and a great sense of responsibility to show my gratitude for the groups I have enjoyed.[3]

Centered in home, meeting, Quaker schools, and Quaker institutions, the life of the Cadburys went on within, but not particularly of, the Philadelphia of the 1880s. The Gilded Age that followed the Civil War was bringing extremes of wealth and poverty to the Quaker city, and corruption was rife in the city government although a reform group, with some Quaker members, had installed an honest mayor at the time of Henry's birth. Immigrants beginning to pour into the city were providing middle-class homes with an abundance of servants and sending the population upward toward eight hundred thousand. City Hall was being built at Broad and Market, and across the street the Pennsylvania Railroad was erecting an unsightly terminal. The architect Frank Furness and the great painter Thomas Eakins were at work. In 1882 the first shipload of Russian-Jewish immigrants arrived.

In 1867 Joel Cadbury had formed a partnership with two other Quakers to create Haines, Jones and Cadbury, plumbing supplies. With the growth of the city, the firm flourished and the Cadburys enjoyed moderate affluence and lived in a quiet, residential part of town, north of Market, where substantial red brick and marble-trimmed houses lined the streets and many Quakers lived. A few years after Henry's birth the family moved from Mount Vernon Street to a larger house at 1502 Green. Each summer the Cadburys rented a house in Moorestown, New Jersey. Henry Cadbury remembered clearly his excitement as a small child when workmen would load the trunks and household goods onto a huge cart while the family itself made a trip to Moorestown by streetcar, ferry, and train.

In Moorestown, Anna Cadbury managed the household consisting of six children and two servants, while her husband commuted
by horse and buggy to the train and by train and ferry to the city. It
was an era of absentee fathers. Anna Cadbury was a strong, some
say strict, mother. She controlled her lively brood by asking the children to conform to a common schedule. Winter or summer, there
was a time for everything. In a letter to his brother John in the summer of 1894, Henry, aged ten, said of the epistle, "I guess this will
do for my afternoon reading." In the evenings all children were expected to gather in the living room and spend time with their parents, the girls sewing or preparing their lessons, the boys doing
homework or taking turns reading aloud.[4]

The five oldest children, though all strong individuals, accepted
this routine, but Henry did not care for it. He became good at
inventing reasons why he had to do something elsewhere in the
house. This and other small rebellions won him the family nickname of Upstart Kid or USK. Anna Cadbury for a time tried the
ruse of asking him to do the very thing she wanted him not to do,
but he was far too clever to be long trapped by this device. Eventually she decided she would have to be somewhat less demanding
of her youngest child. Henry evidently had a strong inner sense of
his own needs and purposes and a diplomatic way with people, even
as a child. The urge to retreat and to guard his own privacy remained with him throughout his life. Despite the schedule, there
was time for play. The four Cadbury brothers, Benjamin, William,
John, and Henry, liked to canoe and bicycle together. In Moorestown they had gardens and rabbits or chickens that they raised together. Humor was a strong element in the Cadbury family. The
father, Joel Cadbury, Jr., was sometimes stern but "always carried a
twinkle in his eye," according to one grandson, Benjamin Bartram
Cadbury, and often brought home amusing stories for the family to
share. A visitor to the Friends Asylum (now Friends Hospital) of
which he was a director, Joel Cadbury met a patient who called himself an octagon, explaining that he had a front side and a back side,
a top side and a bottom side, an inside and an outside, a right side
and a left side. Mr. Octagon became a family legend. The children
collected and told each other jokes and stories. In the letter to his
brother John, Henry included a sample of ten-year-old humor:
"What does the donkey say when he goes to grass? Oh e oh e oh e
oh e oh."[5]

As the children grew older their humor grew more sophisticated
and they wrote jingles to celebrate family birthdays and graduations
and recounted wry stories of human foibles to each other. Although

Henry became the acknowledged wit of the family, both Ben and John were known for their sense of humor. Through the years family reunions were times for side-splitting hilarity.

As the youngest of the family, Henry was cared for by his two older sisters. When he was very small, Anna put him in the special care of Elizabeth, the oldest, born in 1871, twelve years his senior. The warmth of their relationship lasted throughout the years. When he was ready for first grade, Emma, born in 1875, had the duty of taking him to and from school his first year. Henry particularly remembered a time when he was naughty and Emma had to take him home from school in the middle of the day while he stepped on the bricks with the most mud under them to splash mud and vent his anger. [6]

Education was an important value to the Cadbury family. The Cadbury parents studied the Quaker schools in the Philadelphia area and decided that the best schools were in the city. The two girls attended Friends Select, at Sixteenth and Race, and the four boys were sent to Penn Charter, on the corner of Twelfth and Market, next door to the Twelfth Street Meeting House. Both schools traced their origins to the earliest days of the settlement of Philadelphia and the charter of William Penn. After a year at Friends Select, Henry entered Penn Charter at age seven, two years early, and graduated at fifteen. When the school attended midweek meeting at the meetinghouse, all four hundred boys would line up by class and each class by size. Henry, as the smallest boy in the youngest class, was the first to enter and the last to leave.

It was to this same meetinghouse that Henry came on First Days. There was no Sunday School in those days, and children were expected to sit quietly throughout meeting. Henry remembered an occasion when another child about his age sat nearby: "Evidently he was rebuked by my example of quiet sitting. When his mother unwisely after meeting mentioned my quiet behavior I heard him reply, 'Mother, I noticed Henry moved twice.'" [7]

The Cadburys attended meeting twice on First Day. In between, the children were supposed to be quiet, resting, or reading improving literature. Anna Cadbury allowed one-half hour for relaxation before suppertime. Henry remembered jumping around on one foot, bumping into his siblings, or playing tag. Otherwise, he thought, there was a little too much restraint. First Day was also a time for Bible study. When Anna decided that her youngest needed some biblical training she learned what Bible verses John Ruskin's mother had taught her son and insisted that Henry learn them. Later in life Henry thought it had been a good selection and was grateful to have those verses engraved on his memory.

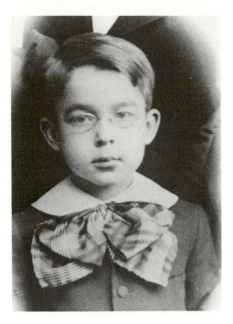

Henry Joel Cadbury as a child. From the private collection of Mary Hoxie Jones. Photo copied by Theodore Hetzel.

In addition to the First Day observance, the Cadburys had regular family Bible reading and prayer. The family religion was evangelical and Christocentric, as befitted Gurneyites. In common with other Orthodox children, Henry grew up believing that the Hicksites denied the full divinity of Christ, or at least his redemptive power. His mother once came home from a Hicksite funeral which she had attended (against the discipline of her meeting) disturbed that the Bible text used had been "Awake thou that sleepest and arise from the dead" (Ephesians 5:14) without the additional phrase, "and Christ shall give thee light." His father also attended a Hicksite funeral and brought home the impression that the deceased had been congratulated on his good works as though these, and not faith in Christ, would save him.[8]

At some point in his adolescence, Henry Cadbury began to question the concept of salvation through faith and to feel that obedience to the teaching and the example of Jesus was for him the prime emphasis of the life of the spirit. Years later, speaking to a group of students at Harvard Divinity School, he tried to trace the beginning of this divergence from his family's evangelical creed. Unfortunately, only his own brief notes for this talk survive. He spoke of the influence of the higher criticism, of having "adolescent problems of all kinds," of being put off by the "morbidity of religion," of a developing skepticism, and of reacting against the claims of the very conservative. In a similar lecture four years later, he said that he had experienced no particular crises in faith, but that it had been a gradual development over a period of years.[9]

At Penn Charter, Henry Cadbury enrolled in an academic course. The curriculum was classic, and he began the study of Latin and Greek, as well as French, history and English literature. The faculty, under headmaster Richard Mott Jones, was selected for their academic qualifications; several had been trained abroad. Henry Cadbury blossomed in this environment. He was an excellent student; throughout his life he was curious about everything and eager—at times avid—for information. Learning was always a pleasure.

There were extracurricular pleasures as well. Henry Cadbury was too slight of build for heavy sports, but he began to play tennis enthusiastically at age ten and became an excellent player. He also wrote for the student publication. But the most exciting event he later remembered was the day that John Wanamakers, then a wooden structure at Thirteenth and Market, burned to the ground and the school was let out early so that the boys could watch the flames and the firefighters at work.[10]

In June of 1899, Henry Cadbury graduated from Penn Charter, second in his class, and prepared to enter Haverford College, a Quaker institution on the Main Line, as his three older brothers had done before him. Penn Charter at that time did not give final examinations, and Haverford had not given entrance examinations until the fall Henry Cadbury entered. The result was that Henry, totally unaccustomed to taking exams, failed algebra and all but failed geometry. Had he turned in his work sheets he would have been given a passing grade, but not knowing this, he simply threw them in the wastebasket.

The news that one of his star pupils had failed the exams upset Headmaster Richard Mott Jones very much. He insisted that Henry be given a second chance and allowed to take the University of Pennsylvania entrance exams the next week. Meanwhile, Henry Cadbury was given instruction on exam procedure. As a result he passed and was permitted to enter Haverford. The experience evidently spurred his competitive instincts. Years later he told a Haverford gathering about it: "I was never a great mathematician but I made a point of taking mathematics till the end of the sophomore year in College in order that I could be a candidate for the prize offered in mathematics at the end of the sophomore year, which I did and won the prize. After that I dropped the subject."[11]

Haverford had been founded in 1833 and became a degree-granting institution in 1856. Formed by members of the Orthodox branch of the Society of Friends in Philadelphia and New York, it was established to give the sons of affluent Quaker families a classical education without forcing them to attend institutions under the care of other religious societies such as Yale, Princeton, or Harvard. The principle of coeducation, so important to Quakerism, was evidently not considered applicable in this context. Following the Wilburite/Gurneyite tensions of 1855, Haverford came under the influence of the Gurneyites, with emphasis on an evangelical faith, on education, and on social concerns. There was, however, also enough quietist influence on the Board of Managers to keep them involved in a constant effort to maintain Quaker speech, dress, and patterns of behavior.

Isaac Sharpless, a former teacher at Westtown School, a Quaker boarding school in nearby Chester county, became president in 1887 and began to expand the size of the student body from 94 students when he took office to 195 in 1917 when he left. The expansion was gradual; during Henry Cadbury's four undergraduate years the entire student body could still meet in one room, and there were only 19 students in his class. Sharpless also brought in a small group of first-rate scholars as faculty. These men helped to move the school away from the excessive concern with standards of behavior and toward a desire to nourish the intellectual life of the students.[12]

Among the teachers under whom Henry Cadbury studied was Allen Thomas, college librarian and Quaker historian, who shared with his students his love of books and of the Quaker documents in the library's collection. Francis Gummere, educated at Freiburg and Harvard, taught English literature and German and inspired in his students a love of clear composition and of Goethe and Shakespeare. He helped Henry Cadbury develop the clear, precise style that became characteristic of his writing. President Isaac Sharpless himself taught a senior course in ethics. Rufus M. Jones, a Maine Quaker who had graduated from Haverford in 1885 and returned in 1893 as assistant professor, taught philosophy and psychology. Both Isaac Sharpless and Rufus Jones taught Bible study.[13]

Rufus Jones, still a comparatively young man at the time he was Henry Cadbury's teacher, was to become the most widely known and best beloved of Quaker leaders in the coming years. He was a prolific speaker and writer, an excellent teacher, and a man of action, deeply involved in the founding of the American Friends Service Committee, Pendle Hill, the *American Friend,* and many other Quaker organizations with which Henry Cadbury's life also became entwined. Embracing the positivism of the turn of the century, Jones was a leader in urging Quakerism to adapt itself to new ideas. He was an exponent of a modern interpretation of Christianity, based on the higher criticism, on studies in the psychology of religious experience, such as those of William James, and on new findings in the study of mystical religion. He advocated a "positive mysticism," which stressed a direct personal relationship between humans and God and led to better human relationships and thus to social reform. He believed this was the view and the experience of the first generation of Quakers and that they drew inspiration from a group of earlier spiritual leaders who came out of continental mysticism. His studies on mysticism, so defined, became an important aspect of his life.[14]

In March of 1902, Rufus Jones, a widower, married Elizabeth Cadbury, Henry Cadbury's older sister. Becoming thus an older brother as well as teacher, Rufus Jones was one of the most important influences on the developing mind of young Henry Cadbury. The younger man came to share many of Jones's enthusiasms: for healing the divisions within Quakerism and helping it find its place in the modern world, for conserving Quaker history, and for bringing the tools of modern research methods to bear on the study of the Bible. But they also differed in many ways: Jones ebullient, full of faith and confidence, given to advancing large themes; Cadbury cautious, skeptical, modest, interested in the particulars, the building blocks of history. These differences would emerge over the years. As a student, Henry must have found Jones stimulating, opening up new vistas to his inquiring mind.

In addition to the resident faculty, the Haverford student body had the privilege of hearing a group of important scholars speak at regular intervals in a series of endowed Library Lectures. In 1900 J. Rendel Harris, a former teacher at Harverford, then professor of paleography at the University of Cambridge, England, gave four such lectures. In 1903 Francis G. Peabody, dean of the Harvard Divinity School, delivered the lectures, taking as his theme the relationship of religion and the scholar. The belief that further discoveries in the sciences and humanities, wedded to the values of a liberally intrepreted religious background, would permit young men such as the Haverford students to create a better world was implicit in the lectures, reflecting the intellectual climate of Haverford and of the day.[15]

Aside from its intellectual challenges, Haverford did not represent a sharp break for Henry Cadbury. For the first year he had roomed with his older brother John, and throughout the four years he commuted home over weekends to visit his family and managed to have two Saturday dinners as a result. After Elizabeth's marriage to Rufus Jones, he had another, second home on campus. Many of his classmates were boys he had gone to school with or known in Quaker circles. Campus life proved congenial, as he would have said. In addition to his studies, he was an editor of the *Haverfordian*, an undergraduate monthly, for three years, and editor-in-chief his senior year. In his junior year he wrote a series of six articles on William Makepeace Thackeray, which revealed his growing literary skill. In an article titled "Thackeray as a Humorist," he wrestled with the distinctions between wit, satire, and humor, the very distinctions latter-day students of Henry Cadbury's own humor have tried to untangle:

Joel and Anna Kaign Cadbury and family. Left to right, William Warder, John Warder, Benjamin, Elizabeth Bartram (Jones), Henry Joel. Emma junior, seated. From the private collection of Mary Hoxie Jones.

Humor—when found in its more perfect form—as I believe it is in Thackeray's novels—is a very subtle and intangible matter, eluding our grasp like a flying feather. . . . Someone has made the laconic distinction that "wit laughs at you while humor laughs with you." I think that Thackeray's wonderful philanthropy being granted, it is not hard to see which term best characterizes his attitude. Throughout his whole works the spirit of playful humor prevails without a single wasp sting of direct personal attack. To be sure he ridicules your weaknesses through those of his characters, but he loves both you and them so heartily and he teases you with so little offense that you finally succumb.[16]

Another new interest was the YMCA, at that time at its peak on college campuses. Virtually every member of the Haverford College student body attended Y meetings. Henry served on the cabinet and in the summer of 1902 attended the Northfield Student Conference under the direction of the International Committee of the Y and found it spiritually uplifting. From Northfield he went to Boston for his first visit to that city.

Henry was also a member of various student clubs. His love of the outdoors, encouraged by his summers in Moorestown, manifested itself in his role as president of the Campus Club, a group interested in the plantings and maintenance of Haverford's beautiful grounds. He was secretary and treasurer of the Classics Club and the Tennis Club. He became interested in gymnastics and proficient at club swinging. He led the club swinging at a joint Haverford-Yale Gymnastic Exhibition. He liked to sing college songs and to play the mandolin, forbidden in his Quaker home.

Girls did not figure very prominently in the Haverford experience, at least on campus. Bryn Mawr College, a short distance from Haverford, had been founded as a college for women by a group of Orthodox Quakers from Philadelphia, Baltimore, and New York in 1880. Its president was M. Carey Thomas, a strong feminist who discouraged Haverford boys from hanging around the Bryn Mawr campus. During Henry Cadbury's days at Haverford she wrote a letter to Haverford's president, Isaac Sharpless, complaining that Haverford boys kept appearing on campus and that the less she saw of them, the better it suited her. " I don't want to be too unfriendly, and I don't want anything to disturb the arrangements under which Bryn Mawr secures our milk from the Haverford College dairy," she concluded the letter. Isaac Sharpless read it aloud to the student body, much to their general amusement.

M. Carey Thomas's desire to keep the Haverford boys away from the Bryn Mawr girls was further frustrated by a major fire in Denbeigh Hall on the Bryn Mawr campus during Henry's days at

Haverford. The fire happened in the middle of the night, and a number of Haverford boys hurried off to see the blaze and to meet the Bryn Mawr girls who had been routed by the flames. Unfortunately, Henry slept through all the excitement.[17]

Despite his many interests, Henry continued to be a deeply committed scholar. He won a scholarship, received a prize for systematic reading, was elected to Phi Beta Kappa, and graduated with special honors in Greek and Philosophy in June of 1903. At the time of graduation he was class treasurer and class poet. He was also just nineteen and a half.

In later life, Henry Cadbury was to say that his choosing the profession of teaching was one of happenstance: "I accidentally fell into the profession of teaching and became a teacher. I think it was largely because I didn't have intelligence enough to know that there were other perfectly good things to do, but being brought up in a school and a college the only thing I knew was going to a school and a college and studying books. So when I went to college and got through I decided I would be a teacher."[18]

It seems an extremely modest statement for a man who was known to generation after generation of students as the most gifted of all their teachers; nevertheless it was the way Henry often saw himself. Having made the decision to teach, on whatever basis, he decided to apply to Harvard, following in the footsteps of his brother-in-law, Rufus Jones, who had received an M.A. from Harvard in 1901. It was a departure for the Cadbury family. Benjamin and William had both earned master's degrees at Haverford, and William his M.D. from the University of Pennsylvania in 1902. The two sisters had attended Bryn Mawr, Elizabeth for one year before she was needed at home, Emma graduating in 1898. Venturing from the provincialism of Philadelphia to the provincialism of Boston can be daunting. Henry Cadbury evidently did not find it so, for he spent much of his life between the two cities.

His first year at Harvard was spent in study of Greek, Latin, English, and classical philology. His intense curiosity found a true field of delight in examining the origins and shifting shades of meaning of words. Like an archaeologist, he learned to dig through strata of history to find out how those meanings changed with changing customs and epochs. But having won his M.A. in the spring of 1904, there was no excuse to continue the joys of study. It was time to become a teacher.

In September of 1904 Henry Cadbury signed his first teaching contract. He was to teach classics and history at the University Latin School in Chicago for $1,000 per year. For a Philadelphia Quaker, albeit one who had spent a year at Cambridge, it was a venture into the unknown. He was not yet twenty-one and looked young for his age. His students evidently took advantage of his youth and in-experience. In a letter to his brother-in-law, Rufus Jones, in January of 1905, he alludes to troubles in the classroom: "Perhaps the fault may be my attitude toward the boys." He sounded lonely but said he was beginning to attend meeting and that "the young people are very cordial in admitting me to their interests." [19] He was also be-friended by a Chicago Quaker family, the William Matchetts. Yet, at spring vacation, he was obviously pleased when an invitation came to teach the next year at Westtown School, thirty miles from home in the rolling farmlands of Chester County. His mother, who was a member of the Westtown School Committee, wrote to encourage him to accept: "Thee says the question is, whether thee will be able for the position. Well of course thee cannot tell that in advance, but I am inclined to think thee will. Thee has never been used to co-education but the children there seem to take it quite naturally." [20]

CHAPTER 2
Teaching and Learning

Established as a coeducational boarding school under the care of the Philadelphia Yearly Meeting in 1799, Westtown had managed its adolescent boys and girls through the years by enforcing a strict separation of the sexes. The long brick school building was divided into a "boys' end" and a "girls' end," boys' grounds and girls' grounds. In the early days there were separate classes, and boys and girls sat at opposite ends of a long dining room. Boys and girls in fact were never supposed to see each other, except at meeting, or when brothers and sisters or first cousins were allowed chaperoned visits once every two weeks.

After the Civil War, some of these rules had been liberalized. Boys and girls began to have meals together in 1881 and classes together in 1889. When the pond was frozen they were allowed to skate together. Still, social segregation was very much in place when Henry Cadbury arrived as a young teacher in the fall of 1905. For a boy to make an unauthorized trip to the girls' end was a punishable offense.

As a teacher, however, twenty-one-year-old Henry Cadbury was not subject to any of these regulations. He was just becoming interested in the opposite sex, and the situation was delightful.

> When you are about as young or younger than some of the senior boys you can have pretty good fun if you are at a boarding school and have the run of all the grounds with none of the restrictions that the students had. So I had a great deal of fun with other teachers and the boys and girls at Westtown School. I had the privilege, which no other young man had, of taking young women out canoeing in the afternoon. They were very strict about these things, but being a teacher I was myself the chaperone, you understand, which made everything perfectly valid.[1]

One of the young students he took canoeing was his first cousin once removed, Leah Tapper Cadbury, whom he had known as a child in her father's house while he was attending Haverford. Leah (now Mrs. Carl Furtmuller) remembers a delightful afternoon going up and down the Chester Creek, in apparent defiance of Westtown rules. She also remembers Henry Cadbury as a stimulating Latin teacher, who treated his students with respect and gave them adult examinations. She did poorly on one such examination because it was open book, and she had never before been allowed to look up words while translating a passage and did not know this was permitted. Another student in the same class who remembered his teaching as excellent was Edith Farquhar, now Mrs. Francis Bacon.

Henry Cadbury also spent time with the family of his first cousin, Caroline Cadbury Brown. Born in 1851, thirty-two years his senior, Caroline had married a much beloved Westtown teacher, Thomas K. Brown, and was the mother of six children, all nearer in age to Henry Cadbury than was she. Besides advanced mathematics, Thomas K. Brown introduced Westtown students to the pleasures of camping, fishing, and figure skating. He was away from his family a good deal, and Caroline was a permissive mother, unwilling or unable to discipline her boisterous brood. The children were delightfully uninhibited, and their home was an oasis in the highly regulated life of Westtown.

Lydia Caroline, the youngest of this family, was known throughout the larger Cadbury clan for her habit of saying exactly what came into her head. Some of the other cousins were always a little frightened of what Lydia might say next, but they knew there was no unkindness meant by her frank utterances.

Henry Cadbury, with a strong streak of the rebel in him, was amused and delighted by Lydia's audacities. During her senior year at Westtown she often drove the family horse and carriage to market in West Chester, priding herself on piling the carriage high for the return trip. On one occasion she and her mother picked up cousin Henry Cadbury, then her Latin teacher:

> We invited him to ride back to Westtown with us, but when we three reached our sequestered buggy, he suggested that there was no room. "Lots of room," we assured him, and brought out a folding stool which fitted between the two on the seat and on which I sat aloft to drive. On the way out of West Chester we stopped at a mill and bought a bale of hay. This was propped up on the groceries right across the front where our feet were. My mother hung her feet out the right side and Henry removed his to the left. Then we stopped again. "What now?" my cousin asked in some trepidation. Only some ice, we assured him.

A hundred pounds of ice were stowed in the rear, where it dripped a trail all the way home. Safely arrived, Henry assisted me to put away the ice, unharness the horse, feed and bed him, and open the bale of hay, after which I have no doubt he was invited to supper.[2]

Westtown students had always been called "scholars." Since neither Henry Cadbury nor any of his sisters or brothers went to Westtown, they had to confess, "never a scholar" when the topic of Westtown was broached. There may have been a tinge of regret as well as humor in "never a scholar." Generation after generation of Quaker families had gone to Westtown, had met their future spouses there, had sent their sons and daughters to the school. There was and is today a strong sense of tradition and shared memories among Westtown graduates not to be matched by any day school.

By the time Henry Cadbury began teaching at Westtown his parents were both serving on the Westtown committee and visited the school in that capacity. In addition, his brother Benjamin fell in love with a Westtown teacher, Anna Moore, and made frequent trips to Westtown ostensibly to see Henry but in fact to court Anna. Henry Cadbury was therefore very much in the bosom of his family during these happy years.

While enjoying social life at Westtown, Henry Cadbury was also expanding his intellectual horizons. During Sunday afternoon the teachers were off duty for one hour, and they decided to spend that hour in a self-taught Bible class. Each member of the group took his or her turn preparing a lesson for the coming Sunday. Henry Cadbury found the process intensely interesting. He had studied the Bible at Haverford and heard such biblical scholars as Rendel Harris lecture, but this was his first experience in teaching. Years later he told his Harvard Divinity students of the impact of these studies: "My interest and curiosity were aroused. I saw the desirability for youth to know data in regard to the Bible and reflect on religious subjects in an atmosphere of searching for the truth."[3]

Henry Cadbury's growing interest in Bible study reflected a trend in liberal Protestantism of the day, a growing belief that the tools of higher criticism, and of textual criticism, developed in the middle of the nineteenth century, particularly by German biblical scholars, would lead to a fresh understanding of Jesus, and of the New Testament, based on historic truth. It was generally assumed that the Christian message that would be revealed by such studies would support the Social Gospel, which flourished in the United States in the latter part of the nineteenth and beginnings of the twentieth century. Francis Peabody of Harvard, who influenced Henry Cadbury at Haverford, was an exponent of the Social Gospel, stressing the commitment of Jesus to issues of compassion and peace; so was Rufus Jones.

Early Quakers had been taught to read the Bible not as a source of authority in itself but as a confirmation of their own divine leadings. Robert Barclay, the first Quaker theologian, had likened the Bible to a looking glass, in which one might compare one's experiences with the Holy Spirit to that of the saints of old. Later movements within Quaker thought had seesawed between a more literal and a more liberal interpretation of the Bible. Henry Cadbury's own family had been under the influence of the Gurneyite, or evangelical approach, with a more worshipful view of the Scriptures. But Henry Cadbury's own experience at Haverford and his contact with Rufus Jones had moved him in the direction of a seeking, scientific attitude.

He decided, therefore, that he wanted to return to Harvard and continue his biblical studies in some depth. But would there be a way of using this background in college teaching? He had no wish to become a preacher. He consulted Isaac Sharpless, the president of Haverford. Sharpless assured him that there was a new interest in the scholarly study of the Bible on college campuses. Some of the women's colleges were already starting to have professional courses in teaching the Bible, and he thought other colleges would follow. He did not say that Haverford would be interested, but that was perhaps implicit.[4]

Thus encouraged, Henry Cadbury resigned his post at Westtown and enrolled in Harvard for study for the Ph.D. in the fall of 1908. First, though, came a great adventure: a summer in Europe. Years ago, as a boy retiring to his room to think and dream, he had devised a kit that would include a folding bicycle and a folding boat with which to see the world. Now, a twenty-five-year-old Latin teacher, he was willing to settle for a steamship and the train. He toured Rome, Florence, Pisa, Venice, and Milan before meeting Rufus and Elizabeth Jones and their small daughter, Mary Hoxie, in Grindelwald, Switzerland. The four of them took a walking trip in the Alps, then returned to the United States sharing a cabin. En route they experienced a hurricane at sea and bouts of seasickness none were ever to forget.[5]

Back in Cambridge in the fall of 1908, Henry Cadbury began his studies in earnest. Besides courses in Hebrew and in Syriac he studied in the Divinity School under Professor William Ryder (New Testament exegesis), William Arnold (the religion of Israel), and James Hardy Ropes (introduction to the study of the New Testament). In his second year, he continued Professor Arnold's course in the religion of Israel, studied the Epistles of John and the Apocalypse with Professor Ryder, and began study of the Acts of the Apostles under Ropes.[6]

Founded in 1811 by Unitarians, Harvard Divinity School had always been committed to a liberal, historical, "scientific" approach to the study of the Bible. In the mid-nineteenth century it had come very much under the influence of the new German scholarship with its objective approach to the origins of the biblical texts, and this link remained strong well into the twentieth century. In 1880, Harvard President Charles W. Eliot had undertaken to make the school "unsectarian" by appointing a Baptist to the faculty. The school also attempted to be "broad," permitting elective courses and encouraging exchanges with other divinity schools in the area.[7]

Emphasis on objective inquiry into religion was seen at that time as running counter to the teaching of systematic theology, which was deemphasized. For some years, later on, the schools's only professor of theology was an avowed humanist. Except for liberal Unitarians, few denominations sent their prospective ministers to train at Harvard, preferring them to be grounded in the theology of their particular church. The exception to this rule, curiously enough, were fundamentalists, who were attracted to the school as a place where they could keep faith and history separate. Individuals who were for one reason or another dissatisfied with their denominational schools also came, but their numbers were few. Although the Harvard Divinity School also drew many students from the college and university who wished to take courses in religion, it was plagued from time to time by a dwindling student body.[8]

In 1908, the year Henry Cadbury came to begin his graduate studies, Harvard Divinity School and the Andover Theological Seminary had decided to affiliate. Andover had been founded in 1808 by strict Calvinists as the first school for the professional training of clergy in New England, in reaction to the perception that Harvard was coming under the influence of the liberal Unitarians. To prevent the further spread of such liberalism, the charter of the school specified that every faculty member must subscribe to the Andover Creed, promising that he would "maintain and inculcate the Christian faith . . . in opposition not only to Atheists and Infidels, but to Jews, Papists, Mohametans, Arians, Pelagians, Antinomians, Arminians, Socinians, Sabellians, Unitarians, and Universalists." Few modern theologians were willing to subscribe publicly to this creed, and by 1908 it was in abeyance, though still in place. During the second half of the nineteenth century the school had swung to a liberal position, much in accord with Harvard Divinity. Like Harvard, it was suffering from a shortage of students, and affiliation with Harvard Divinity School would give it access to Harvard's fine library as well as to the riches of Cambridge and Boston. At this time of the importance of the Social Gospel, it was necessary for future pastors to have some experience in center city life.

Two of Henry Cadbury's teachers, Ryder and Arnold, were actually on the Andover faculty, and the new combined Andover–Harvard Theological Library was being planned during his two years at Harvard, along with a new building on Francis Avenue. Francis G. Peabody, the exponent of liberal Christianity and the Social Gospel whom Henry Cadbury had heard speak at Haverford, had resigned as dean the year before, and William Wallace Fenn, another liberal Unitarian, had taken his place. There was a spirit of new beginnings and a great hopefulness at the school. Liberalism, optimism, and faith in the role of objective inquiry were hallmarks of the day.[9]

James Hardy Ropes, under whom Henry began his study of the Book of Acts, had graduated from Harvard College and from Andover Theological Seminary and studied in Germany for two years before joining the faculty of the Harvard Divinity School in 1895. A well-known philologist, he was best remembered for his work on the book of James. Studying the Acts of the Apostles under Ropes during his second year at Harvard, he found his interest stimulated in the unknown author of both Luke and Acts. Ropes became Cadbury's mentor and friend, served on his doctoral committee, and helped him plan his dissertation, which was titled "Studies in the Style and Literary Method of Luke."

Henry Cadbury had originally expected to receive his degree from Harvard in 1912, but in 1910, after he had finished most of his course work, Isaac Sharpless asked him to fill in for one year as instructor in Greek at Haverford while a staff member was absent, and then, by Christmas, to continue on a permanent basis.

Ropes encouraged him to take the position:

> Your chief need in the way of hearing lectures is in the Espistles of Paul, and for that the books are so adequate that I think you can get by your own study the exegetical equipment you need. Our students hear too many lectures, anyhow. In case you found yourself not ready, you could take another winter for it, but I do not believe that would be necessary. So, I would advise you to accept the position. But I hope you can stipulate for a year abroad very soon. It would be of great—almost indispensable advantage for you to come in contact with the German scholars and their methods of work—not so much to see how they teach

as how they themselves work—I should advise you to go to Dobschütz at Strasbourg.[10]

Thereafter Henry Cadbury continued his studies over winter and summer vacations, sometimes staying at the Ropes house in Cambridge. His plan to study abroad was cut short by the outbreak of World War I, but he was able to spend some time with Ernest von Dobschütz, who came to this country in 1913 to attend the Society of Biblical Literature professional meetings in New York during the Christmas holidays and took time to examine Henry Cadbury on the New Testament.

Returning to the Haverford campus was coming home again to the family circle. The Cadbury parents had moved permanently to Moorestown, but Henry Cadbury could easily visit them over weekends. At Haverford, Henry Cadbury spent a great deal of his spare time with his sister Elizabeth, her husband, Rufus Jones, and their daughter, Mary Hoxie, at their home at 2 College Circle. The latter was always very fond of, and close to, her Uncle Henry. She remembers her awe and pleasure when he allowed her to try to type with his typewriter, outfitted with Greek letters.[11]

Also living on the Haverford campus was Henry Cadbury's much older first cousin, Richard Tapper Cadbury, with his children. Every Friday night the Cadburys entertained cousins on campus, including Henry Cadbury and sometimes Carroll Brown, son of Caroline and Thomas K. Brown of Westtown. Leah Cadbury, the young cousin whom Henry Cadbury had taken canoeing at Westtown, was now a Bryn Mawr student and sometimes rather lonely. Many of the Westtown boys with whom she had studied were Haverford students, but because of the attitude of Haverford toward Bryn Mawr girls they never asked her out. Leah tried not to show that she minded, but she did, and cousin Henry Cadbury noticed. After she had to stay home the night of the junior play because she had no escort, he invited her to go with him to a dance at the Merion Cricket Club. Although he himself did not dance, he arranged for her to have partners throughout the evening. Leah always remembered the event as an example of the sensitivity which she saw in cousin Henry.[12]

The sensitivity was allied with acumen. Henry Cadbury was aware that a new, young teacher like himself was regarded as fair game by the students. On his first day in the classroom he decided to arrive early and look about. Shortly he became aware of a suspicious ticking. He searched and discovered four alarm clocks hidden in different places and timed to go off at intervals during the class hour. He also found four other alarm clocks, dusty with age, that had evidently once been planted to trick some predecessor of his. Henry Cadbury gathered up all the clocks, took them to a secretary's desk, and taught the class to a silent but baffled looking group of students. At the end of the hour he announced innocently that if anyone had recently lost personal property it could be reclaimed at the secretary's office.

The return to the Haverford campus after his mind-stretching study at Harvard was the occasion for a time of intellectual and personal growth for Henry Cadbury. One strong influence upon him in this period was the translation into English of a book by a young Alsatian theological student, Albert Schweitzer, titled *The Quest for the Historical Jesus*. The book, a review of more than a century of exacting scholarship, summarized the recent findings of Jewish apocalyptic literature and the growing evidence that Jesus himself had believed in and proclaimed the imminent end of the world. Scholars who refused to face this fact were permitting their own unconscious expectations, based on cultural and psychological influences, to color their findings about the historical Jesus. Schweitzer himself felt that the belief in the apocalypse, although proven historically mistaken, was the essence of Jesus' message. One had to abandon a rational, objective approach to the search for Jesus and respond on faith alone to his message, "Follow thou me."

The Schweitzer book came to have a great influence on New Testament scholarship. Led by a famous German scholar, Adolf von Harnack, a group of savants held that the apocalyptic elements in the gospels were the result of the early Christians' misunderstanding of Jesus. This view influenced the later work of German scholars on the question of the degree to which the early Christians had selected and shaped the stories and sayings of Jesus. It was the birth of what became known as motive criticism.

American liberal theologians, led by Francis C. Peabody, argued that the apocalyptic utterances could be understood if read in light of the passages that describe the Kingdom of God as a spiritual and already present reality. For Peabody, for Walter Rauschenbusch and many others, this interpretation helped to confirm their commitment to Jesus' ethical teachings as the basis of the Social Gospel. In Germany, England, Holland, America, and France, a group of scholars developed the hypothesis that Christ had never lived at all, the Christ-myth theory. Still others psychoanalyzed Jesus. For a medical degree which he earned in 1911, Albert Schweitzer refuted three writers who had claimed that Jesus was "paranoid, morbid, ecstatic, given to chronic delirium, delusion and hallucination."[13]

Henry Cadbury himself took none of these courses. Instead, he was stimulated into a lifelong quest for more information on what sort of person Jesus actually was and how he reflected the time and Jewish culture in which he arose, quite apart from how he was perceived as Savior. He was ready to accept Jesus' apocalyptic views as reflecting His Jewish training and heritage. He did not feel the compulsion to prove Jesus infallible. In other words, he took up the very search that Schweitzer seemed to abandon. There was, Henry Cadbury felt in himself and others, an inevitable and perennial curiosity about the person of Jesus: "I met it when I came as a young teacher fresh from graduate school to this Haverford campus. A group of non-academic men and women in the neighborhood came to me with an informal request. They said, 'We believe something of importance happened in Palestine in the first century. We want you to tell us what it was.'"[14] In response to this request, Henry Cadbury gave a series of popular lectures on the New Testament to the Haverford community in addition to his classroom teaching in Greek. To prepare for these lectures he read widely and then summarized his discoveries and the fresh puzzles they raised in his mind in clear and simple language accessible to the layperson.

Another influence on Henry Cadbury at about this time was some readings in the psychology of religion. At Harvard he had heard William James lecture on the varieties of religious experience and the development of character. Back in the Haverford community he was interested in the thought of a professor at Bryn Mawr, James Leuba, who lectured and wrote on the psychology of religion. Dr. Leuba believed that religion was entirely subjective, a product of the human imagination, a projection and a dramatization on a universal stage of the values of a human society. Nevertheless, he argued, it had always been a vital aspect of civilization.[15]

Although very close to Rufus Jones and many others who believed that Quakerism could be understood only as a mystical religion, based on a direct experience of the Divinity, and who themselves had "openings," Henry Cadbury was beginning to feel that he was somehow incapable of such moments of revelation. Raised to seek Divine guidance in every one of life's decisions, he felt he had been unsuccessful in this effort. Perhaps God, like an earthly father, laid down general rules and left the particulars to the individual to work out, he sometimes reasoned, revealing, perhaps unconsciously, his own experience with a rather distant father. But at other times, he expressed a wistful longing for a more ardent life of the spirit and wondered if the fault lay in himself and his powers of discernment. Perhaps others would call "revelation" the moods into which he occasionally fell, but which, cautious and humble by nature, he would not so describe.[16]

Moreover, his studies in philosophy had left him with "no assurance for or against the existence of God and of immortality." Intellectually he saw no way out of the classic agnostic position, "I do not know." Some questions, he concluded, he would have to leave unanswered, perhaps for a lifetime.[17]

Yet he knew himself to be a religious person, and he was becoming aware that there were others like him, within and without the Society of Friends, who felt themselves somehow inadequate because of their inability to experience moments of direct revelation. To reach out to such persons, to help them feel that their inarticulate urges toward moral behavior and social action were as valid an expression of religion as any other, became a goal. He thought "the correlation of ethical behavior with theological views was small and unimportant." What mattered was the fruit of the religious life. If one could not oneself experience what others called revelation, one could study the lives of the men and women who had been touched by the Spirit, whatever its source, and whose lives had been transformed. One could pattern one's character after such persons, beginning with Jesus, and try to make automatic those habits of ethical behavior which such persons taught with their very lives.[18]

In this period of growth and questioning, Henry Cadbury was ready to look with new eyes at the Hicksites, members of the other branch of Quakerism, or, as Henry Cadbury once said, "those who have been somewhat cadaverously styled 'Bodies Bearing the name of Friends.'" In a flush of enthusiasm for revitalizing the Society of Friends, young Friends in both the United States and England were looking for ways to bridge the gaps created by their ancestors, both between Hicksites and Orthodox and between Philadelphia Friends who had remained in splendid isolation all these years, and the Five Years Meeting, a group organized in 1902 to represent some of the other yearly meetings in the United States with an Orthodox background. Many of these had pastoral meetings and a more creedal approach than either of the East Coast groups.

In the summer of 1911 the Whittier Fellowship Guest House was opened in Hampton Falls, New Hampshire, for young Friends of all persuasions. From it emerged the Whittier Fellowship Guest House movement with extension conferences held in other areas. Both Henry Cadbury and his sister Emma Cadbury became active in this movement. In July of 1912, Henry Cadbury traveled to Indiana to attend the Winona Lake Peace Conference organized by the Five Years Meeting. It was a serious gathering, but Henry Cadbury brought to it his own puckish sense of humor. When an official photograph was taken of the delegates, he ran from one end to the other, managing to appear in the same picture twice, wearing a bathing suit. The next year he returned in more solemn mood to represent officially the Arch Street Yearly Meeting at the conference, thus making one small step to reestablish ties between Philadelphia Orthodox Friends and the rest of Quakerism.

The summer of 1912 was an important one for building bridges. The fall before, a young British Friend, John Hoyland, had come to the United States to study at the Hartford Theological Seminary. Among his fellow students were Clarence Pickett, Moses Bailey, and Alexander Purdy, all young Friends from the Five Years Meeting, but having wide informal connections with other Young Friends. John Hoyland began to reason that the separation of 1827 was in part the fault of British Friends and that therefore British Friends had some responsibility to heal the gap. The following summer he brought a party of ten young Friends from England to travel among their counterparts in the United States. In turn a group of six young Friends from the United States visited British Friends in August. Henry Cadbury joined the group for part of its stay, visited Cadbury relatives near Birmingham, spent time in London, then traveled to Switzerland, where he and a friend from Philadelphia stayed in the little town of Saas-Fee and climbed the Dom. Henry Cadbury recalled his former trip to the Alps with Rufus Jones, but felt this trip exceeded his fondest memories of the first:

> The chief thing is the view. The mountain is not only very high, but is centrally situated so that the great mountains are on all sides—not merely on one side as is the case with Mt. Blanc and Jungfrau. It must be hard to beat that view. Zermatt lies way down one side. On the other our guides looked and yodeled down to their own little village of Saas Fee. . . . We were most fortunate to find it warm and not very breezy on top—so we anchored our ropes to our axes and sat on the snow, took photos and drank in the view.[19]

The drinking was purely figurative. At a particularly arduous stage of the climb, the party of guides and tourists, roped together, paused on a narrow ledge of rock for a breather, and the head guide decided it was a good time to offer each climber a swig of wine. When the goatskin was passed to Henry Cadbury he felt a stop in his mind about passing it on, so strongly had he been raised to abhor alcohol. But the guides clearly wanted a drink, and his basic kindliness overcame his scruples. He passed the wine.

Returning to Haverford after a summer of high points, literally and figuratively, Henry Cadbury was interested in working seriously to heal the breach between Hicksites and Orthodox. With Samuel Bunting, Jr., a Hicksite, he organized a group of twelve young Friends, six from each branch, to study the separation of 1827. They began meeting weekly early in 1913, taking turns between the Twelfth Street and Race Street Meeting Houses. Each reported to the group on some aspect of the separation, its aftereffects in long-term prejudices, or how their religious views differed in the present. An undated article among Henry Cadbury's papers entitled "The Relation of Jesus to Spiritual Life" appears to have been prepared for this group. In it he outlines his concept of the variety of religious experience and tells why he believes that Jesus speaks to the condition of all:

> But it is my privilege to speak here of a force for deepening spiritual life that is of almost universal application because it works, in different ways upon every type of religious temperament. That force is Jesus Christ. Judging from the experience of the church in many ages he held a permanent place in the spiritualizing and revitalizing of religion for all sorts and conditions of men. To the mystic he is the way to God, the medium of beatific vision; to the thoughtful person he is the key of knowledge, the teacher and incarnation of truth; to the practical idealist he is the pattern, the goal and the realization of "the life that is life indeed." In this sense he is "the way, the truth and the life," so Jesus Christ draws all men to him. But how does Jesus come into relation with and influence our spiritual life? One way of speaking of this connection is in the form of a parable. Jesus's career is a type of allegory of our lives. Our moral nature undergoes transformations like those of his life. Sin must die in us, be crucified as he died. Virtue must rise in us as he rose from the dead. His career was a historical drama, a mystery play— in which he is the pattern of the real career of the human soul.[20]

After a year of such reports and speeches, the group was ready to prepare a joint report. Henry Cadbury was the author, but each member carefully reviewed and corrected the text, which was published in 1914. Their chief conclusion was that it was not matters of doctrine but the assumption of authority on the part of a few Philadelphia Quaker families in yearly meeting affairs that had caused the split initially.[21]

Through the study group and his attendance at the Winona Lake Peace Conferences as well as his travels, Henry Cadbury found himself in a position of leadership in the young Friends movement. The path of action in behalf of this work deepened his enthusiasm and his religious commitment. In an article in the *Friends Intelligencer* in the spring of 1914 he wrote that "the young Friends movement is further significant in showing that the Society of Friends is not yet dead, not even moribund." Paraphrasing Mark Twain he said that rumors of the death of the Society had been greatly exaggerated. He spoke of the organizational and intellectual aspects of the movement but emphasized its role in the development of the spirtual life: "We have been rediscovering the Quaker way of satisfying that spiritual hunger and we have found it adequate to our wants".[22]

The year 1914, with its momentous events on the world scene, was in many ways a year of change and triumph for Henry Cadbury. In January his brother-in-law Rufus Jones undertook a monthly publication *Present Day Papers,* merging it with the *British Friend.* For two years Henry Cadbury wrote articles and book reviews and edited manuscripts for this forum for Quaker thought. In the summer he was secretary-manager of a summer school at Haverford. In August he was present at the opening of Woolman House, later called Woolman School, a study center for Quakerism on the Swarthmore campus, later to evolve into the present-day Pendle Hill. As board member, lecturer, and mainstay, Henry Cadbury was connected with this adult school for the revitalization of Quakerism throughout the rest of his life.

It was in August, too, several weeks after the outbreak of war in Europe, that he journeyed to Sandy Spring, Maryland, to be present at the wedding of his first cousin once removed, Carroll Thornton Brown, and Anna Hartshorne, a graduate of Bryn Mawr. Carroll's youngest sister, Lydia, was now grown into an accomplished young woman. She had graduated from Wellesley College in 1912 with a reading knowledge of German and was working at a Philadelphia publishing company.

The two had, of course, seen each other many times at family gatherings, but this wedding was the beginning of Lydia Brown's special interest in Henry Cadbury. She admired him for his erudition, his modesty, and his fervent interest in the Society of Friends. He seemed much more committed than the detached Latin teacher she had known at Westtown, and she wondered if he had experienced a religious conversion. At any rate, she decided that he was the man for her.

It took some months, according to family legend, for that interest to be reciprocated. Some say he was interested in another woman. But Lydia's exuberance had always been attractive to him, and their being cousins was a plus. As a boy, he had always been interested in the story of his grandparents, Joel and Caroline Warder Cadbury, and their love, which surmounted the disapproval they had to endure because of being first cousins. And was not his middle name Joel and Lydia's Caroline? Family tradition played a part in his falling in love.

One source of Henry Cadbury's good spirits in 1914 was his recently acquired Harvard Ph.D. He had completed his examinations successfully in the fall of 1913 (Professor Ropes wrote that they had a hard time making the questions sufficiently difficult for him), and his brilliant thesis had been accepted for publication by the Harvard University Press on the recommendation of Ropes and George Foote Moore. Henry Cadbury was then an exponent of simplified spelling and wrote to ask the press if he might use the new style in his manuscript, but was told a frosty "no." With the help of suggestions from his committee he began to prepare the manuscript for publication, little dreaming it would take six years. The delay was at least partly caused by war conditions and the shortage of paper.

In *The Style and Literary Method of Luke,* Henry Cadbury examined the language of the unknown author of both Luke and Acts, in contrast to that of the author of Mark and to that of an earlier Greek written source, which scholars called Q. To understand the words and phrases used in the gospel he compared them to the available writings of nonbiblical authors of the day. In his preface Henry Cadbury stated: "As a rule the linguistic study should precede rather than follow the theological and history study. Instead of explaining a writer's language in the light of a theory about his identity and interest we should test the theory by an independent study of the language." He saw himself as the patient and careful assembler of facts from which other scholars might draw conclusions, but he warned against drawing those conclusions too quickly. In one chapter he discussed the role of the religious motive of the author in selecting what was recorded. This was to be a frequent theme. In another, he discussed the alleged medical language of Luke. Luke had been called "the Beloved Physician" because of his use of medical language, but Henry Cadbury demonstrated that many of his contemporaries used the same terms although they were not doctors. Indeed, from Luke's use of nautical terms, and his knowledge about sailing, one could just as well argue that Luke was a mariner. Henry Cadbury's argument was decisive. Years later it was said at the Harvard Divinity School that he won his doctor's degree by taking Luke's away from him.[23]

Although publication was six years away, Henry Cadbury's thesis was discussed by other scholars, especially those who belonged to the Society of Biblical Scholars, of which he was now a member, and he was increasingly invited to write papers and review books.

The German scholars heard about Henry Cadbury's thesis through Ernest von Dobschütz, and he was invited to participate in a revision of Wettstein's edition of the New Testament, published in 1751. Henry Cadbury was asked to undertake to comb the writings of the Greek author Lucian for anything pertinent to the New Testament. Henry Cadbury eventually undertook this project and corresponded with various German scholars about it through the 1920s, but the work was abandoned in the 1930s, perhaps with the coming of Hitler.

In the world of Quakerism, too, his fame was spreading, and he was invited to speak at the Westtown School Assembly and the Germantown Monthly Meeting Tea Meeting, both important marks of distinction in the bosom of Philadelphia Quakerdom. His Westtown talk, entitled "Quakerism as an Experiment Station," appeared in the *Friends Intelligencer* in 1915. In it he made an appeal which he was to make over and over that the Society of Friends must not rest on past laurels but continue to make discoveries of the truth—such as its testimonies against war and slavery—to which it was uniquely fitted because of its small size and its experimental past: "I believe it may still be said that the world has yet to see how great things God can do through a small denomination wholly devoted to his will. May it be the aim of Quakerism, by the grace of God, to show the world what he can do through us." [24]

In the summer of 1915, Henry Cadbury attended the Winona Lake Peace Conference once more, then stayed afterward to meet with a group of young Friends from the Five Years Meeting, the Philadelphia Yearly Meeting (Arch Street), and the Friends General Conference, the latter group made up of the various Hicksite Yearly Meetings. With two other young Friends, Vincent Nicholson and Garfield Coxe, he had called the gathering. This was the birth of a new organization, the Friends National Peace Committee, which was to play an important role after the United States entered the war. Jane Addams of Hull House, the daughter of a self-styled Hicksite Friend, had been traveling in Europe with a group of women who later formed the Women's International League for Peace and Freedom and reported that they found a longing for peace among the warring nations. The conference concluded that its task was to rouse one hundred thousand Friends to the challenge of the hour and to urge the president to try to intervene in the world struggle for the sake of peace.

Earlham College in Richmond, Indiana, had invited the brilliant young biblical scholar to spend the first semester of the year 1915 on campus, and Henry Cadbury had agreed to do so. The midwestern Friends, under the influence first of Joseph John Gurney and then of other evangelists of the second half of the nineteenth century, had come to be far more traditional in their approach to the Bible than the Hicksites and the Wilburites, who insisted it must be read in the light of a continuing revelation. Henry Cadbury's own views about the Bible were certainly not those of a literalist. His philological studies had convinced him that it was dangerous if not impossible to draw literal interpretations from Bible verses. He was mischievously fond of pointing out to his Quaker friends in particular that though we are told to turn our swords into plowshares and our spears into pruning hooks (Isaiah 2:4) we are also told to beat our plowshares into swords and our pruning hooks into spears (Joel 3:10). Nevertheless, his vast knowledge of and respect for Scripture made him acceptable to the latter-day Gurneyites, and they were willing to hear views from him they would normally regard as too liberal from a less distinguished scholar.

As a teacher, whether at Haverford or at Earlham, Henry Cadbury was careful never to insist that the students ingest and repeat back to him his own views. Rather, his method was entirely Socratic. By asking skillful questions he helped his students to examine the material for themselves and to draw from it logical conclusions. One freshman from that period, Wilbur Kamp, remembers Henry Cadbury as a stimulating teacher who aroused in Wilbur a desire to know fully the teachings of Jesus and to understand and commit his life to the peace testimony of the Society of Friends. Wilbur also remembers that Henry Cadbury had a visit from a young lady, Lydia Brown from Philadelphia. The two were now secretly engaged.[25]

While at Earlham, Henry Cadbury spoke in a local country meeting about the social service movement—he called it social "servis" in the interests of simplified spelling. "We can no longer, therefore, separate social work from religion," he said. "It is part of religion. Child labor laws may be more edifying than all the creeds. A living wage may lead to eternal life. Some votes speak louder than prayers."[26] He went on to speak of the conflict between capital and labor, of poor housing and inadequate child care, and to urge the meeting to become the center for social change. The war was beginning to have an increasing effect on Henry Cadbury's thinking, causing him to begin to examine more deeply the social order and the relationship between its inequities and war. In November he went with his friend Edward Evans to the founding meeting of the U.S. branch of the Fellowship of Reconciliation, FOR, an international nonsectarian pacifist organization formed in Great Britain the year before. There they met Norman Thomas, socialist, pacifist, and editor of the *World Tomorrow,* for which Henry Cadbury often wrote.

Following the organization of the Friends National Peace Committee in the summer of 1915, Henry Cadbury worked on a letter to be sent to all meetings of the Religious Society of Friends urging that they take action in the cause of peace. One form of suggested action was a petition to congressional representatives asking them to work for peace and to report back to the undersigned on their efforts. The issue of peace was taking hold of his feelings with unexpected strength. "I did not know I cared so much for peace," he wrote a friend from the young Friends group.[27]

In a lighter vein while at Earlham, Henry Cadbury remembered his early interest in humorous writing and produced a spoof on Charles Lamb's "Roast Pig." He called his piece "Fried Chicken" and asserted, tongue in cheek, that in Indiana it was not unusual to see a plate of fried chicken served on an American flag. He concluded, "Don't put all your eggs in one basket is a good motto for the children of men as well as those of feathered bipeds."[28]

There was time for recreation, too. Henry Cadbury visited the home of Edgar Nicholson, editor of the *American Friend,* his son, Vincent Nicholson, and daughter, Caroline. Caroline taught high school in nearby Knightstown but came home for the weekends. A younger brother, Francis, played the piano while Henry, Vincent, and Caroline sang. A boarder in the house, Thomas E. Jones, often joined them for an evening of music.

The interlude at Earlham was a pleasant one, but it was just that, an interlude. Haverford had offered Henry Cadbury an assistant professorship in biblical studies, starting in the fall of 1916, with a raise in salary. He felt that now with his degree and the offer to teach his favorite subject at his favorite college, the pattern of his life had at long last fallen into shape. He had even saved a little money. He was ready to buy a house and be married, in that order.

CHAPTER 3
The Anvil of War

Over the Christmas holidays of 1915, Henry Cadbury and Lydia Caroline Brown announced their engagement to be married, first to their respective families and then to a wider circle of friends. People had begun to be a little concerned that Henry Cadbury, now thirty-two, would never get around to marrying, and the news about the approaching wedding was generally met with rejoicing.

There were, however, a few pockets of reservation. That they were first cousins once removed worried some of Lydia Brown's relatives, and a few of the more sophisticated Cadburys were concerned that the boisterous and outspoken country Browns were not of their social standing. How would uninhibited and plainspoken Lydia function as the wife of a rising scholar who had to attend social events and entertain? The two were in love now, obviously, but would Lydia come to annoy or even embarrass him in public?

By the time of the wedding in June the family had ceased to ask these questions, but they persisted for years among people who did not know Henry and Lydia Cadbury very well. The two were different socially, and as the years passed this difference was accentuated, Lydia Cadbury becoming famous for her outspoken, sometimes outrageous remarks, and Henry Cadbury known for his gentleness and sensitivity. Everyone who was close to the couple, however, saw that the two loved each other very much indeed and rejoiced in their differences. Each was the alter ego the other might wish to be. Lydia said the things Henry was unable to say; Henry's courtly manners pleased Lydia although it was not her nature to emulate him. In public, they pushed each other to extremes. In private they met on equal and quieter ground.

Although Lydia gloried in Henry Cadbury's erudition, she had scholarly interests of her own. Her religious beliefs and her approach to the Bible were her own, too, reflecting a more evangelical and conventional view than her scholar husband. And although she had originally been attracted to him by his fervor in the young Friends movement and his hopes for the revitalization of the Society of Friends, he turned increasingly to her for the enthusiasm he sometimes felt he lacked. In one letter to her during the engagement period he described himself as "a man who needs every spark of idealism he can get." In another, he spoke of her inspiration: "As I look back over the past few days I realize that every time I have thought of thee it has been not to remind me of material things or of physical things but of my own love and especially of thy inspiring ideals for us. And while thee has this effect upon me I look forward with increased assurance to our life together growing better every day by the grace of love."[1]

The wedding took place on June 17 at the Cadbury home at 254 East Main Street in Moorestown. Henry Cadbury's mother, Anna K. Cadbury, was now confined to a wheelchair with arthritis, and because of her infirmity the Twelfth Street Meeting had appointed a special committee to oversee the wedding in her home. Since Lydia Brown's mother had died in 1914, the senior Cadburys had taken on the part of the bride's family in arranging for the wedding. Thomas K. Brown, Lydia's father, and a cousin of Caroline Cadbury Brown, Susan Shipley, sat with Lydia; the rest of the bridal party was made up mainly of Cadburys. The folding doors between the parlor and the sitting room were opened, and the bride and groom came down the wide stairs facing the open parlor and took their places in a double seat in the open parlor door, where all could see. The rooms and the hall were decorated with white flowers, but Lydia carried none, nor wore any jewelry or lace. "The wedding was of conspicuous simplicity," Henry's aunt Sarah Cadbury wrote to the English branch of the family. After the service the guests were offered strawberry lemonade on the porch, then were ushered into the dining room, where they were served breakfast—chicken salad, chicken croquettes, sweetbread patties, "rasped" [hard] rolls, ice creams, cakes, and coffee. Afterward came photography on the lawn. It was, Aunt Sarah reported, a perfect June day.[2]

For a honeymoon, or perhaps one should say instead of a honeymoon, the young people went directly to work at Back Log Camp at Sabael, New York, in the Adirondacks. This camp, established by Lydia's father in 1899, first at Racquette Lake and then at Indian Lake, had become a major Brown family enterprise. Paying guests were invited to join the extensive Brown family in living in tents,

Henry Joel Cadbury and Lydia Caroline Brown. On their wedding day, June 17, 1916, Moorestown, New Jersey. From the private collection of Mary Hoxie Jones. Photo copied by Theodore Hetzel.

eating in a common dining tent, and exploring the mountains in canoes or on foot. "Plain living and high thinking" was one of T. K. Brown's mottoes. Every night guests were expected to gather at the Focus Tent for a campfire and for uplifting conversation.

Family members were taught to put the guests' interests first at Back Log, to take part in opening or closing the camp, and to work without pay if the summer was not a remunerative one. Every family member had his or her own role. Most of those on the "distaff side" were expected to sew or mend the tents, order the food, and supervise the meals. The men were more likely to have the pleasant duty of taking the guests on overnight paddles or hikes. Mothers were not expected to spend too much time with their own children because they were to enter into the camp life wholeheartedly.

It was a way of life one either loved or disliked intensely. Lydia's mother, Caroline Brown, always disliked it and had her own little cabin built so that she did not have to live in a tent. As a child, Lydia was very lonely at Back Log, but later she came to enjoy it. She was often the one to do the camp laundry and to order the food. Having grown up in a family several members of whom were deaf, she had a high, ringing voice. When she tried to talk over the defective telephone lines, she raised it still higher. Generations of Westtown students who worked at Back Log in the summers remember Lydia Cadbury shouting her orders to "Mr. Groceryman."

Henry Cadbury became a popular addition to the Back Log staff. As an in-law he was not quite the equal of the Brown brothers in making decisions, but when there were differences about decisions he was often able to play a peacemaking role. He was extremely popular with the guests, and his Bible readings in the morning and talks at the Focus Tent at night became highlights of the Back Log experience. His love of nature was nurtured by the long days in the woods. He came to know the flora and fauna intimately and to be known for his tireless strength in carrying heavy packs, climbing mountains, and paddling long days on the lakes or rivers.

After the summer at Back Log, the young Cadbury family returned to the house at 3 College Circle, next door to Rufus and Elizabeth Jones, which Henry Cadbury had purchased for his bride. It turned out to be a fortunate arrangement; Lydia and Elizabeth, though many years apart in age, formed a bond that lasted through the years. Lydia was also always fond of Mary Hoxie Jones, their only daughter. She admired her famous brother-in-law, Rufus Jones, but when she felt people were taking a too worshipful attitude toward him, she liked to prick the balloon:

"Oh, Mrs. Jones, it must be wonderful to be married to Rufus," an admiring woman said.

"Humph, ought to see him when he has a belly ache," Lydia answered.[3]

Like Henry Cadbury, Lydia Cadbury felt she was not cut out for the sort of mystical experience of which Rufus Jones spoke so often and so eloquently.

"Are you a mystic?" she asked a campus friend.

"Well, I'm not. Rather do a big load of laundry any day."[4]

Laundry was one of Lydia Cadbury's favorite forms of self-expression.

In the fall, Lydia discovered she was pregnant. Henry's new teaching was going well, and at Christmas he was chosen as secretary for the Society of Biblical Literature, one of the youngest men to be placed in this important position. The following spring, President Isaac Sharpless offered him the post of associate professor for a five-year term. Haverford did not have tenure as such, but an associate professor could not be fired unless a special committee of the faculty met with the Board of Managers and agreed. The future seemed secure. It should have been a triumphant year for the young couple, but continuing bad news from the war front and the growing likelihood of American involvement cast a deep shadow over their happiness.

Aside from his teaching and his home, Henry Cadbury's efforts were almost wholly devoted to peace. He continued a series of public lectures on the psychology of war and peace, begun the year before. He prepared a lecture for the Young Friends movement on the Christian view of peace and war. And he wrote an article titled "Christ and War" in which he rejected the arguments being advanced by leading theologians to sanction war:

> It is no surprise therefore to find those who sanction war and military methods now attempting to support their position by appeal to the Gospel. On the contrary, these efforts are an encouraging sign, for they show that now as never before the need for such defense is felt by militarists to meet the growing conviction that war is wrong. Similarly, just before the complete abolition of slavery certain preachers made desperate efforts to justify the holding of slaves by reference to Scripture.[5]

After demolishing one or two of the more inane justifications of war currently being made, Henry Cadbury wrote that he did not believe that the case for or against Jesus' attitude toward war could be deduced from a few isolated or obscure texts. Jesus made no categorical judgments about war, taxation, slavery, or the right of private property. Rather, he set an example of a total way of life and left it to the individual Christian to apply those principles:

> Jesus' life and teaching were devoted to the propagation of a certain type of character, a type including sincerity in religion and life, neighborliness beyond local and conventional limits, spontaneous kindness to one's fellow-men. These ideals of human character were, he believed characteristic of God, who loves his enemies, seeks the lost sheep, is kind toward the unthankful and evil. And he boldly urges men to aspire to this divine ideal of unresisting but irresistible love.[6]

He offered this article to the *Biblical World,* a leading publication at the University of Chicago, and received a rejection from the editor, who frankly stated his position: "Face to face with the alternative of national and idealistic loss and war, it seems to me that the only thing to do is to choose war."[7]

As the war came closer, more and more people were caught up with the war spirit, even including members of the Society of Friends. Some 125 members of Hicksite meetings signed a letter published in the newspapers entitled "Some Particular Advices for Friends and a Statement of Loyalty for Others: Being the Views of Some Members of the Society of Friends Regarding Its Attitude toward the Present Crisis." Their view was that in this particular war all Christians must give support to the national cause.[8]

Just before the entry of the United States into the war, Henry Cadbury wrote the first of a series of letters to the *Philadelphia Public Ledger.* President Woodrow Wilson had urged cooperation, mutual trust, and the restraint of violence in relations between capital and labor. Henry Cadbury suggested that these same methods might work on the international scene.

On April 6, 1917, the joint congressional resolution declaring a state of war was signed by President Wilson and the *Ledger* ran a lead editorial declaring the necessity for the loyalty of all citizens and expressing the hope that pacifists would cease and desist from treasonable and pro-German activities. In a long letter to the *Ledger,* Henry Cadbury identified himself as a pacifist and insisted that it was not treasonable to suggest a change of policy for one's nation. He was opposed to capital punishment even though it was the law of the land. Did that make him a traitor?

> I also gather by being a pacifist I am considered in effect pro-German. It is, however, because I oppose methods that in August, 1914, were called Prussian that I am a pacifist. I oppose conscription and a large

standing army. I oppose aggressive war when we are not invaded. Sometime ago we all opposed these things and called them German because we thought Germany practiced them. When I oppose them in America I am called pro-German.[9]

Now that war was declared, Henry Cadbury coupled his letter writing with action. Along with Edward Evans of the Fellowship of Reconciliation and others of Philadelphia Yearly Meeting (Arch Street), he drafted a questionnaire to send to young men facing the draft. He also called a meeting of young Friends to consider what to do in the face of conscription. At Haverford some young men were already training for possible overseas service with the British Friends. At George School, headmaster George Walton was encouraging senior students to enroll as farm workers and suggesting a conscientious objector farm labor corps.

To many Friends it was becoming apparent that there was an urgent need to bring Hicksite, Orthodox, and Five Year Meeting Friends together to agree upon some joint means of providing service for conscientious objectors. The draft law had not yet been completed in regard to provisions for conscientious objectors, but Friends reasoned that having a workable alternative to drafting them into the army might affect the regulations. It was decided that the Friends National Peace Committee, of which Henry Cadbury was chairman, was the logical organization to convene a meeting of all Friends groups to consider this issue. On April 30, 1917, Henry Cadbury opened a meeting composed of representatives from each of the three groups at the Young Friends offices, Fifteenth and Cherry streets, in Philadelphia.[10]

At this historic meeting Alfred Scattergood was selected as temporary chairman, and the group decided to call itself the National Friends Service Committee. They discussed a permanent headquarters and outlined various plans for service. Because it seemed at that time possible that Friends as well as Mennonites and Brethren might be exempted from the draft, the group expressed its resolve to participate in some way in the great crisis facing the world. Some were more specific about expressing loyalty to the United States and stated their point of view in a patriotic minute: "We are united in expressing our love for our country and our desire to serve her loyally. We offer our service to the Government of the United States in any constructive work in which we can conscientiously serve humanity."[11] At a second meeting, held on May 11, the committee was renamed the American Friends Service Committee, and both Rufus Jones and Henry Cadbury were added to its membership. Shortly thereafter Vincent Nicholson, Henry Cadbury's friend from Richmond, Indiana, was named executive secretary, permanent quarters were established at the Friends Institute, 20 South Twelfth Street, and Rufus Jones was chosen as chairman.

The new committee immediately set to work at a swift pace. Two members were sent to France to explore the possibility of establishing a Friends Reconstruction Unit in France under the wing of the civilian service of the American Red Cross. Money had to be raised and a group of one hundred volunteers selected for training. Henry Cadbury served on a small committee to develop an application form, decide upon the qualifications of the applicants, and make selections.

This proved a difficult task. Few of the young Friends who applied had wrestled with the questions of conscientious objection and thought through all its implications. They knew they were against war, but what specifically was their duty now that the country was at war? Not since Civil War days had the question really confronted members of the Society of Friends. The committee therefore had to try to weigh the sense of conviction expressed by the applicants, as well as judge their qualifications to render the sort of service needed in France. Should they select young men who most needed an outlet for service, or those who would be most useful in meeting the needs overseas? Applications flooded in, and each needed to be considered carefully.

Women applied, too. In late June, the committee sent six women to southeastern Russia to join English Friends who were providing relief for the flood of refugees fleeing invading German armies. Henry Cadbury arranged for this team to be sent and supplied. As a result, he was named to the Women's Committee, a fact he was fond of bringing up in later years.

In the midst of all the excitement over the AFSC, Lydia Cadbury produced some excitement of her own. On June 14, Elizabeth, nicknamed Betty, was born. Henry Cadbury stayed with Lydia through the last hours of her labor and administered gas when Lydia asked for it. When the doctor arrived to deliver the baby, Henry left the room but was near enough to hear Lydia's cries. After the baby was born, and he was summoned back to see the mother and child, he sank to his knees beside his wife's bed and burst into tears. "What is the matter, dear?" asked Lydia, triumphant now that the trauma of birth was over.

"Thee seemed to suffer so," Henry said.[12]

A few days later Lydia wrote to her mother-in-law to describe the birth: "Isn't it wonderful that it is all over—and a little daughter! She is as soft as a flower. I wish Henry were feeling this beginning of affection as a new mother does; a father so slowly learns to love. He has picked her up gingerly, and watches her yawn and stretch with a curious air, most amusing to behold."[13]

Was Henry Cadbury really slow to learn to love the new baby? Or was this Lydia's expectation, based on her experience with her own busy father? The concept of the distant father was widely accepted at the time. Lydia Cadbury was surrounded by nurses and female relatives, and Henry Cadbury was needed by the AFSC. Perhaps this was the beginning of a tension—AFSC versus family—that was to be with the Cadburys for many years. Lydia Cadbury was proud of Henry Cadbury's public service, as she was proud of his scholarship. But with the ambivalence of most mothers of the period, she both resented the competition of outside interests and defended her own right to control decisions relating to the children.

For the Service Committee, problems were beginning to multiply. The original optimistic view that members of the historic peace churches would be exempted from the draft proved false. In a letter to Rufus Jones, the U.S. provost marshal made it clear that pacifists were not exempt from noncombatant duty. Furthermore, no man was to go overseas to work with the Friends unless he had received a permit from his local draft board allowing him to apply for a passport and to receive his physical examination and apply for conscientious objector status.

This was a major blow to the plan for sending the first one hundred men to France in September. A number of these had been called in the first draft, and it was crucial to process their cases. To expedite this strategy, it was decided to ask the men to request transfer from their local boards, scattered all over the country, to those in the suburbs of Philadelphia. Henry Cadbury was asked to undertake the major share of this work. He became an expert on dealing with draft boards and in helping the young conscientious objectors to articulate their positions. By the end of the summer all but eleven of the men had been given permits and received passports, and the rest were processed within a few weeks.

Worse problems were to follow. New regulations made it clear that all draftees must report to mobilization camps and there be assigned to noncombatant service under military authority. Medical work was the only such service to be officially named as noncombatant. For many young Quakers the concept of being assigned to a military camp and of having to wear a uniform and salute officers was unacceptable. Some went to jail, some were seized and inducted forcibly, some took their stand inside the army camps and were imprisoned and treated roughly. In many cases, torture is not too strong a word. A young Quaker boy wrote to the AFSC from

Camp Cody: "I have been stripped and scrubbed with a broom, put under a faucet with my mouth open, had a rope around my neck and pulled up choking tight for a bit, been fisted, slapped, kicked, and carried a bag of sand and dirt until I could hardly hold it and go, been kept under a shower until pretty chilled. If this information will do no good for others thou may just burn this letter and let it go."[14]

Henry Cadbury kept the three Quaker papers, the *American Friend,* the *Friends Intelligencer,* and the *Friend,* supplied with the increasingly gloomy news of the draft law. To prepare draft-age young Friends for what might lie ahead of them he wrote a letter and a questionnaire, stating the AFSC's concept that there could be no division of military service into combatant and noncombatant, but asking the individual to make his decision at the "high tribunal of his own conscience," then let the committee know if he had decided to go voluntarily to a mobilization camp.

> If thee has been drafted and has been ordered to mobilize it is particularly important that we have this record of thy situation so that we can keep thee informed of any developments affecting thy case and be of any further assistance to thee. . . . If thee goes voluntarily or is forcibly taken to any military camp try to find someone in the camp who will be willing to write to us and to receive communcations from us for thee in case we are not able to communicate with thee freely.[15]

This letter, mailed in a plain brown envelope from 20 South Twelfth, fell into the hands of the Philadelphia *Press* and was published under the headline "Quakers Prepare for Acts Which May Violate Law." "On several occasions statements have been made by Dr. Henry Joel Cadbury, chairman of the Philadelphia Young Friends Committee which has shown the willingness of Friends to ignore the law if it does not coincide with their own ideas of what should be done," the newspaper reported accusingly. Henry Cadbury was becoming notorious as a spokesperson for the pacifist position.[16]

While he tried to cope with the mounting problems of the draft, Henry Cadbury had spent the month of August acting as volunteer executive secretary for the new AFSC, while Vincent Nicholson attended a conference in the Midwest, then stayed on to rest on the advice of a physician. Letters flew between them. Should the AFSC adopt the red and black star used by the British Friends or choose blue and red? Ought a second unit of one hundred men enter training? What could be said to the War Department about the status of conscientious objectors?

Eventually Vincent Nicholson returned, in time for Henry Cadbury to resume his regular teaching load at Haverford, although he continued to commute frequently to the little office at 20 South Twelfth Street and to visit Washington to talk with people in the War Department about the status of the conscientious objectors. More and more young men were being drafted into army camps where sergeants had never heard of exemption for pacifists and sought to break the resisting spirit of their puzzling new charges.

Moreover, it seemed to Henry Cadbury that too many of his colleagues within and without the Society of Friends were rejecting the peace testimony. When he spoke at a church in Bryn Mawr in December of 1917 on the Christian opposition to the war, George A. Barton, head of the Department of Biblical Literature at Bryn Mawr College, publicly attacked him as biased. In January of 1918, an article he wrote on the prophet Amos, "Ruthlessness at Home and Abroad," was rejected by *Biblical World* for its pacifist sentiments. (Later it was published in Henry Cadbury's first book, *National Ideals in the Old Testament.*)[17]

The war hysteria seemed to be threatening academic freedom. In an article published in the March issue of the *Haverfordian,* "Freedom of Thought and the Colleges," Henry Cadbury argued that such freedom was not so much a right as a duty, for students as well as for faculty. New ideas had to be explored with a certain detachment if new solutions to world problems were to be obtained. And how were minds to remain free if hysteria against all things German was permitted to prevail?[18]

In June he wrote an article for the *Friends Intelligencer* asking "Are we honest?" and pointing out that though Friends bodies had unanimously approved the peace testimony, individual Friends felt free to disregard it, and some representatives of the Society had actually encouraged participation in the military: "To a certain extent any representative of the Society who by word or example commends as justifiable for Friends any form of participation in war, either voluntary or compulsory makes if not himself, at least others guilty of perjury."[19] There was a definite note of sharpness and frustration in this piece. Henry Cadbury lived by his own high standards. He did not expect the same of everyone, but he certainly expected it of members of the Society of Friends and of those who professed to follow Jesus. The anti-German passions in which the nation was indulging seemed to sweep aside all logic. Even the Society of Biblical Literature was affected; one scholar suggested that biblical scholarship in this country break its dependence on the German scholars: "We can no longer go to school to a nation against which we feel a moral aversion."[20]

Was the whole world going mad, Henry Cadbury was beginning to ask. To add to the vexations of public affairs, he was experiencing keen frustrations over the publication of his thesis. Written in 1912, it had finally been prepared for the Harvard University Press in 1915. But one delay had followed another, and in June the director of the press wrote suggesting that publication be postponed because of a shortage of paper and poor prospects for sales during the war. Henry Cadbury wrote back to point out that the job of keeping the information current and incorporating new research was increasingly time-consuming both for him and for Harvard Professor George Moore, who was supervising the publication, and urging that the book be published on schedule. The press agreed, and Henry Cadbury spent much of the summer of 1918 correcting galleys at Back Log Camp, whenever he could get away from camp duties to do so. The book was published finally in 1920.

In 1917, Isaac Sharpless resigned and William Wistar Comfort, a Haverford graduate of 1894 and the head of the modern language department at Cornell University, had come to Haverford as the new president. He walked into a unique situation. The AFSC was using the Haverford campus to train men for overseas duties, and two of his professors, Rufus Jones and Henry Cadbury, were constantly away from the college, working for the AFSC in Philadelphia and in Washington. Rufus Jones kept a low profile in the press, but Henry Cadbury seemed to see himself as the David of pacifism to the Goliath of war sentiment. Many of Haverford's alumni were not pacifists, and they did not relish seeing the college's name linked publicly with the pacifist position. In addition, during the summer of 1918, they were angered when Haverford turned down the invitation of the War Department to establish an army training camp on campus. Inevitably, the new president found himself in the heat of the controversy.

In July, Rufus Jones wrote to President Comfort to say that Vincent Nicholson, the executive secretary of the new AFSC, had been drafted, and the need to find a replacement for him was urgent. Could Henry Cadbury be spared for the coming academic year to serve as executive secretary? Comfort wrote back that Haverford could not release Henry Cadbury unless he was willing to carry on with twelve hours of elementary Greek while heading up AFSC, "but I suppose he could not do so." The AFSC should look in other directions, Comfort urged. The tone of the letter revealed some of the frustrations of the past months.[21]

Wilbur Thomas of the New England Yearly Meeting was already at work at 20 South Twelfth Street, having volunteered to spend July and August helping the AFSC. Although there were some questions about him, the board decided to ask him to take Vincent Nicholson's place. Vincent Nicholson urged that Henry Cadbury be appointed also because he thought the two would make a good team, but as Henry Cadbury wrote later, the college discouraged him from doing so.[22]

Back at Haverford in late September for the fall term, Henry Cadbury read the newspapers with growing despair. The hatred expressed against Germany seemed to be cresting to unbelievable heights as the allied armies advanced toward the Rhine and Germany made peace overtures. All the frustrations of the past year and all his sense of outrage at the abandonment of Christian principles or even human decency toward the enemy, he poured out in a letter to the *Philadelphia Public Ledger,* written on Haverford College stationery:

> As a Christian and patriotic American may I raise one cry of protest in your columns against the orgy of hate in which the American press and public indulges on the receipt of peace overtures from the enemy. Whatever the immediate result of the present German request for an armistice, the spirit of implacable hatred and revenge exhibited by many persons in this country indicates that it is our nation which is the greatest obstacle to a clean peace and the least worthy of it. Never in the period of his greatest arrogances and successes did the German Kaiser and Junkers utter more heathen and bloodthirsty sentiments than appear throughout our newspapers today. Intoxicated with the first taste of blood and flushed with victory, the American public hastens to condemn in advance the soberly phrased pleas of a conciliatory foe. While the English press wisely refrains from comment until an official answer can be given, Americans with insatiable lust for vengeance cry More! More! Every concession on the part of the enemy is counted as a mark of weakness and is made an excuse for more humiliating and unreasonable demands. While the war-weary people of Europe long for peace, we conceited newcomers into the fight prefer to sacrifice their youth and ours by the millions in order that we may dictate a peace to suit our insane hysteria. Surely it behooves us at this hour, when not retaliation for the past but the assurance of a safer and saner international fellowship is the world's need, distinguishing justice and mercy from blind revenge, to keep ourselves in the mood of moderation and fair play. A peace on other terms or in any other spirit will be no peace at all, but the curse of the future. Signed: Henry J. Cadbury.[23]

Although Henry Cadbury had written strong letters to the press all through the war years, this one published on October 12 was uncharacteristically angry, and it produced an immediate angry response. Many letters were written to the *Ledger* denouncing Henry

Cadbury as neither a Christian nor a patriot and reiterating all the tales of German outrages, which he was seen as condoning. Similar letters poured into Haverford from angry alumni. By using college stationery, was Henry Cadbury not implying that his views were those of the college? Even some Quaker alumni supported the war. Now they joined with the majority in demanding that Henry Cadbury be dismissed immediately to make it clear that Haverford did not share his unpatriotic views. A group of twenty alumni met with former President Isaac Sharpless to press for his dismissal. Henry Cadbury also received anonymous threats to lynch him and to burn his house down.

Both Lydia and Henry Cadbury were stunned by this response. Henry Cadbury immediately went to see President Comfort to explain that his letter had not been intended as an attack on anyone, but only a call to Christian principles. The interview was apparently not a great success, and afterward Henry Cadbury put down some of his thoughts in writing:

> The letter was intended to bespeak the same Christian freedom from hate and revenge which President Wilson and Secretary Lansing so finely expressed in their recent speeches. It was not intended to express an opinion on the relative guilt of the belligerents, on peace terms, or on any other matter of national policy. Owing however to the present tense state of public feeling and the vigor of the language in which my views were expressed it has caused more comment than I anticipated. I freely confess this error in judgment, and so far as the results affect myself I shall bear the personal disadvantage as deserved. I can make this confession the more readily as I know thee will construe it as no surrender of cherished Quaker principles but as the confession of one whose judgment is fallible and whose zeal is not always wise.
>
> Equally surprised am I at the way some persons have associated the position of an individual on matters of national morality with the institution in which he teaches Greek. For this I have the deepest regret.[24]

Regret, unfortunately, turned out to be not enough. More criticism poured in to the college. Rufus and Elizabeth Jones came next door to confer with Henry and Lydia Cadbury. No one knows exactly what was said at that interview, but Rufus Jones clearly had no alternative to offer to the mounting pressure for Henry Cadbury to resign. At the thought of having to part from the college where he had been a student for four years and a teacher for eight, Henry Cadbury wept. On October 21 he submitted his resignation, and on October 24 he wrote a letter to the faculty saying that his attitude was one of "confessed indiscretion and sincere penitence."[25]

A special meeting of the Board of Managers had been called on October 22 to consider the situation. President Comfort defended Cadbury's scholarship and integrity but said that "certain personal characterstics and combative tendencies lessened his usefulness." Former president Sharpless spoke to the same effect. Members agreed on "their unanimous emphatic disapproval of the letter," which they described as "this indiscretion on his part, following, as it did, numerous similar but less serious ones." They were, however, divided about equally between those who thought Henry Cadbury's resignation should be accepted immediately and those who feared that such action would be a blow to academic freedom. A sub-committee was appointed to consider the case and make a public statement. As a result, an article appeared in the *Philadelphia Evening Bulletin,* which reported that "Henry J. Cadbury, who bewails the fact that America is not ready yet to shake hands with the Huns . . . will have to give up his college position" and that no one on the Haverford Board disagreed: "'There was absolutely no division on the question of the impropriety of Mr. Cadbury's public statement,' said Asa S. Wing, president of the Haverford College Board. . . . There was a division, however, on the question of academic freedom and the dignity of taking too precipitous action on the matter.'"[26]

At a second special meeting of the board held November 1, the committee recommended that Cadbury be given a leave of absence for the rest of the academic year and his resignation be reconsidered no later than March. The board accepted this recommendation, along with the statement:

> The precious privilege of free judgment and utterance where the conscience is truly concerned, Haverford College respects and maintains. But the habit of temperate judgment and consideration for the feelings of others with whom one has associated oneself should always characterize the utterances of a scholar, especially upon matters touching the public conscience. We hold that Professor Cadbury in his letter to the Public Ledger of October 12 reflected upon the integrity of the present spirit and aims of a vast majority of our fellow citizens, and used intemperate and unjustified language, which Haverford College repudiates.[27]

Apparently, neither the faculty nor the students raised any protest to this decision. They knew that Cadbury was being given leave with pay and the opportunity of being reinstated in March. Technically, one could not say that he had been dismissed, and the question of tenure was therefore not involved. Many stressed his insensitivity in appearing to speak "for the whole." Since he had annoyed at least some of his colleagues with his strong pacifist stand, the general view seems to have been that he had created the situation. By apparently accepting the board's decision, and keeping a low profile, he helped to confirm this view.

The swiftness with which these events took place and the speed with which his erstwhile friends seemed to be deserting him turned Henry Cadbury into a shaken man. He regretted his strong language, but he did not want to back down abjectly from a principle he still believed right. He had one comrade in adversity to whom he now turned. This was Clarence Pickett, a Friend from Kansas whom Henry had known at the Winona Lake Conferences. Clarence was now a Quaker pastor in the town of Oskaloosa, Iowa. His pacifism was so unpopular there that his house had been painted with yellow stripes, and members of his own meeting had offered to buy a war bond for him to prove his loyalty. Hearing of Henry's troubles Clarence wrote to express sympathy. Henry's response reveals that he was not yet settled in mind about the experience:

> Dear Clarence, Your letter of sympathy was needed and appreciated and I hear you are having troubles of your own. Well, let's "stick it." Of course I don't wish to defend myself. I was said to be intemperate and indiscreet. But as thee says we mostly err on the other side. I am impressed with how different the penalties are for missing the golden mean on its two sides. Overcaution rarely gets what thee and I get.
>
> I am most concern [sic] to convert it all into good—with thy assistance and friendship.[28]

Meanwhile, the Selective Service agents had reported Henry Cadbury to the United States District Attorney, Francis Fisher Kane, as a traitor, and Henry Cadbury was asked to appear at Kane's office to defend himself. Fortunately, Kane took a liberal view of the Espionage Act, and he may also have felt that Haverford's Greek professor had suffered enough.

In the midst of the furor a scholarly article by Henry Cadbury, "The Basis of Early Christian Anti-Militarism," was published in the *Journal of Biblical Literature*, stating that though Jesus made no specific pronouncements on war, the whole tenor of his life and death was a choice of love over force. Recognizing this, the early Christians refused to fight and were willing to accept death rather than to kill: "They did not succeed in demilitarizing the Roman empire. Instead, the church itself was ultimately militarized—and Christian pacifism was left to the dissenting sects. . . . But for the spread of Christian character, ideals and influence, the sword has never been more effective than the non-resistant faith of the ante-Nicene church."[29] The article was acclaimed for its scholarship as well as its message. A professor from the McCormick Theological Seminary in Chicago, George Robinson, wrote to thank Henry Cadbury for writing it and to say he had "enjoyed it as I have seldom enjoyed anything since the war. I wish I might meet you." [30]

Feeling that no one in Philadelphia much wanted to meet him at that point, Henry Cadbury must have found the praise bittersweet.

Throughout the rest of his life, Henry Cadbury reflected on his suspension from Haverford as a turning point in his life. Had it not occurred, he might have gone on quietly teaching at Haverford and never been known outside Quaker circles. But in a deep sense it changed him and shaped his emerging view of himself and of the role of religion in his life. He had never known that he would feel so deeply about pacifism and that he would become—though inadvertently—known as one of the martyrs to academic freedom. The depth of the conviction that led him to take an unpopular stand seemed to well up from the bottom of his being, beyond his conscious choice. The experience of bearing the brunt of so much public anger, and trying not to be angry himself, in turn deepened his sense of conviction and of leading. Taking action, taking a stand, then could be seen as itself a road to spiritual growth. He had helped young men who had an incoherent feeling that they could not kill find service with the AFSC, and through that service articulate an increasingly clear sense of what religious pacifism might mean. He would see himself thereafter as a traveler on that same road. Action, he was to say over and over, could lead to belief and to the nurturing of religious life, as well as belief to action. It was another way of reiterating the Quaker faith that if one takes a step in the light, more light will follow.

The experience was a turning point also in his developing interest in the history of the Society of Friends. The delicate balance between the individual's freedom to seek and articulate the truth—which left unchecked would lead to anarchy—and the group discipline of corporate decision making—which could and often did lead to inertia and conformity—became a theme of his. He himself represented the two tendencies—what one might call the yin and yang of Quakerism. He had grown up in the heart of the Society, eager to please and to conform but harboring a questioning mind and a seeking heart. By vigorously advocating the peace testimony—just what a young Quaker should do—he had somehow overstepped the invisible line between appropriate and inappropriate behavior. To his intense surprise, he found himself in the ranks of the small number of men and women whose prophetic voices had moved the Society forward in such testimonies as the abolition of slavery and the equal treatment of women, but who had suffered at the hands of the Society as a result. Henry Cadbury never saw himself as a radical, but he became interested in the lives of the Quaker radicals of the past and supportive of those of his day, and he nudged the Society forward on many issues. At the same time, his interest in arriving at a true sense of the meeting grew, after the Haverford incident, until it became one of his characteristics. Never again did he risk the accusation of speaking for the group unless he knew that the group was indeed with him.

CHAPTER 4

On Quaker Service

During the summer of 1918, when Henry Cadbury had considered volunteering to work for a year with the newly formed AFSC, Haverford College had discouraged him. Now, abruptly, in November he was forced to take the leave of absence he had once sought. The irony of the situation did not escape him. The positions at 20 South Twelfth Street were already filled, but there was need for someone with Henry Cadbury's gift with words to convert the unfolding story of Quaker service abroad into articles for the Friends publications and other friendly magazines. Henry Cadbury became a volunteer publicist.

The end of the war on November 11 meant that AFSC reconstruction work could begin in earnest. Most of it was located in the Verdun area, where much of the fighting had taken place. Here AFSC workers helped to erect prefabricated houses, to assist in the development of cooperative stores, and to reestablish agriculture. A series of army dumps were turned over to the Quakers for the salvage of useful materials, among them rifle butts, which were literally turned into plowshares. The French government provided the Quakers with groups of German prisoners to assist with this work. Rather than accept free labor, members of the unit kept track of the hours the prisoners put in and later gave the appropriate amount of money as a gift to their families. Elsewhere, Quaker workers ran canteens and hostels for refugees. When the term of service of the original volunteers ended, many decided to stay on for another year, and other Quaker men and women, who had missed work in wartime, volunteered to join.[1]

All of these activities made excellent copy for the *Friend* or the *Nation.* In addition, exciting stories were coming in from the Russian group with which Henry Cadbury had a special affiliation as chair of the AFSC Russian committee. Having spent several years in the village of Buzuluk in the Samara region, the Quaker unit, with its American women volunteers, left before the advancing Bolsheviks, who did not welcome foreign relief teams, and worked in the winter of 1918–19 in Siberia in informal alliance with the American Red Cross, trying to respond to conditions of starvation and of disease.

By the first of January 1919, however, the committee had decided to hire a full-time secretary to handle the publicity among other duties, and Henry Cadbury declined the position because of the uncertainty of his future. He wrote to his brother-in-law Rufus Jones, then briefly in France on AFSC business, to say that he was thinking of volunteering to spend a year as a member of the Reconstruction Unit. He thought it was important for new volunteers to go to see the work through, and he felt that the personal contact would do him good. Lydia Cadbury was willing.[2]

He wrote at about the same time to his Harvard friend and mentor, James Ropes, saying that perhaps he and Lydia Cadbury would spend the semester in Cambridge if there was scholarly work for him to do. Ropes wrote back that he would welcome Henry Cadbury's help with the task of editing the texts of Acts for the commentary which F. J. Foakes-Jackson and Kirsopp Lake, New Testament scholars, had undertaken as part of a monumental study on the beginnings of Christianity. Neither it nor any other jobs Ropes could think of would be very remunerative, he warned, and rents were high in Cambridge. Nevertheless, Henry and Lydia Cadbury would be warmly welcomed if they came.[3]

In the end, Henry Cadbury decided against going either to France or to Cambridge. Instead, he stayed at Haverford, lectured, volunteered at the AFSC, and wrote voluminously. He continued with his popular articles on conscientious objection to war. One of these, "Conscientious Objectors in Europe," appearing in *Young Democracy* that spring, was a compilation of information about the conscientious objectors in Russia, Holland, and England. Most of his energy, however, went into writing a remarkable book, *National Ideals in the Old Testament*, published by Scribner's the following year. In a relatively short volume of essays, some of them already published, written in a clear and popular style, Henry Cadbury undertook nothing less than a survey of the entire history of the Jewish people from the exodus to the time of the Maccabees, emphasizing the effect of their evolving national ideas, as articulated by the prophets, on that history. Historical theories had rested on the supernatural, the military, and more recently the economic analysis of events, Cadbury argued, but had rarely been approached from the point of view of collective human idealism: "Ideals as well as expectations of profit have guided the course of events and animated national conduct. Providence has found expression through patriot and prophet, and through the developing experience of nations, no less than by miracle and military intervention. History must be interpreted spiritually as well as materially, naturally as well as supernaturally."[4]

Tracing the revolutionary fervor of the people of the exodus, the impact upon their nomadic values of settling among the Canaanites, the consequent development of a sense of turf, then of the institutions of monarchy and war, Henry Cadbury put his chief emphasis on those prophets, who were far ahead of their own time and were seen as treasonable in their day:

> And it is the same quality—a neutrality toward parties and an insistence on principles—that gave the prophets an aloofness even from national partisanship and an almost international viewpoint. Gradually and incompletely, yet in striking degree, the prophets surpassed even the claims of patriotism. As a god of justice, Jehovah seemed to them superior to national prejudices and partisan. He was no respecter of persons. His covenant was not a preferential treaty. By their own superpatriotism the prophets contributed to a supernational religion. Frequently, as we have said, this neutrality appeared in the eyes of their opponents as nothing less than rank treason, but as a higher loyalty it created in the prophets the highest ideals of national allegiance and service.[5]

Among the prophets about whom Henry Cadbury wrote was Jeremiah, "The Unpopular Patriot." His article on Jeremiah, which appeared in the *World Tomorrow* in October 1918, just when Haverford was in uproar against him, appears startlingly apropos:

> Upon Jeremiah there fell the unique sorrow—the sorrow of the unpopular patriot. Sharing all the suffering of his fellow citizens in the ravages of war and siege, even to the extent of voluntary self denial, he must bear besides the intolerable burden of an outcast, misunderstood and unheeded, maltreated and abused, and above all, falsely accused of disloyalty and treason.[6]

He also wrote about Amos, who preached against both the atrocities of war and the atrocities of peacetime, including the exploitation of foreign peoples and of lower classes at home. In this essay, "Ruthless Abroad and at Home," published in the *World To-*

morrow after it had been rejected by *Biblical World,* he drew analogies to the current day:

> In international affairs the same lust of conquest, the same relentless vengeance to the bitter end, the same cold cruelty in the name of military necessity, and national interest, continue, and in the social life—greed, oppression, luxury, and indifference to the interests of the poor. Nations still gladly condemn in other nations what they condone in their own history and in their allies. . . . And organized religion is still often merely the ally of the government and of the industrial status quo, more concerned to serve Caesar and Mammon than to "render unto God those things that are God's." It still shelters the self-satisfied, comfortable classes "who are at ease in Zion", but "are not grieved for the affliction of Joseph", while it strives to silence moral criticism or to exile into obscurity as traitors the God-sent prophets who compare injustice within a nation to the universally condemned sins of its foes.[7]

Another prophet, Hosea, had a message for today, he believed, in his call to a higher loyalty, a message of love: "Justice must be supplemented by mercy, law by love, reason by affection. . . . International law must be transformed into international love." President Wilson had recently called for the same standard of conduct between nations as between individuals, Cadbury commented. Surely this was a fulfillment of the prophecy.[8]

It was a young man's book, full of a young man's fervor and moral earnestness, but had touches of that graceful wit which was to come. In a chapter on the Book of Jonah he commented that the incident of the whale had overshadowed the main point of the writer—Jonah's overzealous nationalism, which made him wish not to convert but to destroy the city of Nineveh. Cadbury called the tale a "Cartoon of Nationalism." Even those who took the whale story literally seemed to sense the underlying comic message: "Even those who accept the story of the Book of Jonah as literally true often take it scarcely seriously, but with a smile at the submarine experiences of the ill-starred prophet."[9]

Published in the spring of 1920, the book was well received in scholarly circles. The *American Journal of Theology* reviewed it favorably, and Karl Budde, an internationally known Old Testament scholar praised it: "The book is indeed timely; it has never been as necessary to emphasize the relationship between national and religious ideals as it is today, and in that you have succeeded, it seems to me, in a refreshing and healing manner. . . . I am amazed at your total mastery of O.T. research and the delicate appropriate judgments concerning its problems you develop here."[10]

News that Henry Cadbury might be available for a new teaching post was meanwhile spreading through the academic community during the early months of 1919. In February, Rufus Jones had an inquiry about Henry Cadbury's teaching ability, along with the question of whether his pacifism was "offensive." In mid-March, just before the deadline for Haverford's decision to act upon his earlier resignation, Henry Cadbury received an offer from Andover Theological Seminary in Cambridge to become assistant professor of New Testament for the academic year 1919–20.[11]

To be in Cambridge, where he could work with the finest scholars on New Testament research and have available to him one of the best libraries in the country, was an exciting prospect. It meant that the obscure Quaker scholar was gaining national recognition. Harvard University, with which the Andover Seminary was affiliated, had no pacifist background. Indeed, some of its theologians had been active in war work. Yet the value placed on academic freedom seemed absolute.

Henry Cadbury was, moreover, sure from the attitude of the president of Haverford and some members of the board that the passage of time had not diminished the anger felt against him for his fiery letter to the *Public Ledger*. He believed he should forestall "the decision on my previous resignation, which if I may judge from the attitude of the president of the college and some other members of the board, would have been against my retention, even for the remainder of my unexpired term of service." [12]

He therefore wrote to inform the Board of Managers that he had accepted the Andover position and that they were free to consider this as a new letter of resignation, "unless you believe it to the advantage of the college to act upon my earlier offer to resign upon the basis suggested when that offer was made." Although he may still have regretted the language he had used in the *Public Ledger*, Henry Cadbury was by this time sure that Haverford would eventually be embarrassed by the charge that it had violated academic freedom in placing him on leave the fall before, and he wanted to give the Board of Managers an opportunity to refuse to accept the original resignation and thus clear Haverford's good name:

> I have no personal desire to prevent such a decision, nor to take the matter out of your hands, but rather to offer you the opportunity to avert the unjust criticism which might have been brought upon the college by a disposition that you could have made of my case as postponed from your meeting in the Eleventh Month. Of course I have no desire willfully to cut myself off from service to the college and to the ideals of a liberal religious education which your Board has cherished for Haverford and for the Society of Friends.[13]

President Comfort, however, chose to interpret Henry Cadbury's acceptance of Andover's one-year offer as grounds for severing his connections with Haverford, and the college moved to accept his original resignation. The case, as Henry Cadbury predicted, became famous and was included in a study of church attitudes in wartime, *Preachers Present Arms.*[14]

A former student of Henry Cadbury's, William Henry Chamberlin, wrote about the incident in his *Confessions of an Individualist*, published in 1940:

> The letter would have been generally recognized as elementary commonsense ten years, or even one year later. But the mood in America at the time was suggestive of a Soviet purge or a Nazi pogrom. . . . A chorus of vituperation was raised against Henry Cadbury, and Haverford, to its shame, bowed to the mob sentiment and let him go. This would certainly have seemed to be an issue on which a Friends college should have stood by a pacifist professor, even at the cost of a little, temporary unpopularity. Fortunately, Dr. Cadbury's subsequent academic advancement was not adversely affected by this incident.[15]

Haverford did not apologize for its action, and when *Preachers Present Arms* was being prepared in 1932, it still refused to comment on the incident. But Henry Cadbury never held a grudge and continued close to his old alma mater and his many friend on campus.

With the decision now taken, the Cadburys prepared to move to Cambridge, subletting their house at 3 College Circle and renting a house at 1075 Massachusetts Avenue in Cambridge. Henry Cadbury took part in the Haverford Summer School in June, and the Cadburys spent July at Back Log Camp and August at South China, Maine, the summer home of Rufus and Elizabeth Jones, where they rented a cottage on the lake. Betty was now a bouncing two-year-old, and by the end of the summer Lydia Cadbury was expecting a second child.

Lydia Cadbury had attended Wellesley College and was familiar with nearby Cambridge, whereas Henry Cadbury had spent three years at Harvard full time and had been back and forth frequently. Nevertheless, they were Philadelphia Quakers, and they felt a bit strange at first so far from Philadelphia and its Quaker institutions. Where were they to send Betty to school, Lydia Cadbury wondered? There was a pastoral Friends Meeting that met in Roxbury and a small silent Quaker meeting that gathered in the Phillips Brooks house on the Harvard campus. This group welcomed the Cadburys with joy and provided a nucleus for their social life.

Henry Cadbury settled into his one-year assignment at the Andover Theological Seminary with ease. The affiliation with Harvard Divinity School was working well, the new library was built, and the faculty functioning as a team. Joining Andover at the same time as Henry Cadbury was Willard L. Sperry, the pastor of the Central Congregational Church of Boston, a liberal churchman and a scholar. Professor John Platner, a church historian, was dean, Professor William Arnold, who had been there earlier, still taught Hebrew, and Daniel Evans, trained in theology in Germany and England, completed the small Andover faculty. At Harvard Divinity School was Henry Cadbury's professor and friend, James Ropes; William Fenn, still dean; George LaPiana, a liberal Catholic who taught early church history; George and Edward Moore, brothers, the former a Presbyterian and the latter a Congregationalist; James Jewett, professor of Arabic and Islamic history; Henry Wilder Foote, assistant dean; and Kirsopp Lake, Winn Professor of Ecclesiastical History. Of British background, Dr. Lake had taught at the University of Leiden and was well known as an authority of early Christian literature. His undertaking, with F. J. Foakes-Jackson, of a monumental, five-volume history of the beginnings of Christianity was causing great interest throughout the world of New Testament scholarship.[16]

Aside from teaching his courses, Henry Cadbury began work with Kirsopp Lake on the *Beginnings of Christianity*, concentrating on the Preface of Luke for the second volume. He also published several scholarly articles. "Luke—Translator or Author?" appeared in 1920 in the *American Journal of Theology*. On the basis of his increasing knowledge of Luke's style he demonstrated that the unknown author of the gospel known as Luke had composed his gospel, using certain passages from Mark and another lost source, which scholars hypothesized and called Q, but adding material of his own. He disputed the theory, held chiefly by Charles Torrey of Yale, that Luke had merely translated the gospel into Greek from written sources in Aramaic, the spoken language of Jesus and his disciples. Although Torrey was older than Henry Cadbury and spoke witheringly of his decades of experience, most biblical scholars felt that Henry Cadbury had the best of the debate that surfaced at a meeting of the Society of Biblical Literature in 1920 and again in 1930. The article drew praise from the German scholars, including Adolf von Harnack.[17]

He also continued his series of popular articles with a piece for the *Messenger of Peace* (May 1920) in which he denounced the economic blockade as a substitute for war. He had called for economic sanctions in 1915, but now that the Quaker relief workers were reporting that the results of the Allied blockade were hunger and disease, especially among children, he had decided that "the economic weapon was as cruel as any bomb or gas or cannon that military science has ever dreamed of." Carrying this new point of view to its logical conclusion, he denounced the industrial strike as a means of coercion and a form of violence in a debate with Norman Thomas published in the *World Tomorrow:* "It may be that our attitude toward strikes can be changed only by similar developments . . . you will grant that we have not yet seen the possibilities of the industrial strike, as we had not yet seen the possibilities of the international boycott in 1915." [18]

Norman Thomas answered that violence was already inherent in the economic system, that organized labor had made great strides against the exploitation of children and women with the help of the strike, and that if this method was withdrawn, there was a moral obligation to substitute another. He was evidently surprised by Henry Cadbury's position. Henry Cadbury was known for his mildly socialist leanings and his concern for economic oppression. But his evolving religious pacifism was reinforcing his belief that conversion, not coercion, was the method of Jesus. It was the transformation of individuals, one by one, that would ultimately bring an end to war and to injustice, and shortcuts would bring more harm than good.

News of the results of the Allied blockade of Germany and Russia had affected him deeply. During the summer of 1919, three women representing the American Friends Service Committee—Jane Addams of Hull House fame, her friend Alice Hamilton, and Carolena M. Wood—had entered Germany along with some British Friends and had come home with harrowing reports of mass starvation among the children. The Quakers had begun plans for a small relief operation to meet this need when they were asked by Herbert Hoover, then chairman of the American Relief Administration, to undertake distribution of food among all German children. During the winter he spent in Cambridge, Henry Cadbury received reports of the AFSC's efforts to gear up for this mass feeding, at the same time he read letters from his German scholar friends deploring conditions in the Fatherland. Having objected to an orgy of hate against the German people, he was now seeing the bitter results.

Though their life in Cambridge was pleasant, both Cadburys continued to think of Philadelphia as home. They had planned to travel to Moorestown on December 1, 1919, to help Joel and Anna Cadbury celebrate their fiftieth wedding anniversary but had to cancel their plans when Lydia had a miscarriage. Henry Cadbury paid his parents a visit in the spring during Yearly Meeting week and attended some of the sessions. It was evidently his first visit since the Haverford crisis. "I think it is a pity he feels sensitive about showing himself," his mother wrote to Lydia Cadbury.[19] Henry Cadbury still evidently thought he might be called back to Haverford. When Andover asked him to stay another year, he consulted Rufus Jones, who urged him to stay in Cambridge.

On his trips home, Henry Cadbury visited the AFSC offices and began to discuss his desire to play some role in the German child-feeding mission. Since he could not accept a year's assignment, it was decided that he should go to Germany for the summer of 1920 and combine efforts to write publicity articles about the work with personal outreach to the German intellectual community, which seemed very responsive to the Quaker message.

On June 10, therefore, Henry Cadbury sailed for Germany aboard the S.S. *Rotterdam,* having left Lydia Cadbury to close the house in Cambridge and get herself and Betty to Back Log. Sharing his cabin and sleeping on the upper bunk was Francis R. Bacon, a thirty-two-year-old architect from Haddonfield, New Jersey, who was leaving his wife and two small boys to direct the AFSC work in Poland. The two explored the ship together and shared a table in the dining room. Henry Cadbury wrote a book review for the *Nation* and tried to practice his rusty German on the way over but was slightly seasick and felt "rather dull and dopey." He found a young Harvard professor aboard with a more enlightened attitude toward the war and Germany than he had encountered generally in Harvard Yard and enjoyed several spirited conversations with him. There was also a German family, a Dutch family, and a Japanese journalist with whom the two became acquainted. Francis Bacon wore his AFSC uniform and captured all eyes. People asked about the AFSC star and were intrigued to hear about the Quaker projects.

> It is interesting how the Friends work gives us an entree with various nationalities and at the same time baffles all national partisans by its unintelligible neutrality. A Frenchman knows of our French work but can't understand our German relief, a German-American blesses our present efforts but is amazed that we worked in France all through the war. So the Russian and the Polander both are half credulous half amused at our ideas and experiences. Francis and I go around together but one is bound for a friendly, one an enemy nation.

While they were at sea word had come over the wireless that the Republican party had nominated Warren G. Harding and Calvin Coolidge. "I hope this will kill the Republican party and its reactionaries," Henry Cadbury wrote tersely to Lydia Cadbury.[20]

After their queasy passage, it was good to see the White Cliffs of Dover on the morning of the nineteenth and to land that night at Boulogne sur le Mer. They went by boat train to Paris, Henry Cadbury enjoying the "perfect villages hidden in trees, the red tiled houses and church spires" and the fields of grain and poppies. There were signs of war also—the rotting shelters of British army camps, the rails torn up and stations bombed.[21]

In Paris, Francis Bacon insisted that they visit the Louvre and other sites of artistic and architectural interest. At the AFSC headquarters, they were briefed on Quaker work in Germany by J. Edgar Rhoads, who was now in charge. He told them that the Quakers were feeding 580,000 children six days a week. The feeding was known as Quaker Speisung and was already famous throughout Germany. Some 15 to 25 percent of the German children were undernourished and thus entitled to the meals. The AFSC was short of workers in Germany and might need to divert Francis Bacon from Poland and Henry Cadbury from his university contacts.

Slightly unsettled by this news, the two continued their Paris sightseeing, Francis Bacon insisting that they not only visit Notre Dame but climb to the roof. After a visit to the reopened markets they took a train to Frankfurt-on-Main, passing through many war ruins. In Frankfurt they were greeted by Quaker workers and established in a hotel room. The next day Francis Bacon led Henry Cadbury on a quick trip through the old city before they were taken on a guided tour of Quaker feeding sites. They saw three the first morning, the third called the Kurfurstenschule:

> Here the children were much worse clothed than before and were more obviously under-sized rachitic and thin. The faces had a colorless look, were V-shaped and several children of six were shorter than Betty is at 3. Here also is one of the kitchens—as each kitchen provides several schools. This one cooks for 2,400 children in all . . . each child gets a half-litre of soup, and all schools that day had the same bean and pea soup. The principal took great pride in showing us the school—the classrooms and office and near the kitchen the great cellar vault in which the children were packed tight while the airplanes were over the city. The principal, like all others, was hopeless about the future. In his own class he said 80% of the children are undernourished and many have died.

In the afternoon, they visited Offenbach, a factory town, where 3,500 children were fed. The town was too poor to supply bowls so the children arrived with frying pans, saucepans, bowls, canteens, and every conceivable vessel to get their rations. One little girl asked permission to thank the two for her meal, and a horde of children followed them across town to another feeding station, making them feel a bit like modern Pied Pipers.[22]

At the second Offenbach station, a transformed barn, one of the cooks said that the child-feeding was the first beautiful thing since the war. These children were far worse than in Frankfurt. "It is pitiful to see two bowlegged children bumping against each other as they waddle along hand in hand, holding each other up as best they can," Henry Cadbury wrote Lydia. "One child who is too weak to go to school is carried by its mother."[23]

From Offenbach, the travelers went to Berlin and stayed in a hotel where many British and American Quaker workers were in residence. Henry Cadbury again was taken on a tour of Quaker Speisung centers, in one of which the children were being fed chocolate soup. Through the American Institute, he began to make appointments with German biblical scholars. Adolf von Harnack asked gruffly, "Why do Americans want to talk with us before they have made peace?" He was affable to Henry Cadbury, however, asking about his Harvard colleagues and saying that the Quaker work was making a deep impression on German hearts and minds. He also praised Henry Cadbury's article "The Basis of Early Christian Anti-Militarism."[24]

His host at the American Institute, however, was more frank about his anti-American feelings. He told Henry Cadbury that the only atrocity of the late war was the Allied blockade of Germany, that they were glad that the *Lusitania* had been sunk, though sorry about the loss of lives, and that he personally felt betrayed by the anti-German attitudes of the American church. Were not both churches equally to blame, Henry Cadbury asked. No, the American church was much worse, the professor said.[25]

This was the first of many such mirror-image views of the war Henry Cadbury was to hear during the summer. A week later Ernst von Dobschütz, who received him enthusiastically, told him that "the Kaiser had been falsely accused and condemned, that he was a man of peace, and that the present German government was too weak to govern." He hoped for a return to effective government by Bolshevism and the reaction that followed. He also blamed the Jews economically and the Catholics politically for Germany's present troubles.[26]

There were, however, other voices. The editor of the *Frankfurter-Zeitung* had remained practically a pacifist through the war, and his paper was considered the *Manchester Guardian* of Germany. He was giving the Quaker work a great deal of support. On July 4, Henry Cadbury and Francis Bacon attended a meeting of the German branch of the Fellowship of Reconciliation and found there a group of German working-class people committed to peace. The next day Henry Cadbury met Hertha Kraus, a twenty-three-year-old woman with a Ph.D. in economics, working full time for the Quakers. She took him to see a poor family, in which three of the children were sick with tuberculosis, then to supper at a typical German restaurant, where the meal consisted of noodles and beans, and told him how during the war they had had to survive on turnips. Yet she was not bitter.

A few days later, Henry Cadbury joined a Quaker retreat at Tombach, near Thuringen, in beautiful mountain country, where a number of Germans with Quaker sympathies were present. Some were pastors who had rebelled from the church either because of its formalism or because of its position on the war and were now trying to preach Christianity to the working class, whom the church was not reaching. Some said they were already practicing Quaker principles when they heard about Friends although they had not known such people existed. Some had become interested through the reports of Germans who had been visited by Friends when they were in British prisoner of war camps. One German woman had felt impelled by sheer conscience and humanity to aid English prisoners of war and had thus begun to correspond with Quakers. One was a pacifist, one a doctor who had discovered the power of silence with his patients. And so it went.

Henry Cadbury had been in low spirits during his first days in Germany. He was homesick, and the lack of mail from home made him feel cut off from his beloved family. His German did not seem to be improving, and the uncertainty about his exact assignment weighed on him. Francis Bacon had been a link with Philadelphia, and when he left on July 5 for Leipzig, taking with him his Hammond typewriter on which Henry Cadbury had enjoyed composing letters, he was desolate. He felt that the decision to assign Francis Bacon to Germany rather than Poland was high-handed and wrote to say as much to Rufus Jones.[27] The gloom of the Germans with whom he spoke and the condition of the children added to his depression. He heard a bewildering variety of opinions from Germans and saw many rallies on the streets.

Soon, however, he was immersed in his publicity work, interviewing, writing, translating, and sending manuscripts back to Philadelphia, and his spirits rose. He traveled, visiting both Quaker feeding stations and biblical scholars in Leipzig, Dresden, Marburg, and Hamburg. His German was improving; when he attended a Lutheran church he found he could follow the simple service. There were too many trains to catch and not enough time to do laundry. "I have fully decided I do not want to engage permanently in the business of a traveling salesmen," he wrote playfully to Lydia. But for the time being it was fun.[28]

Everywhere he went, everyone knew about the Quakers. He wrote an article about it for the Quaker publications:

> What is the cause of this gratuitous advertising, it is hard to tell. Perhaps the name itself with its foreign Q has even greater advertising power than in America. Perhaps the energetic Quaker Oats company has already prepared the way. Certainly many fantastic ideas are sure to arise about us. Do we too feed the children mostly oats? Do we dress like William Penn? How many wives have we? But in general the ideals of Friends are understood with surprising accuracy . . . they are coming to see that there is no pill under the marmalade and that even in enemy country—for we are still at war, are we not—there are men and women of good will who can respond to the need of innocent children in the spirit of the Good Samaritan.[29]

When a reporter from the *Philadelphia Ledger* showed up and insisted on interviewing him he was amused. "He wanted to know all about me so perhaps my pro-Germanism will appear on the front page again."[30]

As the pace of his summer picked up, more and more of his letters to Lydia Cadbury were in the form of a journal, which she was to circulate to other members of the family and then preserve. Henry Cadbury apologized for the impersonal tone of his correspondence: "It is partly because I wanted them to serve as a diary of everything, partly because I want one letter to do for all my folks, and chiefly because my personal feelings and private life have become subconscious." He was clearly, however, in increasingly good spirits. In each city he now visited the art galleries and cathedrals eagerly. One constant source of interest was collecting stamps for his brother Ben in Moorestown. As the time to leave Berlin approached, he longed to have another two weeks so he could visit still another art gallery, as well as spend more time in the library and call upon four additional Bible scholars.

> My days in Germany are numbered, but I want to say how great satisfaction I have had in being here for this short time. It is inconceivable that I should have ever thought it not worthwhile. Of course afterwards one's natural inertia seems strange. But the idealism and spirit of this

fine group of workers whom I have seen at the various centers and also together at the monthly meetings, the earnest response of the German people, the personal contact with Germans in the Universities and elsewhere, all these make it very worthwhile.[31]

On August 12 he sailed from Hamburg to Dover and went to London, where he was to speak at the All Friends Conference held at Devonshire House in Bishopsgate, then headquarters of the London Yearly Meeting. At the Great Eastern Hotel on Liverpool Street he joined a bevy of friends and relatives, Rufus, Elizabeth, and Mary Hoxie Jones and Carroll and Ann Brown among them. Two English Cadburys, Barrow and Geraldine, played host and hostess. Henry Cadbury was glad to see them all, but he was tired, had a sore throat from the London smoke, and was beginning to long for home and Lydia. The depression that had stalked his early summer days seemed to threaten him again. Rather than going on a walking trip in the Alps in September, he decided to return home on an earlier passage.

Meanwhile, there was the conference to attend. It was the first such gathering, forerunner of a series of Friends world conferences to be held in succeeding years. Henry Cadbury had been asked to head up a study commission on "The Life of the Society of Friends in View of Present Demands," and he reported on this topic on August 17. In addition to a scholarly survey of the various problems facing American Friends, he talked about the Society's failure in upholding the peace testimony with sufficient force and clarity during the war. He had spent the summer in Germany with the "madman," as people had called the average German: "I will not deny that he is, or at least was, mad. But his madness sounds identical with the bedlam of so-called sanity in which my own nerves have been racked for years in my home across the way. It is my interest to discover the cause of insanity and know how it can be avoided and cured." His experience in Germany had persuaded him that Christ's method could bring the response of sanity, he said.[32]

"People generally seemed to like my paper," he wrote Lydia. The British Friends were on the whole more politically liberal in their views than the Americans, some of whom voiced opposition to the League of Nations because of its use of force. There were many initial disagreements, but the conference ended well: "Divisions of opinion vanished and all was loving and eager. The American Friends raised a fund for buying G.F.'s (George Fox's) journal MS for Devonshire House. We adopted a number of documents—one to all Friends, one to the people of Ireland, one to the League of Nations, one to governments and one to the council of action of the British Labor Party! The latter was to endorse their desire for peace." From London, Henry Cadbury traveled to Oxford, where he attended a Friends Social Order Conference and again spoke. "The Americans are many of them horrified by the advanced economic views held by the British, and equally horrified by their indifference to smoke and drink," he wrote Lydia. "One of the best papers last night was given by a woman . . . who is a public smoker. Imagine the prejudice against her of a WCTU evangelical Friend from Kansas."[33]

He went from Oxford to a Young Friends conference at Jordans, his mood continuing to rise though he remained chilled to the bone by the damp British weather. By the end of his stay he was writing to Lydia that "I have felt very much at home in England. The English Friends are particularly keen because they think I was more of a C.O. than most Americans."[34]

Perhaps he now at last felt vindicated for his letter to the *Public Ledger* and the ensuing uproar at Haverford. His summer in Germany had convinced him of the madness of war, and the British Friends had taken him to their hearts. A chapter had ended. He was ready to return and plunge wholeheartedly into his new scholarly life in Cambridge.

CHAPTER 5

The Life of a Scholar

Henry Cadbury returned to the United States eager to share with his fellow citizens his impression that the method of reconciliation had worked with the German people, many of whom had seen the Quaker service as a form of olive branch extended by all Americans. The melting away of suspicion, distrust, and recriminations in the face of openness and generosity was, he felt, proof that the method of Jesus could work. If the American people could be persuaded to lay aside the remnants of their anti-German attitudes and contribute to a just peace, the process would be accelerated.

He had scarcely reached Back Log Camp for a short rest and reunion with Lydia and Betty when he had his first opportunity to begin this sharing. He was invited to write a major article for the *Survey* on Quaker work in Germany. His article, "A Nationwide Adventure in Friendship," was published on November 27, 1920. It described the effort to provide assistance in a way that was not demeaning to those who received it, involved maximum local participation, and expressed goodwill in deeds rather than words. Much of the article concentrated on specific German responses: the thieves who returned a large store of goods when they learned that they had taken Quaker Speisung; the Jews who were touched that the Quakers provided kosher food for their children; the pan-German professor who changed his tune and began to see hope for world cooperation. He quoted one German New Testament scholar: "The war of 1914 and the following years will be represented in later times as the most awful war of the world's history. But concerning the work of relief which has been inaugurated on a tremendous scale after the war can the historian say, 'such has history never witnessed before.'"[1]

The article was warmly received. He wrote a second article for *La Follette's Magazine* and was interviewed by the *Boston Globe* and the *New York Times.* Unfortunately, the latter article upset some German-Americans in Philadelphia, and Wilbur Thomas wrote to Henry Cadbury to suggest that all such pieces must first be cleared by the Information Department of the AFSC. Henry explained mildly that such clearance was not always possible when the article was not one's own but agreed to do what he could to prevent it happening again.[2]

Another direct consequence of his summer in Germany was his burgeoning correspondence with the German professors he had visited. He sent them books, articles, and food. He assisted Paul Fieburg to raise money in the United States for the publication of a book in Germany, *Jesus' Sermon on the Mount,* sought an American publisher for several articles by Karl Budde, and kept up the spirits of elderly Adolf Julicher of Marburg, who was losing his eyesight and had to work on his documents with overcoat and mittens because there was no coal. "But I must not complain, since I'm counting on progress, although perhaps not in my lifetime. . . . If one person has encouraged me to bear up and carry on as if it were really peace, it is you, dear colleague,"[3] Julicher wrote to him. He also corresponded with Ernest von Dobschütz, with whom he was working on a revision of Wettstein (and who continued to worry about Bolshevism), with Otto Budde, Karl's son, who was helping to collect stamps for Ben Cadbury, and with others.

In the fall of 1921 Henry Cadbury was asked to deliver the opening lecture at Andover Theological Seminary. Thinking still about the failure of the Christian church to take a stand on the war, he chose as his topic "The Social Translation of the Gospel." In this piece, published in the *Harvard Theological Review* for January 1922, were many of the themes he was to develop in later years. To apply the ethical teachings of Jesus (understood in their broadest terms) to our day—to make a social translation—we must first study them in terms of his day:

> We believe that Jesus' attitude was to the problems of his time as the Christian attitude should be to the problems of our time. But his is an algebraic proportion of four terms: $a : b = c : x$; and the unknown quantity we are seeking, namely the true Christian's attitude today, can only be found if the other three terms are known.
>
> So these three are the first objects of study:—the problems of Jesus' time, the attitude of Jesus to them, the problems of our time. Many who attempt to translate the Gospel socially are satisfied to study the last of these three, but the other two factors, involving as they do research

into ancient history and in the evangelic records are at least equally important.[4]

To understand Jesus and his message, it was therefore necessary to understand the culture in which he grew up, the language in which he expressed his thoughts, the way his mind worked, and his assumptions as a Jew steeped in the traditions of the Jewish teachers of his day. His differences from other teachers lay in his emphasis not so much on goal as on method and the need of choosing pure means to obtain a pure end. The story of his temptation, the story of the cross, illustrate his rejection of evil means as a way out:

> This method of Jesus in dealing with evil was, in a word, the over-coming of evil with good. Desiring as he did not the punishment of wrong, nor the defense of right, as we use these terms, but the making right of him who is wrong, he exhibited a strange contrast with the methods of modern law, industry and politics. He was able to draw the line in both his teaching and conduct between rebuke and reviling, between judgment and censure. The present day methods of dealing with evil Jesus habitually eschews. They are forms of coercion, by law, by violence, by external moral authority, by propaganda. Jesus relied on forms of conversion, by rebuke, by persuasion, by individual and inward conviction, and by love. Love is still the best expression of Jesus's chief social principle, though perhaps a less hackneyed word is reconciliation.[5]

Some theologians had evaded the implications of Jesus' teaching, especially during the war, because of his eschatology, his belief in the imminent apocalypse. Henry Cadbury disagreed strongly: "This war has at least taught us to be a little more sympathetic with the apocalyptic mind. The theory of progress as a slow moving development—a kind of escalator forever leading us upward—has been badly jolted." He believed that Jesus intended his followers to live by millennial standards here and now: "Other people may have other standards, but the Christian is to live as though the Kingdom of God had come."[6]

One aspect of the social translation of the Bible was a reinterpretation of Christian pacifism. This Henry Cadbury clearly believed to be his special task. The errors of the church, the errors of members of his own religious society, in declaring a moratorium on Christian principles during the war were very much alive in his mind. Now that peace had come, and with it disillusionment over the results of war, it was time to press on with the task of educating the church and the public so that never again would war be condoned. He used his many opportunities to speak and to write to hammer at this theme. Other scholars used their leisure time to work crossword puzzles, write murder mysteries, or go bird-watching. Henry Cadbury worked for peace.

One constant theme was the stand of first-century Christians against war, a stand based not on any specific text of Jesus' sayings but rather on the whole meaning of his life and death. In "The Christian Verdict on War," he discussed the Christian arguments of using war for a good end: "Or war may be called a method of maintaining justice. But Jesus is . . . indifferent to abstract rights. The reason is that he cared more for righteousness. He was more concerned that men should do justice than that they should get it." [7]

Another article on the same theme was "The Conscientious Objector of Patmos," He wrote of the scholarly conjecture that the Revelation of John, written by a first-century Christian exiled to hard labor on the desolate island of Patmos, was an allegory of the conflict between the Roman empire and the Christians who were in conflict with the state for the sake of conscience. That conflict began over the Roman demand that the Christians worship the emperor as God. This the Christians would not do, and their subsequent martyrdom was an eye-opening, today we might say a radicalizing, experience:

> The book of Revelation is a witness to this new evolution in Christian self-consciousness. It is a contemporary record of the transition of a group of idealists into radical political solidarity. It is the autobiography of a rebel spirit in the making. The minor conflict on a single matter of conscience at once opened Christian eyes to a fundamental problem. The conscientious objector was exposed to a rapid education. He examined the whole system under which he had been living so carelessly at ease. His new experience set it in a new light. Not for personal reasons, not because of personal hardship but because his eyes were opened, John saw the basis on which the system rested. The revolt which at first touched one question spread to others. Evil, which he had never seen before, was now revealed to his eyes. The commercial pomp, the imperial control, the whole brutal fabric of civilization stood condemned. Only the most radical transmutation could set things right.

The Christians, who during the time of Jesus had lived at peace with the powers that be, were now seen and prosecuted as radicals. The common people were taught to believe that they were guilty of atheism, murder, and sexual promiscuity. These are the charges always leveled at radicals (and were now being charged to Russian Bolsheviks, Henry Cadbury added in a footnote), "and yet the pure and idealistic enthusiasm, the warm social fellowship and the high morality of the Christians maintained its powerful witness and finally they won the victory. Then the patient and persevering spirit of the martyrs, the testimony of Jesus, and the word of God which is the sword of the spirit prevailed."[8]

Believing that the sword of the spirit must be the basis of a true pacifism, Henry Cadbury objected to some of the glib panaceas for war being proposed during the early period of postwar disillusion. The concept of establishing peace by outlawing aggressive war belonged to this category. What was needed instead, he said, in an article, "An Inadequate Pacifism," "is a Christian pacifism that recognizes . . . the guilt of both aggressor and defender because of the immorality of their method."[9]

Meanwhile, on a more scholarly level, he was continuing to explore the new concept of form criticism, or *Formgeschichte,* which the German scholars were developing. In an article published in the *Harvard Theological Review* in 1923, "Between Jesus and the Gospels," he introduced that concept to English-speaking theologians in a review of three books recently published by Karl Schmidt, Rudolf Bultmann, and Martin Dibelius. Although each of the three scholars took a slightly different approach, they all believed that the gospels were put together several decades after the death of Jesus from a common treasure of oral material. This was not in narrative, chronological order; instead, it was made up of discrete self-sufficient sayings, parables, myths, and miracle stories. Each tale or anecdote had been through a process of change and refinement as it was passed along orally, used by an apostle to make a point, translated from language to language, or told in a religious service. They might be likened to precious stones upon a beach, shaped by the pounding of the ocean. The gospel writers had reached into this common treasure trove to compose the gospels and had put the anecdotes together more or less at random. Mark, the first gospel writer, had not written in order. The German writers believed that by carefully identifying the literary form of each discrete piece of gospel material, it was more possible to trace its evolution and thus more nearly to make out its origin. The method was similar to that of the archaeologist, who by digging through strata is able to surmise the form of an earlier civilization from examining shards of its more recent past.

Although not all theologians would be inclined to follow the painstaking methods of form criticism, the new approach had much to commend it, Henry Cadbury wrote:

> It is important first of all to recognize that the gospel matter has a history. It is too easy to forget that history does not write itself, like the

recording thermometer, without human intervention . . . in the case of
the gospels the material was subjected to a rapid series of varied developments. Thus while a study of the origin of the gospels serves to dissi-
pate the greatest of all myths—the myth of a Simon-pure tradition—it
assures us that in believing in the historicity of Jesus we are not following cunningly devised fables. . . . We need not doubt that Jesus was
born, lived and died.[10]

This article established the parameters of much of Henry
Cadbury's subsequent work. He continued to use the methods of
form criticism, not only in his study of New Testament texts but in
attempts to identify old Quaker writings. As time went on he added
another dimension, asking himself what were the motives of the
gospel writers in preserving certain texts and perhaps discarding
others. What apologetic purposes were served? He used the same
methods to understand what materials followers of George Fox
chose to preserve and to edit out of the original manuscripts. And
always he insisted that this approach did not diminish but actually
enhanced the opportunity of recovering in time more of the truth
about the historical Jesus. His careful, painstaking, detectivelike
work in studying probable evolution of the language in the gospels
has continued to inspire other biblical scholars. His form criticism
was a precursor of the literary criticism as it is widely used in Bible
work today.[11]

The publication of "Between Jesus and the Gospels" helped to
cement Henry Cadbury's growing fame. In recognition of his increased contributions, he was named to the New Testament Circle
of the Society of Biblical Literature. His career was given a further
boost when F. J. Foakes-Jackson decided for personal reasons to
withdraw from collaboration with Kirsopp Lake on the *Beginnings
of Christianity* and recommended Henry Cadbury to carry on in his
place with Volumes IV and V.

Having worked with James Ropes on the Book of Acts, and studied it himself, Henry Cadbury wrote much of the commentary that
accompanied the English translation of Acts in Volume IV of this
series and a number of the essays in Volume V. He also did much of
the editing, footnoting, and translating for the two volumes, published in 1933 by Macmillan, and known to theological students
everywhere as "Lake and Cadbury."

He was also busy at this time editing and preparing an index for
a book by former dean Francis G. Peabody. But he missed the joy of
having a book of his own under way. Writing to Rufus Jones to con-
gratulate him on a new book—and to point to a few errors in the
footnotes—he said he wished he were working on a book of his

own. He decided shortly to put together all he now knew about Luke into a new study, using the methods of form criticism. By 1923 he was happily at work.[12]

The writing was a backdrop to the teaching. Henry Cadbury enjoyed his classes at Andover and was not infrequently asked to take classes of his Harvard colleagues. There was also an arrangement with Episcopal Theological Seminary in which students could take classes at Harvard and vice versa. He was refining his Socratic method in the classroom, learning to lead his students to new discoveries by asking a series of questions so adroit that they found themselves giving voice to new thoughts. As he grew more relaxed in the classroom, the wittiness of his lectures grew more pronounced. Though this wit could be barbed, when he criticized arbitrary views or sloppy scholarship, he was generally gentle with students, ready to counsel them not only in their studies but in personal affairs. He never expressed disagreement with his students but seemed to have a real respect for their views, even those that differed markedly from his. Not either/or but both/and was the theme of his classroom.

All of this made him popular. He could not be made a full professor at Andover at first because he was not an ordained minister. Dean Daniel Evans wrote to Rufus Jones privately to inquire whether Henry Cadbury could not become a Congregational minister without violating his Quaker conscience.[13] Since as a Philadelphia Quaker Henry Cadbury had been taught to reject the "hireling ministry," the answer was obviously in the negative. Henry Cadbury was kept on a year-to-year basis. In 1922, a more complete merger of Andover and Harvard was somewhat hastily arranged, and under its terms his future seemed secure.

The Cadburys were beginning to settle into their new life in Cambridge as though it were something more than a temporary exile. On September 5, 1921, Christopher Joel was born. Leah Cadbury stayed with Betty, and Henry Cadbury brought his giggling little daughter to see her mother. While Lydia Cadbury remained in the hospital he was rushed with invitations to go out to dinner and play tennis and still found time to visit his wife and new baby.

The house on Massachusetts Avenue had proved large enough to rent a part of it to Friends, Mabel and Moses Bailey. Since Marguerite Bailey was the same age as Betty this was a congenial arrangement. With the advent of Christopher, however, the Cadburys decided to look for a house to buy. They saw several properties in the late fall and early winter. The search was interrupted when Lydia Cadbury spent January and February in Florida with her two children and her father, but on her return she and Henry decided on a compact dwelling on a quiet street. The house at

7 Buckingham Place was forever known to friends of the Cadburys as Buckingham Palace. There was a room in the basement next to the laundry which Henry Cadbury fixed as a study and three large rooms on the third floor which were used for guests and renters. "We feel, now that we have decided, that it is as iniquitous to let your fancy stray over to another house, or even to contemplate the possibility of another, as to view the various young men that turn up once you are engaged," Lydia Cadbury wrote to her mother-in-law about the purchase.[14]

Henry Cadbury wrote to his father for advice on financing the new house, but neither of his parents saw it. Anna Cadbury, still confined to a wheelchair with arthritis, was going through a period of considerable depression at the time. His father at eighty-five appeared sturdy, but in December of 1922 he became ill and on January 25, 1923, he died suddenly. His wife followed him within thirty-six hours. The family gathered in Moorestown to comfort one another and to make arrangements. Henry Cadbury returned home to Cambridge tired and in low spirits. He had loved both his parents, but there had been a particularly deep bond between mother and son. He had sought her approval despite withholding an essential part of himself. The relationship was a paradigm of his relationship with the world of Philadelphia Quakerism, a bond compounded of conformity and rebellion. When he brought the disapproval of the community upon himself he suffered, turning the anger inward. Here perhaps was one of the roots of his recurring depressions.

The death of their parents brought changes in the Cadbury family. Emma, the younger sister, had been staying home to take care of her mother. Now she was free to go overseas for the AFSC, where she was stationed for fourteen years in Vienna. Ben, the oldest son, was already at work in the family plumbing business and now took over his father's place. John, who worked for the Provident Trust Company and also lived in Moorestown, helped to settle the estate. William, a medical missionary in Canton, China, since 1909, and Elizabeth, married to Rufus Jones, went on as before, though sharing the family grief.

Eventually Henry Cadbury recovered his good spirits, cheered by Lydia Cadbury and by a constant stream of visitors to the new house on Buckingham Place. Mary Hoxie Jones, now a student at Mount Holyoke College, came that first year, bringing a roommate and a friend, all three dressed alike in pleated skirts. Otto Budde visited from Germany. Clarence Pickett was spending the year at Harvard with his wife Lillie and daughters Rachel and Carolyn, and the two families were often together. Traveling Quaker ministers and AFSC staff members came and went. Former Westtown and Haverford students at Harvard were invited to board, paying a small amount for each meal if it were a long-term arrangement. Members of the meeting were often invited for a meal. The hospitable Lydia Cadbury entertained a released World War I peace agitator and employed the dashing wife of another as a temporary maid.

Henry Cadbury's reputation as a public speaker was growing, and with it, a constant barrage of invitations to speak. His special combination of erudition and sparkling, disarming wit increased the demand. In addition to his lectures at Andover, he spoke at the Cambridge meeting forum, at local Congregational churches, and at Boston public gatherings. He was invited to Hampton Institute to lecture to black ministers, to the Chicago Divinity School (where he spent part of one summer), and to Union Theological Seminary. "Sperry asked Bishop McConnell [Francis J. McConnell, the Methodist bishop] the other day what suggestions he had for a speaker at the ministers' week of lectures in April, and McConnell said he would rather hear Henry Cadbury than anyone else he could think of," Lydia Cadbury wrote to Elizabeth Jones.[15]

Although this pace of public speaking was to continue for another fifty years, Henry Cadbury never ceased to dread each occasion. He prepared carefully, often reading a new book in advance of a lecture to be sure that he had something fresh to say. He either wrote out the lecture or made careful notes in a handwriting that was increasingly tiny but clear, including quotations and citations he wanted to make and funny stories he wanted to tell.

To illustrate the care one must take in ensuring accuracy in translation, he told one audience it was often necessary to translate back again into the original language. One scholar of Japanese, who had translated a perfectly sensible sentence from English into that language, was startled when it was turned back into English: "I count it a luck if after standing at the end of a snake I get some whey."

Sometimes he gave the same lecture twice, with additions or subtractions, carefully noting the time and place of each delivery. A number of these speeches were subsequently published, either in scholarly periodicals or in more popular forums such as the *Christian Century*.

In this highly productive period of his life he began to speak and to write about Quaker history. In 1924, when the tercentenary of the birth of the Quaker founder, George Fox, was observed, he was asked to give the William Penn Lecture to young Friends. In this lecture, "Faith of Our Fathers Living Still," he talked about the freshness of Fox's vision, his lack of self-consciousness, and his spontaneity: "The primary need of our day lies not in a better understanding of Quakerism, not in the restatement of Quaker ethics or Quaker theology, but in the discovery of the inner-experience of early Friends."[16]

At about the same time he wrote his first paper for the *Bulletin of the Friends Historical Association,* "A Disputed Paper of George Fox." Addressed to Cromwell's army, the paper in question was an appeal against the persecution of Friends. It had been called into question because of certain passages suggesting a more positive view of the army than Fox was supposed to have. Henry Cadbury pointed out that Fox had been as positive in an address to Cromwell and that certain turns of phrase were characteristically Foxian, whereas others might be the result of the collaboration and assimilation of other authors so typical of the day. He used some of his knowledge of form criticism to discuss the issue. The passage was probably Fox's, he concluded, and of special interest to Quaker historians: "It reveals not merely an unwonted vigor of style . . . but a phase in Fox's attitude towards war that is significant even if not consistent. By revealing his sympathy with the early ideals of Cromwell's army it shows how Fox's pacifism was not an extreme and suddenly revealed doctrine but a natural development."[17]

The next year, he published a paper on the Norwegian Quakers who had settled in the United States in 1825. This was a story he would continue to pursue for many years. He was too curious to let a subject go until he had exhausted all information about it, and the result was that he kept a number of research projects going, like so many balls in the air, adding another from time to time.

His growing interest in Quaker history did not prevent him from continuing to publish scholarly articles on the meaning of certain biblical words and phrases and to circulate these among interested scholars for their comments. He maintained a lively correspondence with scholars in France, England, and the United States, as well as Germany. He frequently became interested in helping these scholars publish important pieces of work. A scholar in England had prepared a Lexicon of Josephus, which Clarendon Press in Oxford would publish only if a subsidy was provided. Henry Cadbury felt it was so important that the book be published that he personally raised the necessary sum.

All this time he continued to write his book on Luke, with the patient help of his wife, Lydia Cadbury. "I have read this Luke book so many times that I told Henry I should soon be qualified for a higher degree in New Testament; whereupon he asked me if I knew Ben-Sira. I didn't and was told I should have to wait before getting a Ph.D.," Lydia Cadbury wrote to Elizabeth Jones in 1924.[18] Elizabeth also proofread Rufus Jones's manuscripts, and there was a friendly rivalry between the two couples as to which could find the most errata in the other's output. When one or the other spotted an error, they simply sent off a postcard with no other message than "p. 223" or "p. 307." The recipient immediately looked at the pages in question and groaned over the faux pas.

Although the manuscript was completed by the end of 1924, it was not published until 1927. *The Making of Luke-Acts,* as it was called, summarized all that was known of the Lucan writings to date and added a great deal of new material based on Henry Cadbury's own painstaking original research. This included not only fresh translation of the earliest of the Lucan documents but also an acquaintance with the language, literature, and culture of the Lucan period, which other scholars still find breathtaking.

An example, given by Amos Wilder of Harvard, was his understanding of nautical terms. There is a passage in Acts (27:17) in which it is said that "the sailors took measures to undergird the ship" in the face of a tempest. Biblical scholars had always wondered how it might be possible to pass cables around the hull of a boat in a storm. By studying a variety of ancient paintings and papyri accounts of sailing, Henry Cadbury was able to show that trusses were stretched lengthwise, or thwart, to keep the ship from buckling.[19]

Henry Cadbury was conversant with the writing styles of the day—just as Shakespeare students saturate themselves in the conditions of stage writing in his time—and used this knowledge to demonstrate that the author of the two-volume work he called Luke-Acts, which consists of one-quarter of the New Testament, had an idiosyncratic writing style of his own. A thorough familiarity with Luke's style could help the student who is trying to reconstruct his sources, known and unknown, through the methods of form criticism. Luke's motives also played a role in the material he selected and emphasized. Luke seemed eager to prove that Christianity was not a threat to the empire or to Judaism and that it even was in keeping with the best of pagan beliefs.

Luke-Acts was reviewed in every major religious publication of the day. Writing in the *Journal of Religion,* E. F. Scott of Union Theological Seminary commented on Henry Cadbury's exceedingly clear and simple style and on the originality of the research. "There is more genuine scholarship in it than in nine-tenths of the ostentatiously learned books that are being written today about the New Testament." He remarked that on many debated questions Cadbury took a guarded position. "Perhaps the chief criticism which most readers will make on the book is that it so often avoids definite pronouncements . . . perhaps a full explanation will never be forthcoming, but all future attempts to reach it will have to take account of the material which Dr. Cadbury has placed before us in this book."[20]

Henry Cadbury's interest in presenting the facts and his reluctance to develop theory and interpretation on the basis of those facts were both admired and criticized by other scholars for many years. His discipline was impressive and challenged others to keep asking the hard questions and to avoid predisposing attitudes. But should he not have been more willing to construct some edifices with carefully built bricks of solid fact? Some thought so; others disagreed. As to the reason for this reluctance, there are only a few clues. Henry Cadbury saw himself as a historian and a philologist, not as a philosopher of religion. Like his ancestor John Bartram, the naturalist, he liked the job of making keen observations and putting them down with economy. It suited him temperamentally. He liked to be absolutely right about whatever he said. He was both too humble and too cautious to advance theories he could not fully substantiate. It is possible that the undertone of depression in his nature contributed to this caution.

To stick with facts was in keeping with the strong Quaker tradition of respecting the truth and avoiding what were once called "airy notions," of approaching knowledge experientially. It also had something to do with the ancient Quaker tradition of not putting self forward. When Henry Cadbury wrote and spoke for peace or social justice he could be a polemicist, but in his chosen profession he preferred to provide both his students and his colleagues with the facts, as best he could ascertain them, and to let them draw their own conclusions, always hoping that the authority of truth would lead them to what he might consider the right answers.

One person who appreciated his approach was his old professor and mentor, George Moore. Among the many letters of appreciation he received from scholars for *Luke-Acts* probably none meant more to him than Moore's epistle: "One of the things I like most in it, as in your previous work, is your skepticism perhaps because I am a constitutional skeptic myself. . . . I think it belongs to the conscience of a scholar not to be more confident than the data warrant. . . . A wise old rabbi said: 'Teach thy tongue to say, "I do not know" lest thou make up something, and get caught.'"[21]

Having helped Henry Cadbury finish the production of *The*

Making of Luke-Acts, Lydia Cadbury turned to productions of her own. On January 3, 1925, Warder Henry Cadbury was born, and on June 28, 1926, Winifred joined the family. Henry watched Lydia deal with this growing family with awe: "It is astonishing that she can do single-handed what she just did this evening—put three children to bed while getting supper, besides helping Elizabeth with her lessons or keeping her otherwise out of mischief."[22]

Henry Cadbury helped by doing the marketing, running the laundry through the wringer, and taking Betty with him to meetings and on trips. The summer after Winifred's birth, he took Betty to Back Log Camp while Lydia Cadbury stayed home with the three youngest children. "Warder is ceasing to throw things at the new baby," Lydia Cadbury wrote laconically to Elizabeth Jones. The pattern was now set; the children were Lydia's responsibility with Henry doing his best to support her and occasionally relieve her without interfering with his studies. This was the division of responsibility with which they had both grown up, and close observers of the family felt that this was the way Lydia Cadbury wanted it. It assigned Henry Cadbury to the role of a distant and sometimes preoccupied father to his young children.

Henry Cadbury had special reason to be preoccupied during the fall of 1925. The Visitors of the Andover Theological Seminary had never been informed of, or approved, the merger of 1922 and had taken the matter to court. In September 1925, the Massachusetts Supreme Judicial Court ruled that the merger was illegal and that every Andover professor must subscribe to the Andover Creed. When this ruling was made final in January of 1926, the entire faculty resigned. Most of the professors were subsequently hired by Harvard, but Henry Cadbury was not. Later, there was some discussion among the Harvard faculty as to whose fault it was that Henry Cadbury was let go.

When the word went forth that Harvard's brilliant New Testament scholar was available, invitations were not slow in coming. Benjamin Bacon, dean of the Yale Divinity School, offered him a position and hinted that Henry Cadbury was the man to succeed him when he retired. Henry Cadbury turned down the post, to the amazement of some of his German colleagues, because he said he would prefer to educate biblical scholars than future clergymen. Bacon, who was apparently fond of Henry Cadbury, was also distressed:

> I need hardly assure you that your declination of our invitation, however disappointing, conveys no offense. I am indeed sorry, because you

were for me the best guarantee of such a succession as I could wish. Indeed I should still look forward to it, with possibly a little deferring of the date, but for the fact that our faculty, rightly or wrongly, have received the impression that your decision is based in last resort on your greater interest in our subject from the purely cultural and scientific point of view, than from the practical or evangelical, in other words, that you would prefer to teach persons whose motive was self-development and general culture than young men whose lives are dedicated to using this knowledge for the upbuilding of the Christian Church. If that is the case of course your decision must be accepted as final. It is indeed an appalling situation we confront if men are not to be found who combine this motive with the true scholarship exemplified in yourself.[23]

Fortunately, Marion Park, president of Bryn Mawr College, came forth with an invitation for Henry Cadbury to become professor of biblical literature starting in the fall of 1926. Henry Cadbury wrote to his sisters Emma and Elizabeth that it was an asset to have had them precede him at the college, but they must not expect great things. The house on Buckingham Place was prepared for renters chiefly by Henry Cadbury, who washed every window and cleaned out the cellar. The house at 3 College Circle at Haverford, which had been occupied by a college widow during the interim, was now vacated to make way for its owners. The years in Cambridge had been pleasant, but the Philadelphia Cadburys were very glad to be home again.

CHAPTER 6

The Beloved Community

M. Carey Thomas had struggled for years to make Bryn Mawr a college known for its academic excellence, attractive to women students who were interested and capable of demonstrating that women could perform as well as, if not better in purely intellectual disciplines, than men. Though perhaps less of a crusading feminist, Marion Park had maintained the same tradition of outstanding scholarship. She was eager that as many of her young women as possible should benefit from the influence of Henry Cadbury's teaching, and she personally took upon herself the job of recruiting students for his classes. During the years 1926–27 forty-four undergraduates were enrolled in his department. The number subsequently grew.

Although he was now teaching undergraduates rather than graduates, Henry Cadbury continued to expect academic excellence and to achieve his results by a series of prodding but open-ended questions as well as his famous little stories and witty asides. Both his method and his manner made him a popular teacher. Some of his students were of Quaker background, but like their sisters from other Protestant denominations they were eager to rethink the religious beliefs of their childhood in light of the emphasis on science and behaviorism of the Roaring Twenties. Henry Cadbury's own questioning and skeptical approach helped them to see that they need not abandon a search to find value in religion but could look for those elements in their religious heritage that had some relevance to their lives. One Quaker woman who studied with him at this period remembers the relief and joy she felt in learning about the historic and human Jesus with Henry Cadbury as her guide and mentor.[1] The thirst of these students for religious belief that did not violate their intellectual integrity deepened Henry Cadbury's interest in reaching out to those who were either having trouble with conventional religious concepts or considered themselves outside the circle of religion completely. In the talks he gave during this period he returned to this theme again and again. The conventionally religious had no authority to shut from their ranks those motivated by a deep search for meaning and value who were nevertheless made uncomfortable by rigid theological creeds, declarations of faith, or religious forms. In a talk to a Cambridge bible class in 1929, he said, "Perhaps they would really like to be religious but they cannot and will not identify themselves with religion as they see it. They fail to recognize the spirit of God in the natural elements in their lives and so they lead either a disappointed or a positively anti-religious life."[2]

His Bible students had obviously chosen his course because of some interest in the Bible. When he spoke to the Bryn Mawr Chapel, however, he was speaking to the entire student body. In these talks he often linked religion to some other field of endeavor (revealing unconsciously thereby the enormous depth of his erudition), attempting to build bridges between the various disciplines and religion. In one such talk in May of 1927, he talked about literature and said that religion, like fiction, was a medium of human imagination:

> At their lowest, the belief in God and immortality are projections of the worthwhileness of human ideals, they are the expression of man's confidence in the validity of his preference for right over wrong, as representing a universal and authoritative and permanent kind of value.
> And the best of religion and the great contribution of imagination which distinguishes man from the beast—if imagination is not found in beast—is precisely its confidence in the worth of the individual.[3]

In another chapel service he talked about the limitations of knowledge, the need for the development of values in tandem with knowledge, and the concept that religion and science could be partners in search of a common goal—veritas.

Standing in the way of many searchers were those who identified religious experience with a church environment or with the mystical experience. His sense that not all people were mystics was growing, and, as he preached and wrote about the varieties of religious experience, his own voice was becoming surer. For him and for many others who might never experience a sense of presence, as well as for the mystics who confessed to having long dry spells, what mattered was the habit of Christian behavior in the absence of direct inspiration. In his parables, Jesus often spoke of the problem of the servant whose master had gone on a long journey. The crucial problem facing the Christian was developing habits of right conduct in the absence of God.

His strong sense that the study of the life of Jesus as a whole was the best means of building a Christian character to carry one through dry spells was growing and with it an interest in writing a book about Jesus. He wanted particularly to warn against the danger of reading into the gospel whatever one wished to find and to urge instead the continued effort to understand Jesus against his own time and environment, however difficult that might be. Ever since he had completed *The Making of Luke-Acts*, he had been making notes for a book about Jesus along these lines. In his classes at Bryn Mawr and the Bible classes he gave at various meetings in the Philadelphia area, he was beginning to explore the themes he would develop. "I am giving them rather strong meat, but I am trying to make them say the hard things themselves," he wrote his sister Emma.[4]

Having been a member of the board of the Woolman School, he was asked to serve in the same capacity at Pendle Hill, successor to Woolman, which was opened in Wallingford, Pennsylvania, in 1930. In the summer of 1931, he gave a series of lectures at Pendle Hill on Jesus in which he explored these ideas. Jesus was best understood as a Jewish teacher, steeped in the tradition of the Jewish law, experiencing the religion of a pious Jew, expecting an apocalypse in no way different from other Jewish thinkers. His thinking was not abstract and metaphysical but ethical and practical. He met each person who came to him for advice with a question or a command which would lead that person to right action. He was speaking specifically to the rich young man who came to him to find out how to have eternal life when he told him to sell all that he had and give it to the poor, not to all young men in all time. He was concerned that the individual act in a righteous fashion, not so much that the end condition would be righteousness. In other words, his approach was to the individual one by one.[5]

For the man or woman who wanted to act in a righteous fashion, the American Friends Service Committee was a channel of service. So Henry Cadbury had always conceived it, and so it served in his own life.

During the years at Cambridge he had been unable to serve on the Executive Board of the working committees, which all met regularly in Philadelphia at that period. His name, however, had remained on the masthead as a member of the general committee, and whenever important consultations were held he was urged to attend. In October of 1924, a conference was held to decide whether to continue the work of the AFSC or lay it down. The result was a decision in 1925 to reorganize into four divisions: a European Section, to carry on the continuing work overseas, now concentrated in a group of international centers in the countries where relief had been undertaken; a Home Service Section, overseeing the placement of young volunteers on Indian reservations, in southern black schools, in settlement houses, and in hospitals; an Interracial Section, with the mandate of responding to the situation of lynching in the South; and a Peace Section, to undertake a new program for peace. Henry Cadbury was soon listed by the Peace Section as a co-opted member. Peace would always be the issue closest to his heart.[6]

Returning to the Philadelphia area in the fall of 1926, he was once more able to attend AFSC meetings regularly and to consult more closely with Rufus Jones, his brother-in-law, who was still AFSC chairman, about AFSC matters. His enthusiasm for the work of the committee and his sound judgment soon won recognition. In March of 1928, Rufus Jones resigned as chairman, and in May Henry Cadbury took his place.

To be chairman of the board of the AFSC has always meant far more than presiding at regular board meetings and reaching a sense of the meeting, although in a Quaker organization, this is no mean skill. It involves knowing the programs of the organization and the personnel intimately, giving spiritual as well as intellectual leadership to the staff, speaking for the committee to heads of states, and being a constant resource and adviser to the executive secretary. Henry Cadbury was known throughout his many years as board chairman for his extraordinary grasp of detail and his intuitive understanding of the problems and feelings of staff members.

There are many legends about his tact. One from a later period concerns a junior staff member who was publicly criticized by an older board member. After the meeting was over, the young man went back to his office, crushed, and put his head on his desk. Suddenly, Henry Cadbury was standing at the doorway.

"Bill," he said, "thee and I are going to have to help Howard."[7]

Henry Cadbury's skill in supporting and encouraging staff members made him popular with AFSC staff throughout his many years on the board. Many saw him as their champion in pressing for change against the conservativism of the board. Some tensions of this nature were inevitable; the staff, in touch with conditions in the field of service and moved by compassion for the victims of war and famine, tended to press for a more liberal interpretation of the organization's mission. The board tended to hold back. Henry Cadbury moved gently but skillfully to be sure that all board members were given full opportunity to express themselves, but he was especially concerned that those ready to move with new ideas be heard. This emphasis and his own forward-looking attitude meant that he was seen as weighing in on the side of change and progress.

At the time he became chair in 1928, Henry Cadbury had need of all his knowledge of human nature and all his tact, for he came to the AFSC at a time of growing tensions. Wilbur Thomas had taken the job of executive secretary in the summer of 1918, when the reconstruction unit in France was at full strength and the committee, representing the diverse elements in the Society of Friends, was united in enthusiasm of the period in making the enterprise work. For several years this enthusiasm had remained at full tide, but as it gradually waned, the committee found itself groping for its next step and occasionally wondering if it ought to lay itself down; the unity waned and support from the monthly and yearly meetings fell off. The reorganization had been an effort to solve these problems, giving scope for different people to pursue different interests. At the same time, it sought to broaden the base of those responsible for the committee by putting the work in the various sections under strong subcommittees. Wilbur Thomas unfortunately understood these moves away from centralized management as questioning his authority. "One criticism of him has been that he made the AFSC a one-man concern, with prodigious energy managing every detail," Henry Cadbury wrote to his sister Emma Cadbury in the Vienna Center to give her background.[8]

On December 27, 1928, Wilbur Thomas abruptly resigned, citing lack of creativity on the board. He also considered himself fired: "Members of the Board of Directors have definitely informed me that there was not sufficient unity on the Board to warrant my continuing in the work." At first he spoke of continuing for another three months while a successor was sought, but as the situation deteriorated he decided to leave on February 15. Anna Griscom was made acting executive secretary for four months. Henry Cadbury sought to play the role of peacemaker by offering Thomas an additional two months' salary, but it was also necessary to act quickly to find a permanent replacement. On February 22, he cabled Clarence Pickett, now teaching full time at Earlham, to offer him the position. Pickett accepted for the fall of 1929. Since Anna Griscom's term ended on June 15, it began to appear as though Henry Cadbury was going to have to "babysit" the AFSC as he had done once before. At the last minute, Clarence Pickett agreed to come to the office once a week during the summer, but Henry Cadbury continued to feel especially responsible until September, when Clarence began full-time work.[9]

It was a time of transition for the AFSC in many ways. A bitter textile strike in Marion, North Carolina, had left more than one thousand workers locked out, with no way to survive the winter. Norman Thomas, who was supporting the strike, and James Myers, of the Federal Council of Churches of Christ in America, asked the AFSC as a neutral, humanitarian body to undertake relief for the strikers and their families. The committee had helped briefly in similar situations in West Virginia and western Pennsylvania, feeding and clothing children, but this was a long-range program. Some Friends still felt, as Henry Cadbury once had, that the strike was a form of coercion and there should be a more reconciling way to heal labor disputes. Unionization was still relatively new, and some Quaker businessmen, who were good to their workers in a paternalistic fashion, felt threatened by it.

Yet management could be coercive too. In Marion, company guards fired on the locked-out workers, killing four. The AFSC decided to undertake the project, and the board member who had been most opposed gave the first one thousand dollars for the relief fund. The committee stayed in Marion throughout the winter, providing relief, and helped the workers to look for other jobs. Through the Quaker network another businessman with more progressive views toward labor policy heard about the situation at Marion and decided to buy the plant and run it along less feudal lines.

Drawing on the experience gained in Marion, the committee was soon involved in a major program of child-feeding in the depressed coal-mining regions of Appalachia. Herbert Hoover, now president himself a Quaker, had worked with the AFSC in the German child-feeding. He now proposed to turn over to them $225,000 remaining in the American Relief Administration Children's Fund if they would raise approximately $175,000 to meet the needs. For a small organization with an annual budget of less than $100,000, it was a giant step. Clarence Pickett agreed to undertake the work, with the backing of Henry Cadbury and the enthusiasm of Rufus Jones.

It was in the Appalachia work that the AFSC began to branch out from relief to new experiments. It undertook a self-help housing program, supported by Eleanor Roosevelt. It encouraged local industries such as furniture making, promoted family planning, and brought young people together for a summer of work on community projects, the first such summer work camp to be held in the United States.

Peace work was growing, too. Beginning in the summer of 1927, regular Peace Caravans of young people set out in their "flivvers" to tour the United States and discuss issues of war and peace in small towns and crossroads across the country. In the summer of 1930, an institute was held at Haverford College to train these volunteers and others interested in peace. Henry Cadbury was the chief faculty member, giving a series of lectures. The next year a second institute was planned. In 1932, institutes were held at Haverford College, Wellesley College, and Northwestern University. Called Institutes on International Relations, they became extremely popular and were supported by the Woodrow Wilson and Carnegie foundations. By 1937, ten were being held, and some gave college credit. Henry Cadbury was part of the faculty of one or another of these institutes, whenever he was able to be present.

Being chairman of the AFSC meant attending countless meetings. It also meant being something of a public figure. Henry Cadbury was amazed one day to get a call from a Friend who lived in Washington, D.C., and knew Lou Hoover, the wife of Herbert Hoover, saying that the president wanted to see Henry Cadbury the very next day. Henry Cadbury said he did not see how he could make it because he had classes to teach. Didn't he realize, his caller asked, that when the president made a request it must be treated as a command and given precedence? Henry Cadbury decided to give up his classes and go, still not knowing the subject of the interview.

Herbert Hoover came straight to the point. There were three different Quaker meetings in Washington: a Five Years Meeting, a Hicksite Meeting, and an Independent Meeting, which was now building a new meeting house on Florida Avenue. Would not Henry Cadbury, as chairman of the American Friends Service Committee, use his influence to persuade these groups to unite? "This request took me as much by surprise as the invitation had. I think, however, I succeeded in explaining to him that I had no papal powers, that the AFSC was a relief organization, and that for me or for it to engage in church politics or local problems of Quaker divisions would be resented and would injure the happy cooperative working of all sorts of Friends with the Committee. So we dropped the subject."[10]

The president seemed willing to talk about peace, always Henry Cadbury's favorite topic. He had supported the current naval disarmament conference against the machinations of an agent of the American shipping companies, Hoover said. This gave Henry Cadbury a chance to ask what aspect of their common Quaker heritage Hoover took most seriously. Henry Cadbury hoped he would say peace, but Hoover answered, "individual faithfulness."

In 1932 the American Friends Service Committee was fifteen

years old. Designed to meet an immediate need in 1917, it had continued from year to year as Friends and their friends had seen fresh needs that could only be met by its unique brand of idealism and practical, hard work. In giving the anniversary speech, Henry Cadbury spoke of the effect of the organization of the committee on the Society of Friends, helping Friends and others to see that the Society was neither decadent nor antiquarian, that it had a distinct task in the world, and that the obedience to group decision making that was unique to Quakerism had been shown to work in the modern world. It demonstrated the continuity of Quaker ideals, although the interest in doing so was largely unconscious, he said: "It regards practical questions in a moral light, its value lies in part in its techniques . . . it has the merit of pioneering and experimentation . . . it must be followed by faith into resultant tasks. These include the intellectual working out of ideas . . . fundamental challenges to existing institutions."[11]

A new topic of experimentation and pioneering for the AFSC lay in the field of race relations. Quakers were beginning to feel uneasy about their failure to address the problems of racial discrimination at home while they sought to solve international conflicts abroad. News of lynchings in the South stirred their consciences. Their response was at first tentative: here and there Quaker groups began to arrange for interracial social occasions as a means of bridging the gap. In 1927, the AFSC hired Crystal Bird, a black woman, to speak on behalf of better race relations to clubs, churches, schools, and religious gatherings. The AFSC also sponsored an experiment under which two blacks in leadership roles sought to involve the black community in working for peace. With the Race Relations Committee of the two Philadelphia Yearly Meetings, the AFSC sponsored a series of race relations conferences. At the first of these in January 1932, Henry Cadbury was asked to chair.

In his opening talk on the first day he traced the leadership of the Society of Friends in the abolition of slavery, from the first declaration against slavery made by the Germantown Meeting in 1688, through the slow process of coming to unity that Friends who owned slaves should be disowned, to the more radical movements of the nineteenth century in which the Grimké sisters, Angelina and Sarah, Lucretia Mott, and others were pioneers: "Abolitionists realized in time that every other cause was involved with this one. Oberlin founded in 1833 as an abolitionist college had to admit women in their first year. Any radical attitude on the race problem will always be linked up with other causes." He spoke particularly of Anthony Benezet, a schoolmaster whose tracts influenced Thomas Clarkson of England to become a leader against slavery in that nation, and John Wesley, who incorporated antislavery in his religious movement: "Friends have always developed a group conscience by appeal to the consciences of individuals—no coercions, no harsh words, but quiet, undemonstrative appeal to conscience. . . . Are we ready to make this meeting in Germantown take the first step in another chapter, another book?" [12]

The Negro question was really a "white question" he believed, a problem of prejudice and narrow-mindedness among white people, a lack of individual faithfulness to the real meaning of brotherhood. What would happen if the Society of Friends today were as far ahead of its time in regard to the Negro as it had been in the nineteenth century? Asked to speak at the Friends General Conference held every year at Cape May, New Jersey, by the Hicksite Quakers, he entitled his series of talks carefully, "The Negro Problem—a Study in Whites."

Reinforcing his concern for current Quaker attitudes toward racial discrimination was his increasing interest in the abolitionists. Whenever he could get away from his classes, lectures, book reviews to be written, committee meetings, and AFSC duties, Henry Cadbury was at work in the Haverford library. A chief focus during this period were the letters to Anthony Benezet. He corresponded with a man who was writing a master's thesis on Benezet at Columbia as well as with a minister, George S. Brookes, who was writing a biography of Benezet and depended on Henry Cadbury for help in collecting the letters. Some historians had hoped Henry Cadbury himself would write a biography, but he contented himself with a series of short articles and the weaving of Benezet's contribution into some of his sermons and speeches. It was yet another form of social translation of earlier revelation.

Immersed as he was in the intricate demands and satisfactions of Philadelphia Quakerism, Henry Cadbury might have been content to maintain only a nominal relationship to the wider world of scholarship to which he belonged, going to meetings of the Society of Biblical Literature, and contributing occasional papers to the major journals of religion and biblical scholarship. But that world was as demanding in its way as the Society of Friends, and it did not give up easily. The Divinity School at Yale University had not abandoned its efforts to recruit Henry Cadbury, and he was again offered, and again rejected, a position in 1928. With the sudden death of Professor William Arnold in 1929, the Harvard Divinity School had an opening, and Dean Sperry urged Henry Cadbury to return to that faculty as the Hancock Professor. When Henry

Cadbury refused, Sperry wrote to express his great disappointment and his faith that sooner or later Henry Cadbury would return to the Harvard faculty: "I can understand that it is not a simple question of Bryn Mawr versus Harvard, but even more of the whole Philadelphia-Haverford community with its present claim upon you as against Cambridge. And I can see that there was a very strong case to be made for your staying somewhat longer where you are."[13]

Another invitaton came which he could not refuse. This was to serve as one of nine New Testament scholars to produce a Revised Standard Version of the New Testament for the American Standard Bible Committee. Another seven biblical scholars were to work on the Old Testament. Of those chosen, Henry was the youngest, at a mere forty-seven. But he was now a world-acknowledged authority on Luke-Acts, and his intimate knowledge of Koine Greek and of the way of life of the Greek and Jewish peoples at the time of the writing of the gospels was unparalleled.

The chairman of the overall project was Dean Luther A. Weigle of the Yale Divinity School, and the secretary was James Moffatt. These two men served on both the Old and New Testament committees. Others beside Henry Cadbury on the New Testament team were Millar Burrows of Yale Divinity School, Clarence T. Craig of Oberlin Divinity School, Edgar J. Goodspeed of the University of Chicago, Frederick Grant formerly President of Seabury-Western Theological Seminary and later of Union Theological Seminary, Abdel Wentz of the Lutheran Theological Seminary at Gettysburg, and W. Russell Bowie, formerly rector of Grace Church, New York, and later of Union Theological Seminary. This group, joined later by other scholars, met on and off for almost seventeen years, holding weekend meetings in New York or New Haven in the winter and long fortnight meetings in the summer. Henry got to know the other scholars very well and to enjoy the long sessions of discussion and debate. He became known among the scholars as one of the most exacting. Writing in the *Atlantic Monthly* in August of 1946, W. Russell Bowie described him:

> At the table would be Henry Cadbury, a scholar of the most implacable patience, never content to let any decision be reached until every imaginable point of doubt as to the exact text to be preferred among variant manuscripts and the exact shade of meaning to be attributed to each Greek word or phrase had been pursued to the ultimate. Frequently a point would seem to have been settled when Cadbury, getting up from the table and searching in some book, would find a new query which would stop the whole proceeding and turn the discussion back to its

starting point. "Where is Cadbury?" somebody asked one day when he had gone for a moment out of the room. "Oh," came the answer, "he is out relining his brakes."[14]

Henry Cadbury's membership on the translation committee was the source of a series of jokes within the Cadbury family. One was about the visitor who asked where he could find Henry Cadbury and was told by Lydia Cadbury, "He's in New York rewriting the word of God." Another was about the boy next door, who boasted to Warder of his father's literary exploits. "That's nothing," Warder is supposed to have said. "My father wrote the Bible."

There might have been a slight edge to the jokes. Henry Cadbury's membership on the Revised Standard Committee must have occasionally seemed to his wife and children like one demand too many on his time. During the years at Bryn Mawr, when the four Cadbury children were all young, Henry Cadbury was too busy and preoccupied to have much time to play the role of father, a role about which he knew little in any event. A friend of the period remembers him at work on the dining table with books and papers about him, while the youngest children tumbled unheeded at his feet. Occasionally he would take Betty or Chris for a walk as far as the duck pond. Otherwise, he continued to leave the care of the children to their mother.

Lydia Cadbury, having grown up in a permissive household, was a permissive mother. She also had a few outside interests to pursue. She was an active member of the Women's International League for Peace and Freedom and an enthusiastic participant in the Haverford Friends Monthly Meeting, which the Cadburys attended while keeping their membership at Twelfth Street. She taught Bible classes using her own approach, quite at variance with that of her husband. She loved to read, especially enjoying German novels. Unless the children needed her attention, she liked to read between bouts of laundry and of cooking.

As a result, the children were seen as undisciplined by some of the Cadburys' friends and neighbors. Legends, whether accurate or not, abound. One night Christopher and a neighbor boy managed to awaken themselves at two o'clock in the morning to gather up all the milk bottles from the doorsteps in the neighborhood and throw them in the duck pond. Another time Christopher set out to collect thermometers from all the porches to do an experiment with the mercury. He was prevented by his father, who proved not so absent-minded in this case. Having guessed what Christopher was up to, he followed him, caught him in the act of lifting a thermometer, and told him, not unkindly, that he must put them all back.

Lydia Cadbury once brought all four children to a Bryn Mawr faculty tea and became engrossed in conversation, leaving the young Cadburys to their own devices. "Where are the children?" President Park asked. "Over there," Lydia Cadbury gestured. Marion Park turned in time to see the Cadbury children pulling the tablecloth off a tea table, bringing cups and silver and sugar and lemon with it.

One of the Cadbury daughters was playing in the street at the lower end of Walnut Lane. A well-meaning woman, thinking that it was a dangerous place for a child to play unsupervised, spoke to her about it. Noticing a crushed frog on the pavement nearby, she said, "How would you like to be crushed like that?" The reply was crisp, "It might be very interesting."

These were, on the whole, happy years for the Cadbury family. Both Henry Cadbury and Lydia Cadbury enjoyed being back in the heart of the community in which they were rooted, able to visit with their large extended families as well as their Haverford and Bryn Mawr friends. If Henry Cadbury sometimes missed the stimulation of his Harvard New Testament colleagues, he had other sources of companionship. Rayner W. Kelsey taught history at Haverford and was the curator of the ever-growing Quaker Collection, the manuscripts on which Henry Cadbury devoted more and more of his spare time. Frank Watson, a sociologist, also a Haverford professor, shared his interest in improving race relations. And Douglas Steere, arriving in 1928 as assistant professor of philosophy, lived next door. He and his wife, Dorothy, became close friends of the Cadburys. Douglas Steere and Henry Cadbury differed radically on their approaches to Jesus: Henry Cadbury's cool, objective, and yet searching; Douglas Steere's warm, subjective, and personal. Douglas Steere came to be interested in pursuing the studies on mystical religion which were of great importance to Rufus Jones; Henry Cadbury was never attracted to this line of inquiry. Yet there was mutual respect and affection between the two men.

According to Haverford College rules, the campus residences were reserved for faculty members, and a professor who had left the college was obliged to sell the house back to the administration. It had not been necessary for Haverford to enforce this rule in regard to the Cadbury residence at 3 College Circle until 1931, but in that year because of a shortage of faculty housing, the Cadburys were told they must move. Accordingly, they rented a house at 774 Millbrook Lane for a school term and bought it in the spring of 1932. "So we have a settled home," Lydia Cadbury wrote optimistically to Emma Cadbury on May 15. "Now of course we're going to try to rent it, furnished, starting in July." [15]

Henry, Lydia, and their children. Left to right, Elizabeth (standing), Warder, Winifred, Christopher. Courtesy of Elizabeth Cadbury Musgrave.

The Cadburys were going abroad. Henry Cadbury had completed six years at Bryn Mawr College and was due for a sabbatical. He was to spend two terms at Woodbrooke, the Quaker retreat and study center in Selly Oak, Birmingham, England, where he could combine Quaker research with lecturing in the nearby schools. The family would have a house in Kings Mead Close, and the two older children would go to Quaker boarding schools. The following summer they planned to visit Jerusalem, while Henry Cadbury worked at the American School of Oriental Research for which he served as board member. Then the Cadburys might travel in Europe and have a visit with Sister Emma. It was a great adventure, and both Henry Cadbury and Lydia Cadbury looked forward to it with pleasure.

On the eve of departure, Henry Cadbury wrote to his brother-in-law Rufus Jones to ask that he keep in close touch with the AFSC and Clarence Pickett: "The group who advise policy is small enough and with the recent mood of depression I have found some of the businessmen over-timid and unable to appreciate our work. This was to be expected and yet on the whole all has gone much more favorably than we anticipated. I hope my concern is clear and will not be too burdensome."[16]

He had all but finished proofreading the final galleys of *Beginnings of Christianity,* Volumes IV and V, hoped they would be published in 1932 (actually, it was 1933), and was able to reflect "on the momentous character of our undertaking." He was ready for new challenges, and with Henry Cadbury they were never slow in coming.

CHAPTER 7

A Year Abroad

Lydia Cadbury always said that Henry Cadbury was a different man when he was on vacation. Far from his study and his 3 × 5 cards and the endless claims of scholarship, he embarked with real enthusiasm on the role of tourist, throwing his unquenchable curiosity for the time being into learning about the place he was visiting. This was particularly true when there was a Quaker connection to be made.

In the late summer of 1932 the Cadburys went first to Holland, where they settled in the Hague, put the children temporarily into a Dutch school each morning, and set out to explore the surrounding countryside by train and bicycle. Henry Cadbury went alone to Amsterdam one Sunday to attend meeting and visit the Rijksmuseum (where he spent most of his time studying the pictures and prints dealing with the English-Dutch wars of 1653–66 "since they enter into the story of Quakerism a bit"). Henry and Lydia Cadbury together bicycled to the Hoek of Holland. The whole family enjoyed a trip by canal and river on a little steamer, seeing many windmills. Henry and Lydia Cadbury together went to Leiden to visit a Dutch New Testament scholar. Christopher, aged eleven, set out on a bicycle to explore the Hague, became lost, and finally found his way home by following a trolley line. "It is a good experience for him but makes our landlady nervous," Henry Cadbury commented. In between bouts of sightseeing, Henry Cadbury bought stamps for his brother Ben Cadbury.[1]

Benjamin Cadbury had had a terrible year. The Great Depression had been hard on the firm of Haines, Jones and Cadbury, and the family had had to practice frugality. Then Ben Cadbury's wife, Anna, had become ill and had died in July. Now he was alone in

Moorestown and very lonely. Both Henry and Lydia Cadbury wrote to him often.

The idyll in Holland ended too soon, and the Cadburys moved to Selly Oak, enrolled Christopher in the Downs and Betty at Ackworth, both Quaker boarding schools, and settled down to life in Kings Mead Close. Lydia Cadbury wrote Ben Cadbury that the house was shabby but the cook exceptionally good, that they were meeting the various Cadbury cousins, and that Henry Cadbury had endless invitations to speak. He addressed the board of directors at Woodbrooke, the community itself, the directors of the Cadbury chocolate works, the students and faculty of the colleges in Selly Oak, and various Friends meetings.

In November, he returned to Amsterdam for an international conference of Friends, where he was a principal speaker and was able to devote several delightful days to identifying Quaker sites in Amsterdam. Out of this experience came an article for several of the Friends publications, "Quaker Site Seeking in Amsterdam."[2] He attended the regular, monthly week of Quaker committee meetings in London and spoke to several Quaker groups on the political idealism of William Penn, a topic related to the 250th anniversary of the founding of Pennsylvania.

Still later in the same month, he addressed a group of Young Friends, returning to a topic that was often on his mind: "Could one really know the will of God?" In his lecture notes he wrote, "Possibly God has no intention to communicate in detail. A father does not dictate on everything . . . we may use our own judgment." There were positive conditions for knowing God's will, he told his listeners, including being ready to hear, preparing ourselves, acting upon the insights we already have, and learning from experience. Obedience could become second nature: "Religious life flowers out of fundamental developed traits of character, not magical communications. Such character is the result of patient achievement."[3]

Whenever he could get away from Woodbrooke, Henry Cadbury took the train to London, where he spent the day at the Friends Reference Library at Friends House now on Euston Road. He had originally intended to devote his research during the sabbatical year to identifying books in George Fox's personal library. A list of 108 such books had been found in 1928, most of the titles identified, and the list published in early 1932. Henry Cadbury had written a review of this piece of scholarship for the *Friend* (London) in April.[4] In his first weeks at the Friends Library he set out to search down the rest of the titles. He made some interesting discoveries but in the process came across a new and exciting challenge. The original manuscript list of Fox's books was contained in a huge, unwieldy manuscript catalog of all the papers and books written by Fox from 1643 to 1691. The catalog had apparently been made in the period 1694–97. Each item was dated and coded and the first and last lines given. It was called the *Annual Catalogue* because entries were grouped by year.

At first glance, the catalog was both ponderous and jumbled. Henry Cadbury was permitted to take it home to Selly Oak to study. He wrote John Nickalls, the Friends House librarian, that after six days of exhausting study and eyestrain he was only just beginning to master the meaning of its symbols. There were many duplications and many references to works already published. If these could be eliminated and some order brought to the rest, would it not be helpful to publish the catalog in book form? Nickalls originally was somewhat hesitant: "The interest of your plan as outlined will, except for the definitely bookish few, lie in the amount and importance of unpublished papers by G.F. that are unearthed as a result of the work. They contain the kernel, but in a tremendous covering of shell. The catalogue is only the nutcracker. It is the uncertainty as to how much kernel there is and the difficulty of sorting it out that is disturbing me somewhat."[5]

Henry Cadbury was unsure at first how much he could accomplish. He had only until spring, when he had promised to go to Palestine. But he set to work, with the help of a secretary and the assistance of John Nickalls, and was able to complete a rough draft of a partial edition of the catalog, which he published in 1939.

The original manuscript of the *Annual Catalogue* proved to contain some five thousand items, about one-third already published, about one-third in manuscript form, and another third lost. Henry Cadbury's book, cataloging the two last categories, proved extremely helpful to students of Quaker history, of Fox, and of the religious ferment of the period. Geoffrey Nuttall, an outstanding student of the Puritan era, who later became a beloved colleague of Henry Cadbury's, wrote of the published catalog: "This is an extraordinary volume. Only a remarkable mind would have thought of attempting the detective work necessary to produce it, would have thought this possible, even, or worth doing. Only a remarkable will would have had the stamina to persist with the enterprise, till he had brought order, clarity, and significance out of apparently meaningless jumbled fragments."[6]

In the category of lost papers, Henry Cadbury found some seventy folio-size manuscript pages of 150 separate narratives of miraculous cures made by George Fox, a potential book of miracles which his followers had not published, perhaps out of fear of further persecution, and which was now lost. Because of the first and last line entries it was possible to compare these narratives to other incidents in Fox's known manuscripts and reconstruct many of the entries. To this tantalizing quest Henry Cadbury determined some day to return. It was another opportunity to apply to early Quaker documents the methods he had learned in his studies of form and of motive criticism. Besides, it was fun. This patient detective work, the mulling over of seemingly meaningless clues, was his forte and his love, whether in the study of the books of Acts or of early Quaker documents.

Henry Cadbury had just settled down to this enticing piece of research when news came that shattered his serenity. James Ropes of Harvard had died, and in accordance with his wish, the Harvard Divinity School, cumbersomely then called the Theological School in Harvard University, was offering Henry Cadbury the Hollis Chair of Divinity, the oldest such chair in the United States, and the status of full professor. Willard Sperry sent a long letter outlining all the reasons why Henry Cadbury should accept:

> I know that your Quaker training raises in your mind the whole problem of the "hireling priesthood," but at the same time, if there is a Theological School in the country where an unfettered and honest expression of religious opinion is encouraged, it is this place. . . .
>
> We have for so long taken it for granted that we could persuade you to become Ropes' successor that I am really half-frightened at the idea that there is any possibility for failure. We need you and we want you. The faculty of course is all agreed about it, and President Lowell said to me this morning that it went without saying that we wished Cadbury, and must send him an instant invitation.[7]

For Henry and Lydia Cadbury it was a difficult decision. For Henry's profession, financial security for the family, and a chance to devote himself to research, Harvard was ideal. But it meant turning their backs once more on the many demands of Philadelphia Quakerism and isolating themselves from the community in which they both felt ties of love and commitment.

It was clear that they could not accept the job for another year. Bryn Mawr expected its professors to return for a year after their sabbaticals. Henry Cadbury wrote to Willard Sperry immediately that he could not consider the position until the fall of 1934 and would have to ask for some time to think it over and talk it over with his wife and close associates. He wrote to Rufus Jones to ask for any light he had to share.[8]

When news of Henry's difficult decision became public, many people had opinions. His collaborator Kirsopp Lake wrote to advise Henry Cadbury to wait until the new president of Harvard was announced in April and then to weigh his decision carefully. Lake wanted Henry Cadbury to come to Cambridge but had some questions about the direction the Theological School was taking. He had hoped it would train ministers, not scholars as such, but the break several years before with the Unitarian Association had meant that it got fewer and fewer ministers to train. He had hoped to change the school's direction, but he had resigned for personal reasons at the beginning of the term and now taught in the Harvard history department.[9]

Making Henry Cadbury's dilemma more poignant was a letter from Clarence Pickett, who spoke frankly of missing Henry Cadbury during his sabbatical year: "I feel now and again the desirability of conferring with the chairman in a more intimate and searching way than I can do with those who are now acting." More to the point, he hoped very much that Henry Cadbury would continue as chairman of the board of the AFSC:

> I know the privilege that Harvard offers, which is perfect from the academic point of view . . . but Friends are living these days in a plastic period so far as the social order is concerned, which seems to me to compare to some of the strategic moments in the history of Israel when the prophets were so important a factor in the life, not only of Israel, but of the world. We are weak on vision and ability as individuals, but I think as groups we may be able to give some light. I am constantly cheered by the way the small experiment, based on the conviction that the inner light resides in mining camps as well as in colleges receives attention and the ray of hope that it seems to bring. . . . I have a deep affection for thee and covet more than almost anything I can say to have thee around where I can be with thee.[10]

Torn by conflicting pulls, the Cadburys decided to postpone making a final decision until spring. Lydia Cadbury continued to enjoy life in Selly Oak, although in the damp climate she had trouble with her sinuses and her ears. Henry Cadbury worked hard to complete the catalog of George Fox's writing, played tennis, and accepted speaking engagements.

One of the most interesting of these was an invitation to address the Friends Historical Society in London. Some British Friends had retained unconscious vestiges of an attitude left over from colonial days that they were the wiser older relatives of their young American counterparts; they did not always like to be told that the American Quakers had influenced them. Henry Cadbury was somewhat daring, therefore, when he chose as his topic for his first address to the British Quaker historians the influence of American Quakers on the development of British abolitionism.

This influence, he told his audience, was large. Anthony Benezet had affected a number of public figures in Great Britain and had converted Thomas Clarkson to take a position for the abolition of slavery. Various American yearly meetings had sent epistles to the London Yearly Meeting, asking the British Friends to use their influence with the crown to move toward abolition. John Woolman, the humble tailor from Mt. Holly, New Jersey, known for his lucid journal, had come to London in 1772 to speak against slavery to British Friends. When the latter decided in 1783 to address the king against slavery it was at "the recommendation of our brethren in America to take under consideration an application to those in power in favour of the poor enslaved negroes." In other words, it was the American cousins who had urged the British Friends on to take a stand. It might have been strong medicine, but Henry's talk was so gracefully and tactfully put that it was well received.[11]

It was not possible, however, in the spring of 1933 to concentrate wholly on the history of the past. The worldwide depression and the rise of fascism in Europe were ominous aspects of history in the making. Late in March the Cadburys had a visit from Hertha Kraus, the German woman whom Henry Cadbury had met in 1920, who was now a member of the Society of Friends. Hertha told them as dispassionately as she could of the situation under Hitler, the reign of emotion over reason, the cruelty, the establishment of concentration camps for political prisoners, and the masking of totalitarianism under the name of revolution. She had been expelled from her job as a social worker under civil service in Cologne and accused of inefficiency and corruption while her place was taken by a Nazi stone mason. Hundreds of other civil servants who were not Nazis had also been fired and were to be tried. Hertha felt she had to return to Germany for the trial. Then she hoped to go to the United States with a friend, Gertrud Schulz. Woodbrooke was going to offer them a term in the early summer.

A British Friend, who came out from Germany at about the same time, also reported appalling conditions and described the situation at the Quaker office in Berlin, where political victims flocked, seeking help. What was urgently needed, Henry Cadbury wrote to Clarence Pickett, were British or American staff members to augment the hard-pressed staff to help with interviewing, correspondence, and travel arrangements. He made a list of former

AFSC workers with German experience and German language facility who might be able to fill the gap. "We have individual information about certain Friends or old Woodbrookers ejected, in hiding, escaped, abroad, or lost to view," he wrote carefully, no doubt aware that his letter might fall into the wrong hands.[12]

He did not speak of but he must have wondered about his German theological colleagues. They no longer wrote; some of them perhaps saw the resurgence of German military might as vindication of the humiliation they had suffered at the end of World War I. Others perhaps did not want to risk involving Henry Cadbury in their trials, or perhaps feared that his liberal sentiments might be known to the Gestapo.

There was no time to brood about this depressing development. Henry Cadbury's term at Woodbrooke was over, and the house they had lived in at Kings Mead Close was needed for another family. The Cadburys moved for four weeks to Grasmere in the Lake District, where they had a rustic cottage and could enjoy climbing the stone hills, seeing daffodils dance, and hearing the skylark, in company with the ghost of William Wordsworth, whose Dove cottage was nearby.

During these quiet weeks of retreat the Cadburys made their decision. Marion Park had written that she would be deeply sorry to lose Henry Cadbury from the faculty. At the same time, because of the depression, she had to announce that all salaries were to be cut 10 percent, and Henry Cadbury would receive only $5,200. Harvard offered $8,000. Willard Sperry had continued to urge Henry Cadbury to come to Harvard, though granting that he understood the pull of continuing work with the Friends and the school environment for the children. Finally word came of the appointment of James Bryant Conant, a Harvard professor of chemistry, to the presidency of Harvard. The Cadburys decided to return to Cambridge, and Henry Cadbury wrote to Clarence Pickett that he would continue as AFSC board chairman until 1934, but that a new candidate should be sought.[13]

On the last day of April, Henry and Lydia Cadbury with the two younger children, Winnie and Warder, left England aboard the S.S. *Rotterdam* for a leisurely trip down the coast of France and Portugal, stopping at Lisbon and Tangier, and through the Mediterranean to Egypt. The four spent several days in Cairo, saw the pyramids, then set off by train to Jerusalem.

Henry Cadbury had agreed to be honorary lecturer at the American School of Oriental Research in Jerusalem from mid-May to mid-July. This institution was connected with the Society of Biblical

Literature, and Henry Cadbury had edited its *Annual* for the past five years. At the school the Cadburys were given an apartment. Lydia Cadbury found Jerusalem "thrilling" but very dry and much colder than she had been led to expect. She said she would like to return someday when central heating had been introduced.

Between lectures, Henry Cadbury set off to explore the Holy Land. He visited Ramallah, where an aunt and uncle of Rufus Jones, Sybil and Eli Jones, had helped to start a Friends School fifty years ago and where he spoke several times to the student body, and he made a special trip to Amman, "the oldest Philadelphia," writing an article about the trip for the two Friends papers in his home town.[14]

His major interest in the course of the summer, however, was tracing the old Roman roads. Traveling from Ramallah to Jaffa, passing through Beth Horon, Midieh, and Lydda, he was able to find the nearly obliterated Roman road and to locate three previously unmapped Roman milestones. Later in the summer he followed a similarly faint road from Emmaus to Jerusalem, a distance of twenty miles, to establish that there had been a straight Roman road at the time of Jesus' death, when the disciples walked there on the day of resurrection. "Twenty miles he walked through the heat. He was tired, most unusual for him," Lydia wrote Ben Cadbury.[15]

The news from Germany was increasingly ominous. Henry Cadbury talked several times with Judah Magnes, the Jewish scholar, about the situation of the German Jews and corresponded with Clarence Pickett about what role the AFSC could play. Early in August, the Cadburys once more set sail. Aboard the S.S. *Vienna,* the children roamed the ship, and Lydia Cadbury ordered a tub of hot water from the steward, ostensibly for a foot bath, and proceeded to do a large family wash in the cabin. They stopped at Rhodes to sightsee, then disembarked in Athens and there caught a train to Vienna.[16]

The two older children, Betty and Christopher, had stayed in England all this time, finishing up school and visiting relatives, but they had arranged to meet their parents in Vienna, where their aunt Emma Cadbury was the head of the Friends Center. The reunited family settled down for a few weeks' visit, staying at the Friends hostel and taking a meal each evening at Emma's small apartment nearby. Henry, Betty, and Emma went from Vienna to Bad Pyrmont to attend the Yearly Meeting of the German Quakers. Then the whole family took a walking trip in the Austrian Alps, eating at huts and climbing to eight thousand feet. Even Emma, who was nearing sixty, was able to keep up, and they enjoyed good weather six out of seven days.

From this idyll, the Henry Cadburys went on to Geneva, Henry Cadbury to meet with the Geneva Quaker team and discuss developments in Europe. They stayed in a pension on the south shore of the lake, and the children found their way to bathing beaches, parks, and boat trips. One particularly sparkling day Henry Cadbury took Christopher to see Mt. Blanc and the Mer de Glace.[17]

He found the Geneva team impressive. "There is an element of intellectual depth about them that is already apparent," Henry Cadbury wrote to his sister Elizabeth. Discussion ranged over the situation in Germany, the opportunities for Quaker service, and the bearing of the world crisis on Quaker religion.[18]

In the midst of this visit, Henry Cadbury received a cable from Philadephia pressing him to become the head of the AFSC for a year, while Clarence Pickett took time off to become assistant administrator of the Homestead Act, an outgrowth of the work the AFSC had been doing in the coal fields. As usual in a crisis, the AFSC board turned to Henry Cadbury to fill the gap. "But I did not think it would be fair either to Bryn Mawr or to Harvard to accept, and I have declined," he wrote to Elizabeth. "I do not look forward to doing without Clarence next year, but I hope some arrangement can be made to carry on."[19]

Finally, on September 13, 1933, the six Cadburys set sail for the United States, having been away more than thirteen months. There must have been some poignancy in returning to the new house at 774 Millbrook Lane in Haverford, knowing they would have to leave it again in a year to take up residence in Cambridge. But it was becoming clear that the two-way pull on Henry Cadbury was leading to a peripatetic life for them all.

Haverford College was preparing to celebrate its hundredth birthday, shortly after the Cadburys' return. There was to be a convocation, an alumni dinner, a football game, a soccer match, a tea, and the dedication of a new observatory. In honor of the occasion, three of the college's most distinguished alumni were awarded honorary degrees: Cecil K. Drinker, a physician, Christopher Morley, the writer, and Henry J. Cadbury. The terse citation described him as "Professor of Biblical Literature at Bryn Mawr College, Chairman of the American Friends Service Committee and a recognized authority on the exegesis and interpretation of the New Testament." William Comfort conferred the degree in person. Nothing was said of Henry Cadbury's suspension fifteen years earlier, but many people felt that in a sense Haverford College was making its peace and its apology.

Scarcely was this event over than it was time for Henry Cadbury to take a swing through the South, speaking at a banquet at Duke University celebrating the summer's institute on international relations; to an assembly at Guilford College in Greensboro, North Carolina, on "The Spiritual Traditions and Resources of the Peace Movement," and to a Baltimore Yearly Meeting group on the general subject of peace. He was home in time to celebrate his fiftieth birthday on December 3 with his wife and children and to prepare a series of Christmas lectures for meetings and forums in and around Philadelphia. As usual, he devoted the Christmas holidays to the meetings of the Society of Biblical Literature in New York. On January 7, 1934, he chaired another in the series of annual conferences on race relations sponsored by the AFSC and the two Yearly Meeting Race Relations Committees.

A concern that the Society of Friends must move forward on the issue of race was taking hold of him during this period. He told the Race Relations Conference that he feared the Society of Friends largely shared the standard white attitudes on this issue and was no longer in a pioneering stance. Later in the same year he pressed for the AFSC to take on more work in the field of race relations.[20]

But although his concerns were serious, and he often challenged the Society of Friends in ways that some found annoying, his wit and good humor were becoming more and more evident. In February he gave a talk at Westtown assembly called "The Life of a Scholar." A student, Spencer Coxe, remembered seeing the title of the lecture posted and groaning inwardly. Instead, he recalled having one of the most delightful evenings of his Westtown career. Henry Cadbury compared the life of a scholar to that of a detective, stamp collector, or puzzle maker. He said that Lydia Cadbury could speak, if she would, on the wife of a scholar and told stories of his own absent-mindedness. He touched on the fundamental requisite—curiosity—and said that scholarship might not always have an apparent value to society, but the urge to explore the unknown was like the urge to climb Everest. His droll delivery, his delightful habit of being amused by his own jokes, and his charming asides turned the speech into a delight. The audience was won over completely.[21]

Throughout this year, the AFSC continued to demand a good deal of Henry Cadbury's time. No one had been found to take Clarence Pickett's place while he worked on the government subsistence housing program. Instead, he spent one or two days each week in the office on Twelfth Street and managed with some additional staff support. Still, it was necessary for Henry Cadbury as board chairman to stay in as close touch as possible, especially with the news from Europe growing worse every day. His sister Emma reported from Vienna that after the fighting in early February, when chancellor Engelbert Dollfuss crushed the Socialist opposition, the little Center staff found itself called upon to provide relief for as many as eight thousand families a week. The board decided that it was necessary for Clarence and Lilly Pickett to go to Europe in person that spring to see what Friends might be able to do in the crisis. As chairman of the board, Henry Cadbury wrote a letter commending the Picketts to the Christian care of all they visited.[22]

The efforts of the Quakers to think of ways to help the Jews in Germany brought them to the attention of the American Jewish Community. Henry Cadbury was already well known to a number of Jewish scholars for his studies on Jewish thought, culture, and language at the time of Jesus. It was therefore not surprising that the Central Conference of American Rabbis asked him to address its annual convention in June of 1934 in Wernersville, Pennsylvania. It was suggested that he might draw on Quaker experience in dealing with persecution to help the rabbis consider what might best be the course of the Jewish community in the face of the threat of Hitler.

Henry Cadbury began this historic talk by saying that the Quaker ideal of service was to approach the persecutors and appeal to their consciences. This was the audience to which he should be speaking, the Nazis, not the Jews. But since he had been asked as one member of a persecuted group to discuss the problems of another persecuted people, he would try to do so. He would not concentrate on trying to avoid persecution, which Friends had done through migration, or trying to stop persecution through noncompliance and persistence, or courting persecution through martyrdom; but rather on the maintenance of the highest ideals under persecution, thus winning world opinion:

> A natural reaction to persecution is hatred, reprisal and revenge. With, of course, some failures the Friends have attempted to avoid this. The example of Penn shows this. Retaliation . . . multiplies the wrongs, calls attention to the strength of the persecuting group and increases fear, hate and dislike in the opposite sides.

Remembering how the denunciations of Germany in World War I had simply increased German militancy, Henry Cadbury warned against making emotional appeals to American public opinion that would only solidify German intransigence and could increase the maltreatment of the oppressed in Germany. The boycott of Germany that was being proposed was a form of war without bloodshed, and war in any form was not the way to right the wrongs being inflicted on the Jewish people:

> It is easy enough for us to sit quietly at ease and try to suggest what to do. But the persecuted himself needs more than human resources to endure. . . . Perhaps something can be done by your demonstration of non-partisan good will, by your conspicuous avoidance of whatever evil you are charged with, and your patient and wise philosophical calm and humor. Make clear the ideals for which you stand, so that persecution will be for those ideals.[23]

The *New York Times* covered this speech with the headline:

URGE GOODWILL BY JEWS FOR NAZIS
Professor Cadbury of Society of Friends Says it
Will Gain More than Hate—Decries Boycott as "War"[24]

Not surprisingly, some of the rabbis were upset by what sounded like a plea to give way to Hitlerism. Henry Cadbury's speech had not affected them that way, but the newspaper account would perhaps make the world feel that their attitude was supine. They developed a resolution calling for resistance to "the attacks being made by the Hitler Government upon civilization and upon all the moral and spiritual values which we cherish." Rabbi Stephen Wise gave the resolution to the *New York Times* with some comments: "Although Professor Cadbury is a dear friend of mine and I do not wish to quarrel with him personally, I do wish to right the wrong implied when he asked the Jews not to show hatred toward Hitler and Germany."[25]

Henry Cadbury characteristically did not reply to this criticism. He had been asked to draw from Quaker experience and from his own views, and he had done so. He had not intended to make pronouncements for the Jewish people, but if the speech had been so interpreted, or so reported, he would have to accept the consequences. Perhaps he had sounded more judgmental than he realized. This form of deafness still overcame him at times when he was deeply involved in moral issues. It shocked both him and his listeners, who perceived him as the mildest of men.

But he truly believed that the way of love and goodwill, the way of Jesus, must someday be tried, and if the cycle of war and vengeance and hatred and more war that had produced Hitler was ever to be broken, and for those who, like himself, felt they must live, as his Quaker ancestors had pledged "in that life and power that taketh away the occasion for wars," there could be no turning back, although the pacifist position was painfully full of dilemmas in the face of Hitler.

There were actions, however, that Friends could take. They could begin the long process of helping Jews, and those of mixed ancestry, leave Germany; they could provide what succor they were able to those who remained, and they could remonstrate with the Nazis over their inhumane treatment of political prisoners and Jews. For more than a decade the American Friends Service Committee was to be active in these channels of service, and Henry Cadbury was deeply involved.

CHAPTER 8

Conscience in the Classroom

In the fall of 1934, the Cadburys returned to their house on Buckingham Place in Cambridge. A new family, the Emersons, had
moved in next door in their absence, and there were children for
Winnie to play with. Lydia Cadbury approached her new neighbor
one day when they were both out hanging clothes with the question,
"How is it that you and your husband have such beautiful children
even if you are both homely?" It was the beginning of a friendship.[1]

Lydia Cadbury's reputation for forthrightness was forever ce-
mented in the Cambridge community by an event at a social evening during that first year back. A Harvard professor and a female
colleague had gone to Reno together, filed for divorce from their
respective mates, and subsequently married each other. It was an
unusual enough occurrence in the 1930s to cause tongues to wag,
but in private. At the party Lydia Cadbury saw the couple in question together and asked Henry Cadbury in a voice loud enough to
be overheard:

Henry, does thee know that that woman has committed adultery?
Lydia, I only know that she has not committed it with me, came the
reply.[2]

Lydia Cadbury also became famous for riding her bicycle all
over Cambridge. Once, arriving at a corner where a police officer
was directing traffic, she paused at the light and balanced herself by
resting her hand on his shoulder. Someone took a picture, which
was published in a Cambridge paper and became part of the growing Lydia Cadbury legend. People sometimes wondered if Henry

were embarrassed by Lydia Cadbury, but in fact he enjoyed her escapades. "Has thee been a very bad girl today?" he would sometimes ask her.[3]

Henry Cadbury's own outlet continued to be tennis. He played a hard, fast, competitive game. One of his students of the period remembers playing with him and with Richard Mott Gummere, a classics scholar and director of admissions. The games were memorable: "Henry and Richard would curse each other out in Greek. And they would use the Quaker plain speech. 'This is when I am going to get thee! Richard,' Henry would say."[4]

The children settled into Cambridge life, though they missed their friends on the Haverford campus at first. Betty, having graduated from Westtown, entered Wellesley, following in the footsteps of Lydia Cadbury; Christopher began Westtown in the fall of 1936, Warder in 1940, and Winnie in 1941.

As Hollis Professor, Henry Cadbury was expected to teach no more than eight hours a week and to devote the rest of his time to research. He had a carrel in the Widener Library as well as an office at the Divinity School and spent many hours in happy bibliographical research. With the Hollis chair came a special library of books kept in a closet, about which he wrote an article, "My Professor's Closet." He also studied the history of Harvard Library, wrote about John Harvard's books, and began a long-range project of building up an impressive collection of Quaker books and documents at Harvard.[5]

Enrollment in the Divinity School was at a low ebb when Henry Cadbury joined the faculty in 1934. The Great Depression had taken its toll on the student body in all liberal arts institutions. Harvard had not entirely recovered from the blow of the Andover separation in 1926 and the consequent loss of Congregational ministerial candidates. In addition, the rise of neo-orthodoxy in the late 1920s and early 1930s meant that the liberal tradition in theology was less popular. The new president of Harvard, James Conant, was insisting that the school become more self-supporting. It became necessary for professors to take on several roles. When the librarian of the Andover-Harvard Theological Library resigned in 1939, Henry Cadbury was asked to become library director, with an assistant librarian working under him to supervise the day-to-day management of the library. This might have seemed a double load, but Henry Cadbury's interest in books made it a pleasant duty. Despite the austerities of the budget, he used the opportunity to build up the collection. Since there was never quite enough money to buy books, he urged his colleagues to join him in reviewing books for the *Harvard Theological Review* and subsequently donating the books to the library.

As library director, he moved his office to a large room adjacent to the library and was there most of the time he was not actually teaching classes. This meant he was available to both students and colleagues most hours of the day. Although he was always a busy man, he was courteous about interruptions. Gradually, over the years, he became known as someone to whom one could go with one's problems. He was always genuinely glad to listen and to offer help, often by asking the right questions. It was thus that he earned the reputation as "unofficial Quaker pastor to colleague and student alike."[6]

He was also available to Harvard College students with an interest in the New Testament or Quaker history. Among such students was Frederick Barnes Tolles of New Hampshire, of Unitarian background, who became so interested in Quakerism as a result of his conversations with Henry Cadbury that he ultimately joined the Religious Society of Friends. Henry Cadbury helped Frederick Tolles gather original material about Ralph Waldo Emerson for an honors paper on the Quaker influence on the Concord poet. Frederick Tolles earned an M.A. and ultimately a Ph.D. at Harvard, writing a brilliant thesis on the Quaker colonial mercantile establishment that was published as *Meeting House and Counting House.* In 1941 he became the director of the Friends Historical Library at Swarthmore with the help of Henry Cadbury's recommendation.

Frederick Tolles and Henry Cadbury had much in common: a sincere devotion to painstaking scholarship; curiosity; a probing, objective approach to accepted legend; and a dry wit. Despite the differences in their ages, they became fast friends. They worked together on many projects and corresponded for years to come.

Henry Cadbury's interest in helping Frederick Tolles as a student with his research was characteristic. Throughout his life, he was as much involved in the scholarly pursuits of others as in his own. He answered queries, did original research, collected documents, corrected manuscripts, read proof, and looked for publishers for aspiring scholars and authors. In several cases, when it was necessary, he raised the money for publication. He also gave away material he had collected for his own eventual publication if someone came along who wanted to work on the same topic and asked for help. Some of his colleagues worried about this generosity, for Henry Cadbury was willing to give away material to scholars considerably less able than himself. What seemed to matter to

Henry Cadbury, however, was that the job be done. He responded as generously to the authors of children's books or of novels as to those of serious historical studies. Sunday school teachers wrote to him for help. One wanted to know how many times toads were mentioned in the Bible!

Much of his correspondence was devoted to helping both the Friends Historical Library at Swarthmore and the Quaker Collection at the Haverford Library improve their holdings. He bought books at auction, checked catalogs in England and elsewhere, urged families to donate their letters and documents to the Quaker libraries, and made sure that duplicate copies of pamphlets, publications, and minutes of Quaker meetings and organizations were shared among the libraries and, when possible, with Harvard.

His work with the *Annual Catalogue* of George Fox's works had led to a continuing search for more of the lost Fox documents. In an 1887 copy of the *Friend* (Philadelphia) Henry Cadbury had read a description of an ancient manuscript volume of Fox's epistles copied in a clear, uniform handwriting, but he had no luck finding the manuscript. Shortly after coming to Harvard, he wrote a letter in the *Friend* inquiring about its whereabouts and was rewarded by a letter from its present owners, Edward Wanton Smith of Germantown, and his sisters, Anna Wharton Wood and Esther Morton Smith, describing precisely the volume he sought. Owned originally by Thomas Richardson of Newport, Rhode Island, whose name was inscribed in 1714, the book contained more than forty unpublished letters of Fox, as well as those of other early Quaker leaders, many of them addressed to Friends in Barbados, and many dealing with the issue of slavery.

Henry Cadbury was elated by this extremely valuable find and tried to speculate on its origin. He concluded it was possibly compiled by Thomas Richardson's mother-in-law, Leah Newberry, who, according to Rhode Island Women's Quarterly Meeting minutes, kept a book of Fox's epistles to read to the Quarterly Meetings.[7] He told the owners of the importance of the manuscript and was gratified when, in 1944, they donated the volume to the Quaker Collection at the Haverford College Library.

In 1936, a new curator took over the Quaker Collection and became Henry Cadbury's correspondent and friend. Thomas Drake was a historian with a deep interest in the Quaker testimony against slavery. His book *Quakers and Slavery in America*, published by Yale University Press in 1950, is regarded as a classic in the field. Since the Quaker relationship to blacks from colonial days to the present was one of Henry Cadbury's abiding interests, the two had much in common. Whenever he visited Haverford, Henry Cadbury would look up Thomas Drake, usually with a small addition for the collection and a list of questions to ask. Among the questions was inevitably one addressed to Drake himself: Had he learned anything new lately? What was he into now? Drake sometimes felt this probing had a critical edge: "His enormous drive, his phenomenal card-catalogue memory, his extraordinary output, even his suggestions made one feel a little deficient in enterprise and accomplishment."[8]

Henry Cadbury was apparently unaware that he sometimes had this effect on his colleagues. His curiosity and his memory together drove him to a need continually to gather facts from people or from books, until he seemed like a walking encyclopedia in the making. "What have you learned that I ought to know?" was a standard salutation. Though pleasant, he had little time for small talk. He made notes on endless 3 × 5 cards, sometimes using the discards in a library to save money, but he was also able to refer one to a particular footnote on a particular page in a particular book without referring to his written notes.

His correspondence alone would have daunted the average scholar. To save time and money, he used penny postcards. His trenchant sayings and queries became famous. "You know a man named Cadbury?" the superintendent of the Minnesota Historical Society asked Thomas Drake in 1935. "He simply bombards me with postcards." Henry Cadbury was doing research on the Norwegian Quakers and could not get to Minnesota. Other Quaker archivists experienced feelings close to terror when Henry Cadbury's stream of innocent but pointed postcards began to arrive. He always knew precisely what was needed and where it might be found. One had to be on one's toes to keep up.[9]

The proofreading he undertook so generously had its compensations. Some of the little stories with which he illuminated his lectures came from typographical errors he found in the articles he read, either in manuscript or in printed form. He was fond of quoting one author who referred by mistake to "the power of applied silence" instead of science. And he enjoyed a clipping from a Salem, Indiana, newspaper: "While attending services at Highland Church Saturday, four heifers, owned by Charles and Humphrey Brown, escaped from the pasture and were killed by a train."[10]

At approximately the same time as Thomas Drake came to Haverford, a Quaker couple, Howard and Anna Brinton, became the directors of Pendle Hill. Henry Cadbury had known the Brintons for many years. Howard Brinton had grown up in West Chester, and had gone to Haverford. Both Howard and Anna Cox, his future wife, had attended the All Friends Conference in London in 1920 and had later worked together on child-feeding in Poland. Both had advanced degrees, Howard in physics and philosophy, Anna in classics and archaeology. They had taught together at Mills College in California and at Pendle Hill, and both continued to teach and to write. Frequently, they involved Henry Cadbury in their projects. The three shared an interest in Quaker history, although their approach to Quakerism itself was much different, Howard Brinton particularly being known as a student and proponent of mysticism. The first collaboration between the Brintons and Henry Cadbury came in 1938, when Howard Brinton edited a book in honor of Rufus Jones, entitled *Children of the Light,* and Henry Cadbury contributed a chapter, "Hebraica and the Jews in Early Quaker Interest," mentioning Margaret Fell's and George Fox's books addressed to the Jews and the contact of several Jews with the early Society of Friends.[11]

Henry Cadbury had scarcely settled into the pleasant but demanding academic life of his first year at Harvard when he was asked to give the prestigious Lowell lectures at King's Chapel in

With Thomas Drake. Photo from the collection of and by Theodore Hetzel.

Boston the following spring. William James had given the Lowell lectures when Henry Cadbury was first a Harvard student. Henry Cadbury decided it was the right time to develop the ideas about Jesus and his times about which he had been thinking for some years. He wanted particularly to warn people against reading into the life of Jesus what they might wish to find and to urge instead that the quest for the true historical Jesus, however slow, painful, incomplete, and disappointing that quest, be continued.

These Lowell lectures, published by Macmillan in 1937 as *The Perils of Modernizing Jesus,* are regarded by some scholars as Henry Cadbury's most important piece of work. In reviewing the book for the *Journal of Biblical Literature,* John Knox, a member of the Revised Standard Version New Testament Committee, said that Cadbury had rendered an important and distinctive service: "It is a brilliant analysis of the ways in which we distort Jesus in the very act of seeing him. It is an impressive warning against believing too implicitly what our modern Western eyes tell us about him. For Jesus was a Palestinian Jew of the first century, and between such a man and ourselves there can be no such thing as seeing eye to eye and face to face." [12]

In these lectures, Henry Cadbury developd the theme that Jesus must be understood as a pious Jew of his time, with apocalyptic attitudes, a matter-of-fact belief in the reality of exorcism and miracle, and a submission to the will of God that were very much part of the Jewish and Oriental thinking of his day. His religious experience was not unique: "The religion of Jesus was not centered about a specific religious experience. It was rather the religious interpretation of unspecifically religious experience—his homely knowledge of men and of nature, his native and forthright sense of good and evil, and his personal acceptance of the life that befell him with its twofold prospects of success and failure as the divine will for him." [13]

Jesus thought concretely, not abstractly, Henry Cadbury said, and therefore did not generalize his ethical precepts. He thought in terms of individuals, never of social institutions. Those today who wished to make him the author of a social gospel were guilty of ignoring this fact in their effort to "modernize" his message. He taught that men must act justly, not that justice must be achieved. Yet the religious spirit with which Jesus taught was a prerequisite to social betterment:

> No passion for humanity, no philanthropic sentiment, no program for social betterment can be more effective in producing perfectly socialized persons than the essentially religious spirit such as we find in

Jesus. This religious spirit cannot be put on at will, is not always easy for the modern mind. In fact it must be expressed in different terms in different ages and may today sometimes lurk unrecognized or scornfully denied under the philosophy of sociology or philanthropy. When it does exist it is marked by the same power, insight, instinctive virtue and persistent efficiency which marked the career of Jesus.[14]

Henry Cadbury was aware that the process of demodernizing the figure of Jesus might seem destructive and disappointing. Should we fill the gap with new ideas? Or leave it empty? Or partially fill it with the results of painstaking historical research and imagination? He urged the latter. No leap of faith was necessary; Jesus' authority came from the validity of the truth he taught; the more that could be recovered of that teaching and that truth, the better for humankind.

Among those who were enthusiastic about the lectures was Dean Willard Sperry. "I think it is absolutely first rate," he wrote. "It seems to me to say clearly and unequivocally what badly needs saying and to blow away a vast amount of fog and dust that has surrounded this subject for a quarter of a century. Personally I have been groping for some time for some of the conclusions you have reached and I am grateful for your help."[15]

If it was perilous to modernize Jesus, it was also dangerous to modernize Quaker history. In an article "Friends and Their Social Testimonies," published in the *Friend* (London) in June of 1935, Henry Cadbury asserted that early Friends were very much a part of the social ferment of their day and that many of their social testimonies were held by other minority groups. Friends, however, took their religion seriously, tested it through experience, were willing to suffer for it, and translated individual conviction into group conscience through the unique process of achieving unity in the meeting. Just as Jesus demanded more of his followers than the other Jewish teachers of his day, so Friends demanded more of themselves.

And where did this driving social conscience originate? Henry Cadbury thought it was largely unconscious: "—earlier statements of forgotten predecessors, anxiety for the welfare of one's fellowmen, hostility to the conventions of society. Nearer the surface of consciousness were the reasons given for the position—scripture texts, when such were possible, and assertions of divine revelation."[16]

Friends had also been creative in translating the social ideals of one generation to the next, from the slow development of a Quaker pacifist position in the seventeenth century, to the birth of a Quaker position against slavery in the eighteenth and nineteenth centuries:

Conscientousness at one point has led to new areas of sensitiveness. Our refusal of war service has almost led us to the refusal of war taxes. There has been constant interplay between our insistence on equality in sexes and that in races, and we have recognized the analogous and casual relations between war and competitive industry. The early Friends were "agin" society on many fronts. In our age of specialization one unpopular cause at a time seems all that an individual or a small denomination can handle. But life cannot be so divided.[17]

The article was prophetic. An opportunity for Henry Cadbury to test out and to suffer for his beliefs, and to widen his own sensitivity, lay just ahead. In June, the state of Massachusetts had passed a law requiring all teachers to sign an oath of allegiance to the Constitution of the United States and of the Commonwealth of Massachusetts, and Harvard professors were not exempt. Henry Cadbury found that he had until November 30, 1935, to sign the oath or lose his position.

As a Friend, Henry Cadbury was opposed to oaths. That was easily remedied; he was allowed instead to file an affirmation. But more seriously, he was conscientiously opposed to the very concept of the loyalty oath and its threat to academic freedom. And as a pacifist he was aware that the pledge to support the Constitution implied the use of force. Yet most of his learned colleagues urged him to sign. The contributions he was making to the field of New Testament scholarship and to the education of future scholars and preachers, he was told, were far more important than his uneasiness at taking such an oath.

Several others at Harvard were in the same quandary. Kirtley Mather, a geologist, was refusing to sign on the grounds of civil liberties. (He later signed with qualifications and continued to teach.) Professor Earl Winslow at Tufts, a Friend, also refused to sign and ultimately lost his position. A larger group, consisting of seven teachers at Andover Seminary and Seal Thompson, professor of biblical literature at Wellesley College and a good friend of the Cadburys, urged Henry Cadbury to unite with them in joint action, demanding the right of signing with stated reservations. For the sake of this group, Henry Cadbury undertook correspondence with the American Civil Liberties Union and a Boston law firm on possible courses of action.

After the painful sense of isolation he had experienced when he was suspended from Haverford, he felt the need of consulting widely before making a decision that might change the course of his life. Lydia Cadbury, of course, was supportive, but she had hated the episode at Haverford, and the thought of being again uprooted was disturbing. Henry Cadbury wrote to Harold Evans, a Phila- delphia Quaker lawyer; to Otto Reinemann, a Quaker scholar with a German background; and to Joshua Cope, a Quaker ornithologist teaching at Cornell University, to get their views. Evans felt he had taken a similar oath as a lawyer without much trouble, Reinemann did not see the parallel with the German oath, and Cope confessed he had not given the matter much thought.[18]

Hearing of his quandary, Friends in Philadelphia were fully sympathetic. The Board of Directors of Pendle Hill had offered Henry Cadbury the job of director for that year. The position re- mained unfilled, and several board members wrote to assure Henry Cadbury that if he felt he had to leave his Harvard position they would welcome him with open arms. So would Bryn Mawr. Clarence Pickett thought the AFSC ought to get behind a drive against such laws. The Yearly Meeting Peace Committee wrote that it was "shocked."[19]

After much agony of spirit, Henry Cadbury decided to unite with the Andover group in a joint protest and to try to find a way to make the affirmation without violating his conscience. His first at- tempt was to rewrite the wording on the blank he was asked to sign. It was sent back to him as unacceptable. A second effort was to state his objection to the oath on a sheet of paper attached to the blank. This, too, was returned.

A few days after the deadline, he was called to see President James Conant. Conant himself had objected to the oath but had signed it, stating that "it was unthinkable that Harvard should dis- obey the law" and on that same basis he had urged the Harvard fac- ulty to sign. Henry Cadbury approached the interview expecting the worst. Instead, Conant indicated that Harvard would refuse to accept a resignation and asked if Henry Cadbury would be willing for the officers of the University to use his case as the basis for test- ing the constitutionality of the oath. If they decided to do so, they would carry the case as far as the Supreme Court. They did not be- lieve that they would win, but they thought they might at least gain time for a new legislature to come into being and perhaps to keep Henry Cadbury on the faculty for another two years while the case progressed through the courts. Henry Cadbury wrote his brother Benjamin Cadbury to describe the interview: "This is the first sign of spunk in the University since the law was passed and I am cheered. But of course nothing is settled, still less public."[20]

Immediately after the interview with Conant, Henry Cadbury

went to Yale to deliver some lectures. On his return he heard from his colleagues at Andover-Newton that they had decided to try once more to file with reservations. Seal Thompson was doing the same. Henry Cadbury decided to go along with this last-ditch effort for the sake of the others. On December 26 he addressed a letter to James Conant and James G. Reardon, commissioner of education, outlining his objections to the oath: "Any political control or dictation in education can easily become for a conscientious teacher a form of political interference with the free exercise of religion, and this is especially true of teachers who like myself are teachers of religion or for those who teach in private or parochial schools." He stated that he was signing the attached affirmation conditionally and that if at any time he felt the law was jeopardizing freedom of thought and expression for himself or for others, "I shall be at liberty to revoke the accompanying affirmation and the solemn promise therein contained." This letter must be kept on file both at the university and at the office of the commissioner of education, he stipulated.[21]

On January 2, 1936, came the prompt reply. The commissioner was accepting his affirmation and, although it could not be a matter of public record, was going to file the accompanying letter. The same decision had been made for Henry Cadbury's partners in conscience. For the moment the crisis was past.

This second brush with a threat to academic freedom had a strong effect on Henry Cadbury. He spoke of the need for Quakers to be vigilant for the maintenance of academic freedom at the Friends General Conference the following summer, stating, "Nor can truth set us free, unless men are free to seek the truth."[22] He carefully followed the passage of loyalty oaths by the various states and the attempts to have them ruled unconstitutional and kept files on those individuals who refused to sign, most of them not subversives at all but Quakers like himself.

The experience also deepened his sense that for him the path of religious expression was the path of action. He spoke of it in a lecture given to the students and faculty of the Divinity School in February:

If you could have lived with me through the strain of many weeks this autumn and early winter when I was dealing largely in the secret of my own conscience, with the question of my relation to the teacher's oath, you might have seen what I mean by a living religion. I refer not to questions of my personal welfare, they never bothered me at all. But if real moral questions are at stake (even in the very slight degree) and

if loyalties are genuinely in conflict, and if moral questions are only
too easily confused with merely political or strategic considerations, a
course of right action in personal behavior taxes much more than you
might suppose the genuinely religious elements that any man can bring
to such a problem.[23]

The degree of self-revelation reflected in this statement was
wholly uncharacteristic of Henry Cadbury. He preferred in the
classroom and on the lecture platform to keep his own opinions private and to draw out the thoughts of others. But when he was called
upon to speak of his religious beliefs he accepted the assignment,
however distasteful the task. At Harvard Divinity School he was
asked to make a presentation called "My Personal Religion" in 1936,
1940, and 1944, and he several times complied with the same request from Quaker meetings. The humility that prevented his in-
flicting his views on others evidently also prevented his refusing to
air his views when others felt it was his turn to do so.

In the 1936 lecture he began by confessing he felt he did not
have much to offer in the areas of theology and personal religion:
"My lack of these is a nakedness that I hesitate to expose." He felt
perfectly comfortable, he said, in leaving the metaphysical questions in regard to the existence of God and of immortality open and
unanswered, just as he told his students he was willing to leave open
certain historical questions about the New Testament. And though
he had been raised a Quaker, in what many regarded as a society of
mystics, taught to expect occasional divine revelations, he had never
found that expectation fulfilled. Moreover, he thought this was true
for many others: "Now I am not denying a large mystical strain in
Quaker history, both early and late, but I am quite convinced that it
has never been general and that a large number of non-mystics
have enjoyed religious life under its auspices and have contributed
much that Friends have done for human good."[24]

As for himself, perhaps he failed to recognize what others would
regard as an intimate religious experience. Sometimes the reality of
such experience might be too close to be recognized, he said, quoting Francis Thompson's poem:

> The angels keep their ancient places;—
> Turn but a stone and start a wing;
> 'Tis ye, 'tis your estrangèd faces,
> That miss the many-splendoured thing.[25]

"And I find myself in moods that seem to me closely to resemble
the moods of religious experience. But I do not induce them, nor

quote from them, nor treat them as evidential. I am inclined to think other people would do so. I would regard that as a matter of interpretation."[26]

Both theology and mystical experience could in fact be regarded as interpretations or dramatizations of life. Thus a vivid conviction of duty within a person could be interpreted as a direct command of a personal God. John Woolman had a traditional theology and interpreted experience mystically, but his journal revealed "a sensitive conscience feeling its course in a series of soul searching problems." This was the religious personality in action:

> When a man deals religiously with issues that others settle in other ways, in fact takes seriously the religious implications of behavior . . . tries to practice fully the standards that conventional religion officially endorses, and to make his whole life consistent if not conscious, he is in my opinion practicing religion as much as the one who skillfully builds the dialectic structure of a well rounded theology or as the man who through public and private devotion lives in that mystical drama of a religious imagination.[27]

It was an amazingly frank statement of his dilemma. Many people would find it a damaging confession, Henry Cadbury said. The orthodox might say he was a hypocrite to teach and preach religion from such a point of view, whereas the secular would continue to discount his scholarship and thought because he was suspect of being "for religion." Nevertheless it was where he stood: "I should be willing to let my religion rest very largely on a life of honest thinking, of kindly dealing and of challenging impact upon the social issues and conventions that it comes into contact with."[28] Although many of his students, and some of his colleagues, held a far more orthodox religious view than his, there was no evident reaction to this or to the several equally frank talks he gave. As one Friend recently remarked, people did not always hear Henry Cadbury. They saw Christian characteristics in his humility, his simplicity, his freedom from malice, and his devotion to conscience, and they inferred a conventional concept of faith undergirding his life, no matter how clearly he tried to explain his intellectual hesitations. Eventually he came to see that this projection was almost inevitable, and he would simply have to live with it.

A related and continuing problem was his relationship to fundamentalist students who were beginning to come to Harvard in increasing numbers. He had no wish to attack their beliefs, but he hoped, by asking adroit questions, that he might open their minds a bit. But to his surprise many of these students did well, enjoyed his classes, praised his methods, and wrote to him after they left Harvard, although they seem unshaken in their orthodoxy. Did they interpret what he had to say in light of their own wishes? Should he perhaps write about the perils of conservatizing Henry Cadbury?

One of his early students was Harold B. Kuhn, an Evangelical Quaker who found some of Harvard's theological positions not always congenial. Yet despite their obvious difference, he found Henry Cadbury unfailingly helpful and kind:

> As a teacher he was outstanding for his ability to see issues, recognize legitimate differences of opinion between himself and others . . . his attitude was always personally supportive, open-minded, cordial and fair-minded.
>
> He had a keen but disciplined sense of humor. Always careful not to embarrass the fledgling student, he could use his humor as an ever-so-gentle prod. . . . I never knew him to use a cutting remark, never lacking understanding for those who, like myself came from Evangelical backgrounds.[29]

Harry Meserve, also a student of Henry Cadbury's at this period, a liberal who later became a well-known Unitarian minister, was deeply moved by the respect Henry always showed those of his students who differed with him. "It was more than respect, it was genuine love," Meserve said.[30] A student from a somewhat later period, Leroy Garrett, a minister of the Church of Christ, remembered being shocked when Henry Cadbury spoke of the resurrection in class: "Once in class when we were going over the so-called Apostles' Creed, which reads 'I believe in God Almighty and in Christ Jesus, his only son, our Lord,' and goes on to say 'And the third day rose from the dead.' Just before that it reads 'Who was crucified under Pontius Pilate and was buried.' The old prof, who was sly as a fox, referring to that creed being recited in church, said, 'That's the line I believe, I join in when it says he was crucified under Pontius Pilate and was buried.'"[31]

Harry Meserve remembers Henry Cadbury saying in another class that he believed in the resurrection on Tuesdays, Thursdays, and Saturdays. Yet because of his gentleness and the genuineness of his convictions, the students came away his ardent supporters. Leroy Garrett wrote that he came in time to understand how committed Henry Cadbury was to the ministry of Jesus and learned to love him.[32]

Yet despite his continuing questioning and his espousal of an ethical religion, one sometimes hears in Henry Cadbury's writings and talks echoes of a continued search and continuing longing. In a talk given at several churches in this period called "The Absence of God" he spoke of the sense of Presence enjoyed by the mystics, but pointed out that most of them had their dry, blank periods, whereas nonmystics lived continually in the situation described in the parables of Jesus: the good servant who must do his duty in the absence of the master: "Religion is not only the beatific vision, it is getting on without it." [33]

With *The Perils of Modernizing Jesus* well under way and the crisis in his own career once more settled, at least for the time, Henry Cadbury had a little more time to devote to the pursuit of Quaker history, which he called at this point in his life an avocation. He was still studying the abolitionists and their predecessors. This led naturally to an interest in Negro membership in the Society of Friends. Why had a people who had been so progressive in advocating the rights of the Negro been so slow to admit Negroes to membership? He gave a course on Quaker social testimonies at Pendle Hill in 1934 which dwelt on this problem, and in April 1936, he published an essay titled "Negro Membership in the Society of Friends" in the *Journal of Negro History.*

In a scholarly and yet graceful style he wrote of early Quaker efforts to provide religious instruction for the blacks and the setting up of special black meetings. Richard Allen, the founder of the African Society in Philadelphia, forerunner of the first African Methodist Episcopal church, Mother Bethel, had attended a Quaker school run by Anthony Benezet and had modeled procedures in the African society after those of a Quaker meeting. Occasional blacks were admitted to membership in the eighteenth and nineteenth centuries. Most of these were outstanding people: Peter Hill, the clockmaker from New Jersey; Paul Cuffee, the sea captain; David Mapps, also a sea captain, and his wife, Grace; Cyrus Bustill, baker for George Washington's army, and his daughter Grace Bustill, who married Robert Douglass, and their children, Sarah Mapps and Robert Douglass, Jr., respectively a well-known educator and portrait painter. Robert Purvis, a founder of the American Anti-Slavery Society and the Pennsylvania Anti-Slavery Society, attended Byberry Meeting.[34]

There were, however, many cases in which Friends were reluctant to admit Negroes to membership and treated those who had joined as second-class citizens, asking them to meet apart or sit on a special back bench. The discovery that Arch Street Meeting segregated its black members in this fashion caused Angelina and Sarah Grimké to feel estranged from that meeting.

Henry Cadbury's essay presented no false claims for Quaker attitudes toward equality, nor did it falsely disparage the group. John Hope Franklin, the noted black historian, was impressed. In October of 1937, Henry Cadbury was asked to address the Centennial of the Cheyney Training School for Teachers, now Cheyney University, founded by Friends originally as the Institute for Colored Youth. He chose as his topic "The Contribution of Negroes to the Education of Friends" and made the point that blacks had aided Quakers in the slow evolution of a tender conscience over the issues of slavery and racial discrimination. He spoke of the influence of Fanny Jackson Coppin on his own childhood attitudes toward questions of race. And of Sarah Douglass he said:

> A teacher for sixty years—nearly half of them in the Institute for Colored Youth when this institution was still in Philadelphia—Sarah Douglass by her refined and sensitive personality must have profoundly affected her Quaker associates as she affected those of her pupils who remain alive to bear witness. They still recall how on every Third-day morning she was absent from the school-room to sit apart and in silence in the neighboring mid-week meeting of Friends. Her quiet little bowed figure may have done in that place of worship a piece of education for Friends more effective than her presence in the formal classroom could do with the children of her own people.[35]

Attacking race prejudice at home, like preserving academic freedom, seemed more and more important as the extremes of Nazi totalitarianism were becoming evident. Henry Cadbury had maintained his sense of kinship with the German scholars and his distress that the United States had joined in punishing and humiliating Germany at the end of World War I. He was therefore depressed in the fall of 1936 to hear that on the occasion of the 550th anniversary of the founding of the University of Heidelberg (1386), the minister of science and education for Germany had declared that the "academic enterprise must be carried on under the suzerainty of the state it serves."

Although it should avoid the dangers of modernizing the findings of biblical scholarship to meet present needs, responsible scholarship could not be divorced from the values and problems of the hour, Henry Cadbury believed. It was a matter, not of modernizing, but of translating the message to apply it to modern problems. In 1936 he was made president of the Society of Biblical Literature, which he had served so long and faithfully as secretary, and in his presidential address given at the annual meeting during the Christmas holidays his talk was called "Motives of Biblical Scholarship." He contrasted those who read for revelation with those who looked instead for additional information, confident that "some remote spiritual utility will accrue from the minutest contribution to truth." The scholar must in the long run remain true to the best in the professional tradition, both in piety and open-mindedness, but he must not be indifferent to moral and spiritual values and needs of contemporary life, he said, referring to the recent Heidelberg statement.[36]

One form of social translation of the gospel for Henry Cadbury continued to be nurturing the life of the Society of Friends. In 1937, the Cambridge Friends built a new meeting house on Longfellow Park, not far from the Harvard campus, and declared it an independent body, not affiliated with any yearly meeting or group of yearly meetings. This was part of an effort, then under the wing of the American Friends Fellowship Council, soon to become part of the Friends World Committee for Consultation, to build up new meetings free from the schisms of the past. At the same time, it was a tool to unite the various branches of the Society of Friends. Members of the Boston Monthly Meeting had been worshiping for some time with the Cambridge group. Henry Cadbury worked to persuade them to merge. He and Lydia Cadbury joined the Cambridge Meeting, while keeping close to their family roots by maintaining membership also in the Twelfth Street Meeting in Philadelphia. He played an important role in the Cambridge Meeting for some twenty years, sometimes serving as clerk of the monthly meeting, sometimes as clerk of the committee on ministry.

His fame as a biblical scholar continued to grow. On June 16, 1937, Glasgow University presented him with an honorary doctorate in divinity. With the degree came a marvelous velvet beret and scarlet gown, which he wore ever afterward in academic processions.

Lydia Cadbury came along for the great occasion, and the two had a glorious time, tramping around the lochs near Glasgow, then crossing to Belfast to walk in the green Irish countryside and visit Irish Friends, then back to Birmingham for a reunion with Cadbury cousins. Geraldine Cadbury had just been made a Dame of the British Empire for her work in juvenile delinquency, and another cousin, Edward, had received an LL.D. for his collection of oriental manuscripts given to Birmingham University. The three Cadburys had a hilarious time teasing each other about these honors. Henry Cadbury also visited Oxford, had an hour and a half in the Bodleian, and continued to Friends House in London, where he managed to find two original letters of Anthony Benezet.

Upon his return to the United States in late June, he went straight to an AFSC conference on international relations in Napersville, Illinois. Then it was time for Back Log Camp. In September, the second Friends World Conference was held at Haverford and Swarthmore colleges. The opening night was given over to a panel discussion titled "The Individual Christian and the State," with Joan Mary Fry of London presiding, and T. Edmund Harvey and Henry Cadbury speaking. Henry Cadbury's talk, published in the *Friends Intelligencer* and also as a pamphlet, outlined the Christian and the Quaker objection to the rising tide of nationalism, which put the interests of the individual second to those of the state and stood in the path of the development of world brotherhood.

Through the papers and the reports of AFSC European staff, Henry Cadbury was kept abreast of developments in Europe as the rising tide of fascism crested. In Spain, the AFSC was helping to feed refugee children on both the Loyalist and the Republic sides. Elsewhere in Europe, AFSC staff were becoming increasingly involved in helping Jewish families and those of mixed Jewish-Christian marriages to make plans to emigrate. The Cadburys decided to do their part by helping to sponsor a brother and sister from Belgium, each with a spouse and children. The first family came over in the spring of 1938, but it took many months of exasperating delays and painstaking correspondence to persuade the U.S. consul in Belgium to permit the second couple to come. At one point Henry Cadbury had to state that his salary as Harvard professor was ample to support the entire family if that were necessary.[37]

It seemed to AFSC staff abroad that the U.S. consular service was nightmarishly slow in processing the applications of families trying to leave Hitler's Germany. Low as the quotas were for entry into the United States, they were not being reached. After the Night of Broken Glass in November 1938, when the Nazis attacked Jewish homes and shops and began to terrorize elderly Jews, the AFSC sent Rufus Jones, Robert Yarnall, and George Walton to Germany to intercede for the Jews. They were received in the Gestapo by a subordinate of Reinhard Heydrich and assured that they would be given every assistance in investigating the suffering of the Jews. The Jews themselves, however, urged the Quaker group to redouble its efforts to speed up migration.

In response, Clarence Pickett began to work on a project which Henry Cadbury had first suggested in 1933. He found twenty young men and women, fluent in German, who were willing to volunteer their services to the staff of the overworked American consulates in Germany. A wealthy woman agreed to pay all their expenses. The person at the State Department to whom Clarence originally spoke had been encouraging, but when he returned with the twenty signed up and ready to go, a second official told him point-blank that the consulate service was none of his affair and that if it needed more translators it could go to Congress for authorization. It was, as Clarence Pickett wrote, a hard blow. Henry and Lydia Cadbury, who had helped to recruit young men and women for the task, were very disappointed.[38]

With the mounting tide of nationalism came the threat of a second world war. Henry Cadbury had scarcely paused in his long campaign to convert at least the Christian church, if not the entire public, to the way of peace. Now, as the shadows deepened, he redoubled his efforts. He seized his many speaking engagements and opportunities to talk on such topics as "The Moral Objection to War," "War—The World's Worst Habit," "The Morality of War," "The Spiritual Basis of Pacifism," "Pacifism in the Early Christian Church," "Christians and the War Crisis," and "The Unrepentant Pacifist." In the summers of 1938 and 1939, he gave a course at Harvard Summer School titled "War and Religion." His approach was gentle and good-humored—"Lots of people who are exposed to my instruction feel it is like being exposed to the measles"—but there was real moral fervor in these lectures. In the fall of 1939, following the outbreak of war in Europe, he gave a series of radio talks over a Boston station entitled "The Pacifist in Wartime."

Lydia Cadbury was accustomed to her husband's ceaseless speaking and writing, but she was concerned about the way he was driving himself and the increasing despair he felt. In an October letter to Emma Cadbury, who had been forced to leave Vienna and was now back in the United States, she wrote of her fears:

> Henry is a remarkable being; tho I must say that with this war getting worse and worse I fully expect him to land in jail before long. I fear he will lose his position here, tho Harvard is less likely to fire a pacifist than any college I can think of; and we shall all be scattered and get our living in sundry ways. It is depressing to read the comments as the war goes on; that if we had only finished cleaning up Germany at the end of the last war this would not have happened; Hitler called just what the Kaiser was called 20 years ago; do we ever learn anything?[39]

CHAPTER 9

War and Darkness

With all of Europe embroiled in World War II and the United States on the verge of entering the conflict, Henry Cadbury seemed to his wife and others a driven man. In addition to his endless efforts to speak and write against war, he accelerated his already prodigious output of scholarly articles, reviews, and chapters.

Some of these projects were directly related to his pacifist concerns. In 1940 he developed a special reading list on "War and Religion" for the *Bulletin of the General Theological Library,* bringing together some of the research on this subject which he had been engaged in over the past twenty-five years. And in the same period he wrote a paper for the Civil Liberties Committee of the American Bar Association, preparing its case in support of the Jehovah's Witnesses, who refused to salute the American flag. Henry Cadbury's paper covered the refusal of certain early Christians to wear the laurel wreath when presented by the emperor; the disobedience of Quakers in Barbados, Virginia, and South Carolina to laws governing the holding of slaves; and more recent problems of Christians in Korea and Formosa when asked to participate in Shinto services, revealing something of the sweep of his scholarship.[1]

But there were other projects as well. Howard Brinton was editing a new festschrift, *Byways in Quaker History,* this one in honor of William Hull, a Quaker historian at Swarthmore. Henry Cadbury's chapter was titled "John Greenleaf Whittier as Quaker Historian." Writing to praise the essay, Rufus Jones told of having gone when he was a young man to meet the Quaker poet.[2]

Results of his year's work on the Fox papers were still coming to fruition. In 1940 the British Friends Historical Society published Henry Cadbury's *Swarthmore Documents in America,* a group of letters to and by George Fox, which he had collected and edited. These papers had somehow found their way from Swarthmore Hall in England to libraries in the United States, and their compilation was a service to historians of Quakerism and of other religious enthusiasms of the period.[3]

He had been following up all this time on his intention to reconstruct George Fox's *Book of Miracles* from the first and last lines of the lost documents that appeared in the *Annual Catalogue* and in turn comparing these clues with some narratives in the extant journal. Although the concept of Fox as a miracle worker may have been seen by his earlier followers as further provocation for persecution, and might not be welcomed by all latter-day Quakers, Henry Cadbury explained in a long introduction how very much these attitudes were in keeping with the expectations of the religious leaders of the day. Though the book was not published until 1948, by October of 1940 he had the manuscript well enough in hand to show it to Rufus Jones, who was to write the introduction. "Nobody else on earth could have done it. . . . This will rank as a magnum opus. "The Lord be praised," Rufus Jones wrote back exuberantly.[4]

He was not meanwhile neglecting his New Testament research. His article "The Informality of Early Christianity," which he gave first as a talk at the American Theological Society, was hailed by scholars as another example of Henry Cadbury's capacity to set gospel scenes in their historic context. He pointed out the danger of reading subsequent church history into the earlier accounts of the experiences of Jesus, but even though the gospels and particularly the Acts were written from a point of view, there remains evidence of early Christianity exhibiting the informality of a movement, rather than an institution, just as Quakerism itself began.[5]

But the gathering shadows of war were beginning to pull Henry Cadbury once more toward social action. In April of 1940, he spoke at the Charles Street Forum in Boston in tones as passionate as he had used in the *Philadelphia Ledger* during World War I: "War is an immoral act sanctioned by otherwise moral men. Nations condone ruthlessness as a means to an end and blame God, man, and the devil for their behavior."[6]

In May came a letter from Clarence Pickett suggesting that Henry Cadbury go to central Europe as a roving Quaker ambassador, along with two other men close to the AFSC and friends of Henry Cadbury's, Howard Elkinton and Douglas Steere, to see what might yet be done to ameliorate the situation for the victims of Nazism. Henry Cadbury wrote to Rufus Jones to say that he felt

Clarence Pickett himself would be much more effective because of Washington's confidence in him and that he, Henry Cadbury, would be willing to come to Philadelphia to fill in while Clarence was abroad. "I don't promise to fill his shoes," he wrote.[7]

A few days after this letter was written, Germany invaded the Netherlands, Belgium, Luxembourg, and France. With the separate armistice between France and Germany on June 17, the English Quakers had to withdraw from the work in France, and the American Quakers alone carried on in both France and Germany. Clarence Pickett was soon more heavily involved than ever in trying to persuade the American government to permit the entry of refugee children into the United States. Working closely with Jewish and other religious organizations, he became a symbol of the effort to rescue men, women, and children from Europe. There was no time to visit Germany itself. But Clarence Pickett was near exhaustion, and the AFSC welcomed Henry Cadbury's offer to take his place for the month of August while the Picketts enjoyed a much needed rest on Cape Cod.

With the Battle of Britain under way, there was great interest in bringing British children to the United States. The AFSC cooperated, hoping that the concern could be extended to European children. The Cadburys decided to do their bit by inviting Rud Nickalls, son of John Nickalls of the Friends Reference Library, to stay with them for the duration. He arrived in August with a boatload of British children. Lydia Cadbury managed to intercept the train that was bringing them from Montreal to New York at Fort Ticonderoga and took him in triumph to Back Log Camp.

At AFSC headquarters, Henry Cadbury found himself immersed in preparing for the probable reinstitution of the draft and protesting the blockade of Europe. The Quakers were still working among refugee children in southern France and seeing the results of the blockade in widespread hunger. It was 1917 all over again.

On September 16, 1940, the Burke-Wadsworth bill was approved by Congress, providing the first peacetime conscription in the history of the United States and calling upon young men to register by October 16. Upon his return to Cambridge, Henry Cadbury was immediately besieged by young men wanting his counsel on their draft choices. At the same time, with other civil libertarians, he protested an effort to expose conscientious objectors to public criticism and ridicule by having their names published in the newspapers and over the radio.

Henry Cadbury did not like the role of draft counselor. He had always preferred to lead young men and young women to make up their own minds, using the Socratic method of asking the appropriate questions. It was part and parcel of his firm belief that each person must find his or her own way, own truth. On a deeper level, it was related to his strong feelings about not imposing himself upon others. Yet the young men now facing draft choices had such limited experiences that he felt he had to guide them more than he would have liked, as they came up against the illogic of some of the draft boards.

At the tenth anniversary of the founding of Pendle Hill, he spoke on "Quakerism Adequate for Today" and problems of maintaining an unpopular pacifist stand:

> It is well to recall too that in the matters of conscience, the militarists demand of us a consistency that they themselves are not required to maintain. If you ever hear a C.O. before a tribunal you will notice that the embarrassing questions asked of him could be matched by equally embarrassing questions to be asked the court. I am not pleading for loose thinking or easy self-acquittal, but it is, I believe, unfair to assume that the pacifist has on him the burden of proof, especially when the country is not even at war.[8]

An opportunity to get away from some of these tensions for a few weeks, and to serve the AFSC overseas, came just after Christmas. The Service Committee had decided to send delegates to both England and Germany in an effort to carry on an enlarged relief operation in the war-stricken areas of Europe. The delegates to Germany would contact the German government to obtain permission to enter the occupied areas and appraise relief needs. The British delegation would talk to British foreign officials about lifting the blockade and allowing the entry of food for the children of Europe. Both would visit and do what they could to sustain local Quakers. It was decided to ask Robert Yarnall and Henry Cadbury to be the representatives to Great Britain, and James Vail and Harold Evans were chosen for Germany.

The four men left on January 11, 1941, aboard the S.S. *Exeter.* Wartime travel was dangerous, and Lydia Cadbury was worried, but the travelers encountered nothing worse than a violent storm at sea off Bermuda. Henry Cadbury and Robert Yarnall, with their British visas, were allowed to land on Bermuda. They hired bicycles and rode to visit the aquarium and the historical society and to regain their equilibrium. The rest of the voyage was spent in preparing for their missions to Europe and in getting better acquainted. James Vail could quote poetry by heart, Henry Cadbury discovered, and Harold Evans knew a good bit about navigation.

From Lisbon, Robert Yarnall and Henry Cadbury took a plane to England. They had their papers in order, but before being admitted to the country they were thoroughly searched at the airport. Henry Cadbury was considerably startled to be detained for further questioning. The examining officer had found in his pocket a small book in a strange foreign language, with a German imprint and a series of annotated maps. It must have been clear to the officer that he was dealing with a German spy, masquerading as a Quaker.

Fortunately, the superior officer to whom Henry Cadbury was referred immediately recognized the language of the unknown book as Greek. It was a small Greek New Testament which Henry Cadbury had bought years ago in Germany, and the maps were the various journeys of Saint Paul. The officer, moreover, had once been a student at a Quaker school in York, Bootham, and knew about the Cadbury family. He apologized, and Henry Cadbury was free to enter England.[9]

London in January of 1941 was a city besieged. The blackouts, the bomb craters, the burned-out buildings, the rubble, and the families sleeping in the underground all told a grim story. In 1920 in Germany, Henry Cadbury had seen war's devastation. Here he saw war itself. The British Friends had many worthwhile projects, which he and Robert Yarnall visited. The Friends War Victims Relief Committee, responsible to the London Yearly Meeting, organized and ran some sixty to seventy hostels in all parts of the United Kingdom, providing for the elderly, for mothers and children, and for people bombed out of their homes. The Friends Ambulance Unit, a more autonomous group, concentrated on mobile canteens, on providing feeding and medical assistance in the city bomb shelters, and on giving aid in the hospitals, while training men to staff and run ambulance units at home and overseas. Still, in the midst of devastation, it was hard to make a pacifist witness against the war itself. A heavy cloud settled on Henry Cadbury's spirit.

The two Americans were courteously received at the British Foreign Office, and their plea for women and children on the Continent was listened to with sympathy, but the stark and depressing fact was that in a state of war, aid to the innocent was also seen as aid to the enemy. Their visits with the British Friends were more productive, for they were able to take home to AFSC recommendations for assisting in some of the relief work being carried out by the Friends Ambulance Unit and Friends War Victims Relief Committee. A minute of appreciation for their visit was prepared by the London Meeting for Sufferings held on February 7, 1941.

As usual, Henry Cadbury found an opportunity to slip away from other duties to visit the Friends Reference Library. Friends in the United States were preparing to observe the 250th anniversary of the death of George Fox in January 1691, but there remained some question between historians as to the exact date of that occasion. Henry Cadbury found what he was looking for and sent a cable to Anna Brinton at Pendle Hill.

The result is a Cadbury legend. Western Union called Howard Brinton, Anna's husband, and told him it had some news that must be broken very gently to his wife. Might he be told the contents of the cable, Howard asked. The response was, "George Fox died January 13, Signed, Henry Cadbury." [10]

Returning to the United States by slow stages, Henry Cadbury and Robert Yarnall were delayed for four days in Bournemouth, waiting for a hurricane to abate so they could take a plane to Lisbon. Henry Cadbury amused himself by writing a "Letter from the Past" describing early Quaker associations with Bournemouth. When Robert Fowler was waiting to set sail in the little ship *Woodhouse* with its load of Quakers in 1657, he wrote in his log that "some of the ministers of Christ went on shore and gathered sticks and kindled a fire and left it burning." It was a metaphor, Henry Cadbury thought, for the concept of proclaiming one's message and leaving the results to God. [11]

Eventually the travelers arrived in Lisbon, where they again had to wait for passage back across the Atlantic. Various former and current AFSC workers were in the crowded port city, preparing to travel on to England or unoccupied France, where AFSC relief work was still going on. Henry Cadbury dutifully spent his time in consultation with them but slipped away for a little research into two early Quaker connections with Portugal, a visit from Ann Gargill in 1655 and the arrival of a Quaker ship in port in 1656. The result was a second "Letter from the Past," entitled "Friends at Lisbon." [12]

On March 29, the *Friends Intelligencer* published the first of these "Letters from the Past." It was signed with a pseudonym, "Now and Then." Susan C. Yerkes, then editor of the *Intelligencer*, introduced the new series with an editorial in which she apparently quoted Henry Cadbury himself:

> The writer hopes to show at times mere identity of place or accidental similarity of circumstances; at other times the continuity of distinctly Friendly principles in past and present manifestation. In addition he hopes to share with a wider circle some of the more interesting and entertaining bits of Quaker history he picks up from time to time, especially items which could hardly be dignified by a longer or more formal

article. He feels that in these tense times a little sprinkling of subjects quite remote may be a wholesome ingredient in our reading matter. Just as foreign correspondence is broadening, so history, by extending the perspective of time, is instructive.[13]

Thus launched, the "Letters from the Past" became an important metier. They gave Henry Cadbury a means to use the obscure bits of history he loved to dig up and scope to remind modern Friends of the need for the social translation, not only of the New Testament, but of Quaker testimonies in a former day. "No Friend in his generation so fully bound together Quakers and our history, the Bible and our relation to it, and intelligent hope as we plan the future, as did Henry Cadbury," wrote Moses Bailey, a contemporary Quaker. "If a Quake [sic] should be experimentally cloned, it is he."[14]

Back in the United States, Henry Cadbury spoke on the role of the pacifist in Great Britain in wartime to gatherings of American Quakers and also the Women's International League for Peace and Freedom, of which Lydia Cadbury was now Massachusetts president. He prepared a series of lectures for the Pendle Hill summer school titled "Friends and Their Social Testimonies." He reviewed books and wrote the notes describing ongoing research for the Friends Historical Association, of which he was president, and its journal, while continuing to keep up with his new series "Letters from the Past."

Everyone noticed that he was driving himself harder than ever, and friends were glad to learn that he had applied for a small research grant to spend the months of July and August on the island of Barbados. He wanted to search for remains of four Quaker meeting houses that had been blown down in the hurricane of 1780. Fearing that Lydia Cadbury might be bored as he poked around museums and read old wills, Henry Cadbury suggested that they take their daughter Betty along for company. The three swam daily and visited the islands of Grenada, St. Lucia, Antigua, Montserrat, Nevis, and St. Kitts, looking for Quaker connections.

Henry Cadbury never found any physical evidence of the existence of the old meetings on Barbados, and, in the process of looking for them, he lost a valuable notebook containing all the clues he needed to continue his reseach. There were so many compartments to his life, each discrete and each overflowing with facts, that to lose the key to one must have seemed like a threat to the whole structure. Henry Cadbury became extremely upset by the loss of the notebook, going over the ground time after time. In addition, he developed dysentery. Lydia Cadbury had it, too, but got over it quickly by resting. Henry Cadbury could not rest, and on the trip home he developed a hoarseness in his voice and a continuous ringing in his ears.

The Cadburys returned to Cambridge, and Henry Cadbury tried valiantly to pick up his multitude of duties. News that he had been elected to the Oxford Society of Historical Theology, one of seven honorary members to be added to that society to date, came in October, but did not cheer him. He had been asked to give the Shaffer lectures at Yale the next spring and was looking forward to expanding some of his ideas about Jesus the man. But he was now suffering from persistent vomiting and dizziness, and each engagement seemed like an ordeal.

At Lydia Cadbury's insistence he reported some of these symptoms to the family doctor, but she learned later that he made light of them. It was not until a family friend with a medical background called the doctor and told him how worried everyone was becoming that diagnostic tests were begun. Henry Cadbury's tonsils were removed on the theory that they might be the source of the trouble. All tests proved negative, and Henry Cadbury was finally sent to a psychiatrist for consultation. The diagnosis was that he was suffering from an acute anxiety state brought on by a reactive depression. The doctors suggested a series of electroshock treatments, then thought to bring fast results in depressions associated with mid-life crisis. Henry Cadbury submitted to two such shocks, but he found the disturbance of his memory too disorienting and anxiety-producing. It was like losing a series of compartments. It was suggested instead that he try psychotherapy and a long rest.[15]

Lydia and Henry Cadbury went to the Farmhouse, a guest house on the Westtown property. From there Lydia Cadbury wrote to her sister-in-law Elizabeth Jones that Henry Cadbury was suffering from "a nervous breakdown brought on by years of fevered living continuing right into the dangerous years." Henry Cadbury himself was inclined to tell people that his breakdown was brought on by the war, bringing back to his mind all the trauma he had been through in World War I, plus the physical changes of late middle life. He also told one friend he was sure that the draft counseling had done it.[16]

Yet who knew the true reason? Both Henry Cadbury's father and mother had suffered depressions, as had a good many other members of the Cadbury family. Some continuing research suggests that a higher than usual incidence of depression occurs in families with a good amount of intermarriage, such as occurs, for example, among Mennonites. And there is a school of thought that Quakers and Mennonites may suffer more depression than other groups because of the strong inhibition against expressing aggression and the consequent need to turn it inward.

At Westtown Henry Cadbury played tennis, tried to read novels, and saw a psychiatrist. He was unaccustomed to self-examination, having believed all his life that one could shape one's character to suit one's ideals. Nevertheless, he was interested and intelligent in his approach to the sessions and reaped some benefits. The psychiatrist told him that he could not always expect to be in control of his life. Like an expert canoeist on a strong current, he must expect periods to come when all he would do was dip his paddle into the water from time to time and otherwise go with the flow of the stream. Henry Cadbury also learned from these sessions that it was possible to be too disciplined. "I have over-disciplined emotion out of myself," he admitted in one of his speeches, "My Personal Religion," given to the Harvard students sometime later.[17]

Yet he still seemed to have believed that he ought to be able to make himself snap out of his state of dullness and self-pity. A series of notes he kept during this period are full of little pep talks to himself: "The bad feelings surprise me when they come as disguised and not quickly recognized. Sport of the game is to identify them quickly so as to meet them as familiar and not be feared."[18]

He also wondered if somehow his religious convictions were inadequate to sustain him emotionally at this time. The haunting feeling that he was missing the many-splendored thing, that if he would try harder he might have achieved a sense of God's guidance, seems to have returned. He evidently wrote to Willard Sperry about it, for Sperry replied: "As to religion, my theory is that when you are not well you live off such religion as you have accumulated in the past and you must not expect to get a fresh supply out of the experience itself. It is rather like the animals that eat and drink their own humps in the desert."[19]

In the same letter, Sperry assured Henry Cadbury that he was free to take a six-month leave of absence. His colleagues from the New Testament Revision Committee wrote to excuse him from meetings and to wish him well. The Cadburys drove south in February and spent several weeks on St. Simon's Island off the coast of Georgia, returning to the Westtown Farmhouse in late spring.

By fall, Henry Cadbury felt ready to meet classes again. But the return to Cambridge at first was too much. He sought further psychiatric help and spent several weeks in a small sanitorium in Concord, recommended by Sperry.[20]

Lydia Cadbury was dismayed but not discouraged by Henry

Cadbury's illness. She wrote many letters to his siblings, keeping them informed and urging them to come and visit and cheer up Henry Cadbury. But she herself remained in good spirits, always hoping that he would soon be better. There were times when he felt he was holding on to reality with a fine line, that her cheerful chatter about the children, meals, and social events kept him sane, Henry Cadbury later told one of his children.[21]

In the summer of 1943, two years after the onset, Henry Cadbury was able to write to his sister Elizabeth that he felt well again. "I wonder what Rufus is writing this summer?" he inquired. "I have been thinking that someone ought to write a review of the last thirty years under the title 'Confessions of a Pacifist.'"[22]

As part of the "Confessions" Henry Cadbury may have been thinking about a wartime depression Rufus Jones also had suffered, following a concussion in 1914. Despite Rufus Jones's fame as a mystic, he too had found religion no solace at this time but had felt himself to be high and dry like a starfish above the tide line. To be in favor of peace in a world committed to war was to be a crazy optimist of sorts; what, then, when the tides of optimism roll away?[23]

But now the episode was over, and Henry Cadbury was busy again, writing, speaking, and teaching. Among his duties was that of visiting the Civilian Public Service camps (CPS), established under the draft law, to provide alternative service in wartime to conscientious objectors. These units were supposed to engage the men in projects of "national importance," including reforestation, work in mental hospitals and training schools, firefighting in the West, and medical experiments needing human subjects. The Friends, Mennonites, and Brethren established the majority of the units and ran them throughout the war. Christopher and Warder Cadbury were both drafted to CPS camps, and so was John Musgrave, the man Betty Cadbury married in June of 1942.

Morale was a problem for the CPS men from the first. Set up in hopes of realizing the William James concept of establishing a moral alternative to war, the CPS camps were actually proving extremely frustrating to their occupants. It seemed clear that much of their work was not of national importance but seemed like made work. Meanwhile, were they not cooperating with the very military system they opposed? From some of the depths he had himself experienced, Henry Cadbury addressed this frustration:

> When a great and catastrophic crisis holds the center of the stage, those who cannot conscientiously assist in the war effort, and who find themselves too few and feeble to do anything effective to stop the mass sui-

cide, naturally feel themselves thwarted and frustrated . . . it would be well if more of us could learn to be more earnest and content about the things we may do even though they may seem irrelevant to the more imposing events of our time. It is far more realistic than the ostrich-like absorption of belligerents in their own self-defeating enterprise.[24]

One source of frustration for the CPS men was the hostility of the nearby community. In Big Flats, New York, a local citizen of some prominence regularly attacked the camp in the Elmira paper for holding peace forums and bringing prominent men to speak to the conscientious objectors. Why should the taxpayers have to heat the camps for such purposes, he asked rhetorically. The young director of the camp had decided to confront the man in person when Henry Cadbury arrived for a visit. "Don't go, Bill," Henry Cadbury said, having heard the story. "He is fishing for confrontation. Don't oblige him."[25]

Though he was soon pushing himself as hard as ever, some of his colleagues believed he was less inclined to push others after the breakdown of 1941. Sometimes when he felt others were procrastinating there had been a little sharp edge to his remarks. Now suddenly that edge seemed entirely gone. Within the family it was said that the dark period had mellowed him. He was never a demonstrative man—neither he nor Lydia Cadbury had been raised that way—but he seemed a little more inclined to show feeling from this time on.

Among many tasks he undertook now that he felt well again was writing once more about the relationship between war and Christianity. There was less shrill claim that God was on the side of the Allies this time than there had been in 1917, he noted, but there was still an inclination to justify war as the lesser of two evils. But to the religious pacifist these arguments had little meaning: "Positions like ours do not rest ultimately on dialectic logic or pragmatic demonstration. Religious pacifism is a conviction and a way of life and it is part of a larger Christian conviction and way of life."[26]

Among theologians it was popular to refer to the war as the judgment of God on weak humanity and to search for the source of the sin. In a closely reasoned article, "War as God's Judgment and War as Man's Sin," which he submitted to the *Journal of Religion,* Henry Cadbury argued that to select which sin mankind was being punished for was presumptuous and very much a matter of opinion. He told the story of the Boston Puritans, who believed that King Philip's Indian war in 1675 was a judgment on them for having permitted the Quakers to dwell among them.[27]

Amos Wilder, the acting editor of the *Journal of Religion,* to whom Henry Cadbury sent the article, wrote back suggesting that it be enlarged. Henry Cadbury felt, however, that it might become too cumbersome. He had his file of articles rejected during World War I, and now he would begin to build a similar file for World War II, he wrote. He was busy preparing an article for the *Pennsylvania Magazine of History and Biography* on William Penn as a guardian of religious liberty and a piece for the Colonial Society of Massachusetts called "Quaker Relief during the Siege of Boston," a forerunner to the AFSC's efforts to help both sides in a war situation. A similar article for the Nantucket Historical Association covered the group of Quakers who moved to Dunkirk in 1797 as a result of the American Revolution.

"Henry's mind is bursting with ideas, but tell Rufus they are not the kind of ideas he would like them to be, they are not world shaking books on George Fox or on Jesus but minutiae," Lydia Cadbury wrote to Elizabeth Jones in January of 1944. In the same letter she mentioned being a little apprehensive about a hernia operation Henry Cadbury faced in February, but to everyone's relief he came through with flying colors.

The pain of the period of depression through which he had passed sharpened Henry Cadbury's wit. All his speech notes from this period are adorned with little jokes he planned to use especially with young audiences. He gleefully collected Quaker typos. There was a book of Quarter Saints instead of Quaker Saints, and there was the headline "Jones praised for Quicker Work" not Quaker work. Somewhere he found a line from Shakespeare's "King Lear" transposed: "How sharper than a serpent's thank it is to have a toothless child."

In March of 1944 he gave the annual William Penn lecture to both of the Philadelphia Yearly Meetings. Entitled "Two Worlds," this speech made the case for the two-way influence of faith on action and action on faith. "In spite of striking examples of social pioneering in our history, the Society of Friends has transmitted to us mainly the resources for inner piety. If we are living on this inheritance without preserving it we are prodigal sons. We shall find that if this peters out our social service will become salt without savor," he told his audience. To illustrate his points, he told about Mr. Octagon, the eight-sided man his father had visited so long ago at Franks Asylum, about his own early efforts to design an amphibious bicycle-canoe, and about an oculist developing a new pair of glasses specifically for shaving. "I might summarize our task as finding bifocals for bilateral amphibious bipeds," he told his delighted audience.[28]

In April Henry Cadbury was called upon to chair a joint program of the Race Relations Committee and the Friends Council on Education to discuss the topic "How can Friends schools develop a wider racial policy?" "We want the program to be just right, and nobody can make it quite as right as thee can," Anna Brinton wrote when inviting him.[29]

The war years had helped to sharpen Quaker consciences on matters of race. The relocation of Japanese-Americans from the West Coast, in response to racial hysteria, and their placement in virtual concentration camps had led the AFSC to enter a protest and to launch a program of trying to place the students in colleges and others in jobs in less prejudiced areas. AFSC staff work in finding homes and jobs for refugees from Germany had also taught them lessons in anti-Semitism, and the movement of blacks into northern cities was making it clear that patterns of discrimination had to be ended in jobs and housing. How, then, could Quakers continue to justify having all white student bodies in some of their schools?

Henry Cadbury had been asking this question for many years, and slowly change had begun to take place. Bryn Mawr College had admitted its first black in 1927, and she had lived with the Cadburys when there was question about her acceptance in the dorms. The Oakwood School had followed in 1933, Media Friends School in 1937, and both Haverford and Swarthmore in 1943. These were still the exceptions, however. It was only after the April 1944 conference, led by Henry Cadbury, that the two bastions of Philadelphia Quakerism, Westtown and George School, were ready to move, in 1945 and 1946 respectively. After that, changes came rapidly.

But opening the schools was just the beginning, Henry Cadbury warned in a speech at Earlham College in November of 1944. It was going to be necessary to be sensitive and responsive to enlarging demands: "We thought the principal grievances of the Negro were lynching, segregation (Jim Crow), deprivation of the ballot. We know now it is also (not instead of these) housing, jobs. We need to begin in our own meetings, institutions and businesses today."[30]

The Quakers have a saying, "they proceed as way opens." Not abstract, theological concepts, but the experiences growing out of compassion and relatedness led to the expansion of their social testimonies. This was the true heart of a religious approach to life. Henry Cadbury found different words and different occasions to make this point over and over again.

CHAPTER 10

Translating the New Testament

In October of 1944, Henry Cadbury was once more named to be chairman of the American Friends Service Committee. The little ad hoc committee over the birth of which he had presided in 1917 had now grown to world size. It was known everywhere for its relief work as well as its dedication to peace, and its budget had grown proportionately, swelled by many contributors who were themselves not Friends but who liked the way Friends went about things.

To be chairman now was an awesome responsibility. Rufus Jones was over eighty and could not be expected to keep up the pace of oversight that had become necessary. Clarence Pickett had never ceased to feel that Henry Cadbury provided the wisest possible counsel, well worth the handicap imposed by his living at a distance from the Philadelphia headquarters.

Henry Cadbury first made sure that not only Clarence Pickett but the board and the staff wanted him to be chairman under the circumstances. When he was reassured, he arranged with the dean of the Divinity School at Harvard to be away from his classes on the first Wednesday of each month, when the AFSC board met. He left Boston on the Tuesday night sleeper, spent Wednesday morning conferring with AFSC staff and committee chairmen, chaired the board meeting Wednesday afternoon, and returned to Boston on the night train. To Henry Cadbury's intense delight, the name of the train was "The Quaker via Hellgate." One good thing about being deaf, he told friends, was that he was able to sleep soundly on the train.

The deafness that had begun in Barbados had never left him; in fact, it was growing worse. Henry Cadbury's ability to serve as chairman rested on his capacity to grasp the sense of the meeting and to pull together the various threads of opinion expressed into a consistent whole that seemed like more than the sum of its parts. His keen intelligence and his ability to penetrate human nature at a glance, as one colleague had said, made him outstanding in this role. The deafness could have been an obstacle, but Henry Cadbury never permitted it to be. He never tried to hide his problem but instead brought it to the fore. "Thee and I have a problem. I need to understand what thee is saying," he told people, "and I am deaf." He sometimes roamed up and down the room at the board meetings, to be as close as possible to each speaker. And he appointed the person sitting next to him as his "court ear," to jot down notes on what was being said.

The tradition at the AFSC was strong that the board set policy and the staff implemented it. The all-Quaker board met in a spirit of Quaker worship, seeking the leading of the Light. "The board has the wisdom, we have the skills," staff were taught to think. For this reason, staff members were not encouraged to attend and certainly never to speak at board meetings.

Henry Cadbury, however, believed that the staff had much to teach the board. He was eager not to miss staff meetings or opportunities to hear what AFSC staff members had to tell him. He often said that he thought all board members should listen carefully to the staff, who learned from actual experience what it meant to translate beliefs into action. He arranged his mornings in Philadelphia so that he could spend a half hour with each staff person, rotating those he visited on each trip down. When he did sit down with a staff member, he revealed that he had been keeping up with the person's work and problems in a way that seemed startling. As in his teaching and casual meetings with friends, Henry Cadbury had the ability to make the other person feel that he or she alone mattered, that he had no other agenda than listening with his whole heart to that person's thoughts and feelings. It was Henry Cadbury who noticed that several members of the secretarial staff were so devoted that they were growing old in Quaker service. In the earlier days the committee had assumed most people would give several years of service and then go back to their regular business or professions. There was therefore no pension plan. Henry Cadbury was the first to point out that in fact many people would suffer as a result and to lead the board to decide to institute such a plan.[1]

Being board chairman meant much more than presiding over board meetings. Henry Cadbury once more found himself called upon to represent the AFSC in high places. The Quakers were becoming aware of a need to present their views in Washington more forcefully than the law governing nonprofit groups then allowed. In 1943 a new group, the Friends Committee on National Legislation (FCNL), had been formed specifically without tax exemption so that it could do Quaker lobbying. Henry Cadbury often found himself appearing before congressional committees representing the FCNL.

There was also the need to travel about the country, visiting AFSC friends and donors, Quaker groups, and the regional offices that had been formed throughout the nation, especially during World War II. These offices were supported by local Friends and were somewhat autonomous in operation. Like any Quaker group, they attempted to make local decisions by consensus, rather than rely on directives from Philadelphia. Relations between the national and the regional offices were always a source of some tension and could function only through a system of intervisitation. In 1944 Henry Cadbury journeyed to Kansas for a gathering of AFSC supporters and staff members in that part of the country. The schedule was demanding, but what better way for everyone to meet the new chairman, he wrote home. Referring to the growth of the regional offices of the AFSC and the subsequent tensions between the national and regional offices, he liked to tell the story of a little boy who asked his father, "Why are all those little piglets blowing up the mother pig?"[2]

But though the AFSC kept him extremely busy, there was still much to occupy his time and energies in Cambridge. Ever since he had joined the Cambridge Meeting he had served on a committee the purpose of which was to try to persuade the two branches of the New England Yearly Meeting to join. There were now independent meetings like Cambridge in the Connecticut Valley and in Rhode Island, but their position was like that of "adopted children of divorced parents," Henry Cadbury said. Finally, in the summer of 1945 the parent bodies were united. Rufus Jones was present to give his blessing to the new marriage. "The ring is on the finger, the bridegroom has kissed the bride. Now Friends, make it work," he admonished the gathering.[3]

Henry Cadbury was the most renowned Friend to attend the Cambridge meeting on a regular basis. People sometimes came in the hopes that he would speak. Since he did not speak as regularly as some weighty Friends were known to do, some of these visitors were disappointed. When he did speak, a little rustle and a sign of contentment would spread through the meeting house. He frequently spoke toward the end of the meeting, summing up the message that had been developed through the ministry of others and fitting it to an appropriate Bible text or an illustration from some other time or culture. Yet his messages were never impersonal. Other worshipers said he frequently "spoke to their condition," to use a Quaker term, seeming to sense and understand the depths of their own spiritual striving and insights and expressing them in elegant language.[4]

He was concerned that a worshipful attitude not arise around him, either in the meeting or in the classroom. For this reason he was becoming even less willing to be pinned down about his personal beliefs. He still gave a talk on "my personal religion" for his Harvard students, but he felt that if he expressed himself too openly in meeting he might come to have an undue influence on those who should be doing their own seeking.

His reticence stimulated some to a determined effort to pin him down. It became a game.

"Henry, what would you be if you were not a Quaker?" one friend asked him.

"A Hicksite," came the quick reply.[5]

"Henry, thee speaks like an angel," one enthusiastic fellow worshiper told him.

"How does thee know how an angel speaks?" Henry Cadbury wanted to know.[6]

Now that the Cadbury children had all left home, Lydia Cadbury kept the extra bedrooms rented, generally to AFSC staff or to former Philadelphians studying at Harvard. She still liked to do large laundries and to cook plain food, but otherwise she had little interest in the intricacies of housework. The house was always a trifle shabby and sometimes cluttered; the atmosphere was relaxed, people said. There was always a cat, whom she invariably called "Boozie," and sometimes a rabbit as well. Lydia Cadbury often went to bed when she had done her tasks and read her beloved German novels, laughing to herself. Both she and Henry Cadbury were frugal in their tastes and careful with their money. The daily boarders were charged some small sum—one remembers it was nineteen cents a meal. Travelers were always welcomed, even if it meant moving one member of the family out of his bed and into another in the middle of the night. Lydia's generosity made the Cadbury home often a Grand Central Station. When a black woman came to work in the Cambridge office of the AFSC and could not find appropriate housing, the Cadburys took her in as a matter of course. The beds might sag a bit in the middle, but they were always full. Henry Cadbury himself always looked clean enough but rumpled, as though he had just come out of a clothes basket, his students thought. His study was in the basement, next to the laundry, and he sometimes hung out the laundry between bouts with ancient Greek verbs. He ate everything he was served, avoided coffee, occasionally indulging in a cup of very weak tea. His favorite dish was chocolate pudding. Both Cadburys continued to go everywhere on their bicycles.[7]

Throughout the war years conscientious objectors had continued to come to the house on Buckingham Place in search of draft counseling. Several times representatives of the FBI came, too, looking for information on the young men. Henry Cadbury was unfailingly courteous, but he knew his legal rights and gave away no information that might damage a counselee. He kept in touch with the American Civil Liberties Union, and in 1945 he worked on the case of a young lawyer who was being denied admission to the Illinois bar because of his conscientious objector status. Henry Cadbury supplied the court with a list of Quakers who had been distinguished lawyers or judges. Liberty demanded not only constant vigilance but also constant historical research, it seemed.

With the end of the war in 1945 and the restoration of his good health, Henry Cadbury was able to deliver the postponed Shaffer lectures in the spring of 1946. Published as *Jesus: What Manner of Man* by Macmillan in 1947, the lectures concentrated on how Jesus thought, how his mind worked, rather than what he thought. Assuming that much of what Jesus believed was characteristic of a Jewish teacher of his time, Henry Cadbury made the point that Jesus frequently demanded something extra of his disciples.

> The differentia of the Christian is the extra, that is the extraordinary. We may say that the sign of Christianity is the plus sign. Sometimes when I see the familiar Christian symbol of the cross my fancy simplifies all the historical and theological suggestions of which it is reminiscent into the familiar arithmetical symbol which it often resembles. *In Hoc signo vinces*—in this sign will you prevail.[8]

Referring to Jesus' use of parables he pointed out the frequency with which he referred to the concept of biological growth as a metaphor for the slow process of spiritual growth, rather than sudden conversion. He also pointed out Jesus' frequent use of the motive of the absent master:

> For long intervals we have no contact with the one to whom we are responsible. He is in a distant country and there is no certainty that he will return soon. Our business is to live as we should live, but without

him. Normal rectitude, fidelity, diligence, are expected of us and not emergency behavior. Blessed is the servant whom his master, when he cometh, shall find so doing. This absence goes far beyond the intermittent dullness of contact to which even the mystics confess. It is frankly non-mystical, and holds out no promise of a realized experience of God in this life.[9]

Although much of Jesus' teaching was in line with the Judaism of his day, the hostility he aroused suggests that he had added a new element to old teaching, the plus element. "I have often wondered just how different a man must be to be hanged for it," Cadbury wrote. "The bitterest controversy is often over the narrowest margin." The reason for the wide acceptance of the truth of Jesus' ethical teachings seemed to lie, he thought, not in their originality or religious authority, but in the self-validating character of the teachings themselves: "Like any other words, the words of Jesus find their ultimate sanction in the court of our own consciences. Of course, our consciences have their history, but whatever that may be they are the judges of thought, the august supreme court of our souls. If they concur we simply say, 'We hold these truths to be self-evident.'"[10]

The book was well reviewed in all the major religious journals, and many of Henry Cadbury's New Testament colleagues, from overseas as well as from the United States, wrote to thank him for his continuing contribution to their thinking. As usual, with Henry Cadbury's scholarly works, the book was praised for the questions it raised as much as for the answers it gave.[11]

Meanwhile, another of Henry Cadbury's scholarly projects had come to fruition. In February of 1946 the Revised Standard Version of the New Testament, on which he had been at work on and off since 1930, was at last published. In an article, "Revision after Revision," which Henry Cadbury wrote for the *American Scholar,* he quoted passages addressed to the reader by the translators of the 1611, or King James, version, which showed that they found themselves facing problems similar to those he and his colleagues had faced. They had not wished to disturb the known beauty of the language of the Tyndale Bible, but at the same time felt they needed to make changes resulting from developments in language, knowledge, and custom. These same problems beset the authors of the Revised Version of 1881.[12]

As Henry Cadbury predicted in this article, the new translation was not received everywhere with the same enthusiasm. Some fundamentalists found the new wording too liberal, and there were threats even to burn the new Bible. A Methodist minister, James Laird, remembers hearing Henry Cadbury asked about this in a public lecture. "Well, they used to burn the translators," Henry Cadbury said. "If now they only want to burn the translation, I guess we have made some progress."[13]

Henry Cadbury had thoroughly enjoyed his seventeen years with the New Testament scholars. He reminisced about it many years later:

> It was a very congenial group of people to meet with—undenominational. I was the only Friend but the Lutherans, and the Baptists and Episcopalians and so on had their representatives, all of them outstanding New Testament scholars. These men became our personal friends and we spent time living in comfortable quarters, in winter mostly in New Haven, at the Yale Divinity School there, and in summer mostly at the Chateau at Northfield, Massachusetts, in an abandoned part of the hotel which we had the run of, and we had a delightful time together. When we got in the dining room we made so much noise that we had to be eldered by the head waitress; because we made so much noise telling stories, that's what we did when we weren't at work. The number of stories that my colleagues could tell about the Bible and questions connected with the Bible and religious life were innumerable.[14]

Although he continued to serve on the revision committee and work on other tasks, such as the Apocrypha, he missed the intense fellowship of the New Testament group. Much of the time he had given to the translation group was now, however, taken up with his duties for the AFSC. Someone asked him if the transition had not been abrupt.

"No, I am still trying to translate the New Testament," he said.

The AFSC observed its thirtieth birthday on April 30, 1947. In his message on that occasion, Henry Cadbury referred to the growth of the committee's reputation, budget, and scope, its continuing roots in the religious nature of the Quaker message, its dedication to "that life and power that takes away the occasion of war," and its commitment to experiment and to pioneer:

> Already some needs are clear. For example, after a great war there is and will continue to be intense physical need. If we meet that we shall have some insight into deeper issues. At any rate our choice is today clear as it was on the Jerusalem-Jericho road centuries ago. Either we shall be among the good Samaritans, or we shall be among those that pass by on the other side. As the gospel suggests elsewhere, when food, clothing, and care are concerned it is either "Inasmuch as ye did" or "Inasmuch as ye did not." Beginning from there, we may expect fur-

ther insight. Perhaps the American Friends Service Committee has only just begun. To quote the gospel once more. "And Jesus himself when he began was about thirty years old." [15]

The public interest in postwar relief and reconstruction, at a high point right after the war, was already slackening, and with it funds for badly needed projects were drying up. In the April *Christian Century* Henry Cadbury published an article, "Have Mercy upon Me!" in which he brought up to date the parable of the good Samaritan and described how the religionist, the nationalist, the militarist, the jurist, and the internationalist might today rationalize their lack of response to the man who had fallen among thieves. There was still needed the simple compassion that had motivated the good Samaritan, he urged. [16]

To staff the many programs of relief and reconstruction it had established overseas, and to send volunteers to other such projects, the AFSC recruited a large number of young people to spend a summer in Europe. A former troop ship, the *Marine Tiger,* was used for this purpose in the summer of 1947, and Henry and Lydia Cadbury went along as chaperones and advisers. The trip over was rough, but they found their orientation duties interesting. Henry Cadbury was the president of the Friends Historical Society of London that year and was expected to give the presidential address to the Society the day after the *Marine Tiger* was supposed to land. But the ship was late, giving the Cadburys just time to take the train from Plymouth to London before the meeting began. The British Friends were in something of a flap, with a series of contingency plans, but the Cadburys arrived two hours before the meetings were to take place, calm and smiling. It was their first adventure together since the ill-fated trip to Barbados in 1941, and they were expecting to enjoy it thoroughly.

Henry Cadbury's address, "Answering That of God," was one of his most stimulating efforts to respond to the facile explanation people liked to give about the origins of Quaker social beliefs. The title was taken from the journal of George Fox. Henry Cadbury said, "Be patterns, be examples—that your carriage may preach among all sorts of people. Then you will come to walk cheerfully over the world, answering that of God in everyone." [17]

Henry Cadbury developed the thesis that the operative word was the verb answer. The individual Friend was motivated by his or her need to maintain clearness and sought corroboration in the answer of others. This was slightly different from the neat formulations people liked to make.

Modern thinkers commonly maintain that the Friends emphasized the sacredness of personality, the value of the individual, and the equality of all men (including women) and they assume that recognition of the divine Light of the Spirit or Seed in our neighbors will lead us to the appropriate conclusions for our own action. Logically it should do, yet in so far as Friends actually did maintain these principles, the principles appear to be independent of any such deduction.[18]

The belief of early Friends that there was an inner witness in primitive people, such as the American Indians, who had never received the Christian message, is frequently cited as proof that Friends were eager to speak to "that of God in everyone," Henry Cadbury said, but in fact it was more a matter of seeking a response to one's own actions even in the native peoples. There is some evidence that the American Indians acquired their notions of a natural religion from the Quakers, thus illustrating the efficacy of the self-fulfilling prophecy.[19]

In other words, one should not try to read Quaker history backward and impute a connection between Quaker belief and practice in terms of today's logic, but be willing to understand that the motives for social action were sometimes complex and that belief and action arose together without a necessary cause-and-effect relationship.

After the week of committee meetings in London, the Cadburys went to Woodbrooke, where they visited old friends and attended a family wedding, then on to York, where Henry Cadbury found some important seventeenth-century letters in the Quaker record room. They then crossed to Ireland to visit Irish Friends, among them Isabel Grubb, the historian, with whom Henry Cadbury was maintaining a lively correspondence. Their next stop was Norway. Their son Warder was attending a summer school in Oslo, and Henry Cadbury wanted to visit Stavanger, the home of the Norwegian Quakers who migrated to the United States in 1825 and about whom he often wrote.

From Oslo, they took up their duties of chaperoning returning workers aboard the *Marine Jumper*, another former troop ship. They were soon back in Cambridge and caught up in their normal busy lives. Henry Cadbury was consumed with the publication of *Jesus: What Manner of Man*, while working on another book, *Gospel Parallels*, with Frederick Grant and Clarence T. Craig. Also the Harvard Divinity School was being evaluated, and he was involved in helping Dean Willard Sperry prepare a response to the recommendations of the special commission appointed for this service. Lydia Cadbury had begun a project the year before of getting food parcels to German professors who were connected with Harvard, or with the Society of Biblical Literature, and were now suffering from lack of nourishing food in postwar Germany.[20]

Henry Cadbury was busy in his office in Cambridge one day at the end of October when a call came through from Clarence Pickett in Philadelphia.

"Has thee heard the news?" Clarence Pickett asked. When Henry Cadbury said "No," Clarence Pickett told him, "Well, we've just been awarded the Nobel Peace Prize. Isn't that something?"

The award had been made to the AFSC and its British counterpart, the Friends Service Council, jointly. Henry Cadbury thought that Clarence Pickett ought to be the one to receive it, and if not Clarence Pickett then Rufus Jones, in honor of his long association with the AFSC. But when the AFSC board next met, its members felt protocol required that Henry Cadbury, as chairman, make the trip. The prize was to be awarded on December 10, the birthday of Alfred Nobel. It meant that Henry Cadbury had to be excused from a week of classes at Harvard, and he wrote to the president of the university asking for time off in order to receive the prize. Not unexpectedly, his request was granted.

Now a practical problem arose. To appear at the ceremony, Henry Cadbury was expected to wear a long-tailed evening coat. He possessed a tuxedo but no tails and had no desire to purchase such an item. Fortunately, there was a solution. The AFSC warehouse was collecting old formal clothes for distribution among the waiters and musicians of Europe. They had completely outfitted the Budapest Symphony Orchestra. Henry Cadbury wrote to Eleanor Stabler Clarke, then in charge of the AFSC clothing warehouse, and told her of his need and his measurements. He soon received a long-tailed coat that fitted him perfectly. He wore it to the state dinner in Norway, then sent it on its way to the European drive.

Margaret Backhouse, the chairwoman of the Friends Service Council, was also to be present to receive the award. Henry Cadbury thought it was particularly fitting for a woman to represent Quakers at the august gathering. His niece, Mary Hoxie Jones, then working in England, suggested that he bring an evening gown belonging to a mutual friend. Unfortunately, the dress did not fit, and Margaret Backhouse was forced to purchase a new gown for the occasion. The two had been provided with rooms at a very stylish hotel in Oslo, but they were delighted to be invited to stay with Diderich and Sigrid Lund, Norwegian Friends who had played a role in the non-

En route to Sweden to receive the Nobel Peace Prize, 1947. Photo courtesy of AFSC Photo Archives.

In dress tails borrowed from the AFSC Clothing Room for the Nobel Peace Prize ceremony, 1947. Photo courtesy of AFSC Photo Archives.

violent underground resistance to Hitler, and thus to continue their traditions of Quaker simplicity.[21]

The ceremony itself was simple, Henry Cadbury reported to the AFSC: "Though King Haakon VII and the Crown Prince were present together with the principal officers of the government and the ambassadors of many nations, there was no pomp or circumstance. Between two musical numbers were the speech of award and the very brief words of acceptance on behalf of each of the committees. That was all."[22]

The Friends groups were not exactly sure on what basis they had been awarded the prize. Was it for their work during World War II specifically that they were being honored? Or for their more general long-range effort? Or their commitment to peace?

In giving the award, Gunnar Jahn, director of the Bank of Norway and chairman of the Nobel Committee, stressed the Quaker history of good works over three hundred years, as well as the more recent wartime service of the Quaker bodies. But he also spoke of the peace testimony and the Quaker belief that it is better to suffer injustice than to exercise injustice:

> It is the silent help from the nameless to the nameless which is their contribution to the promotion of brotherhood among nations. . . . This is the message of good deeds, the message that men can come into contact with one another in spite of war and in spite of differences of race. May we believe that here there is hope of laying a foundation for peace among nations, of building up peace in man himself so that it becomes impossible to settle disputes by the use of force. "The unarmed only has inexhaustible sources. Only the spirit can win."[23]

In his response, Henry Cadbury sounded a similar note:

> If any should question the appropriateness of bestowing a peace prize upon a group rather than upon an outstanding individual we may say this. The common people of all nations want peace. In the presence of great impersonal forces they feel individually helpless to promote it. You are saying to them here today that common folk, not statesmen, not generals, nor great men of affairs, but just simple plain men and women like the few thousands of Quakers and their friends, if they devote themselves to resolute insistence on good will in place of force, can do something to build a better, peaceful world. The future hope of peace lies with such personal sacrificial service. To this ideal humble people everywhere may contribute.[24]

In addition to the banquet there was a press conference, teas at the various embassies, and two evenings with Quakers and other relief workers. Henry Cadbury was also expected to give a formal Nobel Peace Prize lecture two days after the ceremonies. In his speech, "Quakers and Peace," Henry Cadbury spoke of the Norwegian Quakers who had been persecuted in the nineteenth century, of his great grandfather's efforts to get rid of money earned through the captured ship, of his own father's struggles with conscience during the Civil War, and of William Penn's edict that the way of Friends was "not fighting but suffering." "It is our hope that the awards of the Nobel Committee to our Quaker Service may enable us and our millions of friends throughout the world to persevere in meeting that deeper spiritual hunger and thus promote the cause of peace, as was the intention of the founder."[25]

On his trip home he took time out to write to his sister Emma. "My trip is one on which I know not when to begin or to stop—a quite unique experience. One nice thing was the contact with Friends," he wrote. It was his beloved Society that had been honored, and though he had been reluctant to be the spokesman, he was glad after all to have been the instrument of that honor.[26]

In February of 1948, Rufus Jones and Clarence Pickett called a small group of churchmen together at Quaker House in New York to discuss the possibility of preserving Jerusalem as a religious center for all faiths under "A Peace of God." On March 12, an appeal which Rufus Jones had drafted was sent to the chief rabbi of Jerusalem and the head of the Supreme Moslem Council of Jerusalem, signed by representatives of all major religious groups. Both the Jews and Arabs agreed to this peace, and in May, when the United Nations decided to set up an administration in Jerusalem on a temporary basis, the two groups united in asking that Clarence Pickett be the municipal commissioner. Since Clarence Pickett could not get away to accept, Harold Evans and James Vail went instead. By the time they reached Jerusalem, however, fighting had broken out, and they were asked to take part in a number of mediating conferences which ultimately proved futile.[27]

Nine days after drafting the "Peace of God" appeal, Rufus Jones suffered a coronary occlusion. He was eighty-five, and though he rallied and was even able to continue writing, his health was not good throughout the spring. In June he had a second, more severe coronary, and on June 16, 1948, he died.

Henry Cadbury was unable to be at the memorial service, held six days later. He was as usual traveling for the AFSC. He wired back a message to be read: "Emerson once said, 'an institution is the lengthened shadow of one man, as Quakerism is of George Fox.' We may now add so is the AFSC of Rufus Jones." Later, however, writing in *Quaker Life* he pointed out that no Quaker institution should be viewed as the product of one man: "The familiar Quaker business procedure is a better indication of how our committees operate. It is always a collective affair, and leadership, no matter how inspired and effective, does not overshadow the joint contributions of colleagues and fellow workers." Rufus Jones himself had made that point.[28]

He had always been a devoted younger brother, an assistant, a colleague. He had made few decisions in his life without first consulting Rufus Jones. The two men, though very different, had complemented each other in many ways, and people bracketed them together.

Thus it came as no surprise when in the fall of 1948 Katherine McBride, president of Bryn Mawr College, asked Henry Cadbury to fill the vacancy created on the Board of directors by Rufus Jones's death. Since a chair in the history of religion was being created in Rufus Jones's honor, it was particularly fitting for Henry Cadbury to be consulted about a scholar to fill it, as well as many other academic matters.

Altogether, 1948 was proving both a painful and productive year. After many delays, the Cambridge University Press finally published his painstaking edition of *George Fox's Book of Miracles*. The British Friends Historical Society also published *Letters to William Dewsbury and Others*, a group of valuable seventeenth-century documents which he had found in the York Reading Room the year before and had copied, transcribed, and edited. A new organization, the North Carolina Friends Historical Society, printed as its second publication a pamphlet based on a speech he had delivered in August at the 251st session of North Carolina Yearly Meeting. Called "The Church in the Wilderness," the speech stressed the solidarity gained by Southern Friends in their witness against slavery: "They did not take the easy view that each Friend should do what is right in his own eyes. Trust in individual guidance and faithfulness did not go so far as to do away with all corporate testimony."[29]

But perhaps his most eloquent statement of the period was a short introduction to the AFSC annual report, which has been widely quoted for many years throughout the Society of Friends and the peace movement:

> If a man call himself a liberal, that means he is free, but the real question is not from what he is free, but to what. Gandhi's life he called an experiment with truth. Nothing less can satisfy the Christian liberal. There is not a bored relief but an active passion in such a quest, an abandon and a devotion. There was once a time when men ran away to

God as boys run away to follow the sea. That time can come again, but it must not be running away from the world to the monastery, to the cynic's seat, to the ivory tower. Only by facing the world with its problems, and man with his failings, and winning through them can men be truly set free. The paths of service and fellowship are two paths that are not ways of escape but ways of conquest. In this cause we may well establish and adopt some priorities: Deeds are more effective than words. Doing good ourselves is more important than containing evil in neighbors. Better than merely helping others is to enable them to help themselves, so that they in turn may help still others. Such tasks are included in the ambition expressed by John Woolman: "To turn all the treasures we possess into the channel of universal love becomes the business of our lives." [30]

Commitment on the part of peacelovers was needed as never before. The short euphoria at the end of the war and around the establishment of the United Nations had given way quickly to the Cold War, just as Henry Cadbury had feared. Lasting peace could not be built on power relationships, he had said at the time of the UN's founding. The United States was preparing to revive the draft or institute universal military training. With what must have been a painful sense of déja vu, Henry Cadbury prepared and presented testimony for the FCNL before the Senate Armed Services Committee against a peacetime draft. "We should not be afraid of communism as an idea," he said. "We should like to think that we had a better idea. We are afraid of communism backed with military weapons, and Russia is afraid of capitalism backed with atomic weapons. The present tragic cycle must be reversed, and we must seek our security through law instead of security through competitive armament." [31]

The law was passed despite this and other protests, and a good many young men decided to refuse to register. Henry Cadbury was soon busy preparing to testify for a number of these in courts of law. In December, he was involved in the case of a young man in Maine who received a stiff two-year sentence. In January of 1949, he appeared in a San Francisco courtroom on behalf of Robert McInnis, a former theology student who had served with his wife as directors of the AFSC Institutional Services Unit in the San Francisco County Jail at San Bruno the summer before and was scheduled to go overseas for the AFSC if he were acquitted. Henry Cadbury addressed the judge persuasively: "This young man stands not in a generation apart from us, sir, but in a tradition far older than we. Near the year 200 Tertullian wrote a pamphlet on "The Soldier's Crown" in which a Christian, like so many Christians in the first years, took the identical position that every participation in war was wrong."[32] Robert McInnis received a minimum sentence of three months, and his wife wrote Henry Cadbury an emotional letter of thanks, praising God for bringing him to them in their hour of need.

Henry Cadbury's appearance for Robert McInnis was one of a series of events planned for him by the AFSC up and down the West Coast. Everyone in the regional offices in Pasadena, San Francisco, and Seattle was eager to have the chairman of the board visit contributors and meet with staff and local Friends groups. "You are good to accept this schedule lying down," Stephen Thiermann, the executive secretary of the San Francisco region, wrote to him. The day before his courtroom appearance, he spoke several times in Stockton. On the day of the trial itself he also gave a radio interview, addressed a luncheon of some two hundred women in Berkeley, then drove fifty miles to San Jose, arriving just in time to address an auditorium full of students before having supper and spending an evening with the San Jose Friends. In Portland and in Seattle he was kept busy every minute. He stopped in Chicago on his way east, then went directly to Atlantic City, where he attended the meeting of the Council of Learned Societies before returning to Cambridge.[33]

Throughout the early months of 1949, he continued to be asked to make appearances for young nonregistrants. Greg Votaw, a Philadelphia Quaker, sought his help. Robert Wixom, a graduate student at Harvard, asked for a "to whom it may concern letter" in regard to his position against the draft. In February Henry Cadbury traveled to Albany to appear on behalf of Ted Norton of Glens Falls, New York.[34]

Older Quakers and pacifists wanted to show their support for the young nonregistrants, and some turned to tax resistance as the way to demonstrate their conscientious refusal to support preparation for war. Ernest and Marian Bromley, who came to play a leading role in the war tax refusal movement, wrote to Henry Cadbury about the merits of such a stand in March of 1949.[35]

The tax issue was puzzling from the point of view of Quaker history. Quakers had consistently refused to pay tithes to support the ministry in England and had been jailed for doing so, from earliest times, and they had been equally clear about refusing to pay for the support of a militia and suffered the removal of their property, or "distraits." But when the tax was "in the mixture," that is, the tax was paid into a fund that was used for several purposes, Friends had been a good deal less clear, Henry Cadbury felt. One of the most famous instances of struggle over this issue occurred when the

Quakers controlled the colony of Pennsylvania in 1755 and 1757 and were asked to approve a tax "for the king's use" that would actually be used principally for the French and Indian wars. John Woolman was one of some twenty Friends who opposed paying the tax.

Henry Cadbury seemed to feel that tax refusal was a logical translation of the Quaker social gospel to the present age, and had gladly supported those who felt so led. He himself never refused to pay taxes, though there is some evidence that he may have considered such a step, but he frequently wrote about it and predicted it would be a new frontier in the Quaker witness against war.[36]

Relations between the United States and the USSR were deteriorating at this time. Concerned over this threat to the peace of the world, the AFSC had used funds donated for the purpose of improving those relations to buy streptomycin for distribution by the Russian Red Cross to tuberculosis sufferers, as a goodwill gesture from the American people to the Russian people. The organization then developed a small working party to create some proposals for easing tensions. As part of that effort, Henry Cadbury and Clarence Pickett met with the current Russian ambassador to the United States to suggest some cultural exchanges. Henry Cadbury spoke of the history of Quaker outreach to Russians and of the work of the AFSC in Samara at the end of World War I. The ambassador said that he came from that region and that his brothers had been assisted by the Quakers. He seemed to open up and did not say no when Clarence Pickett suggested the possibility of a Quaker trip to Moscow.[37]

The results of the working party's deliberations were published in 1949 by Yale University Press: *The United States and the Soviet Union: Some Quaker Proposals for Peace.* A British Quaker group, which included Henry Cadbury's cousin Paul Cadbury and Christopher Taylor, a cousin by marriage, visited the Soviet Union in 1951.

Meanwhile, the establishment of the North Atlantic Pact seemed destined to institutionalize tensions between the East and the West. Henry Cadbury appeared before the Senate Foreign Relations Committee on May 11, 1949, representing the FCNL, to plead for the settlement of disputes through the United Nations, not further cold war: "Let us not acquiesce in a policy that talks with equanimity about another World War. The people of Europe do not do so. We have 'won' two such wars already, and they have proved even with our victory colossal disasters. The only adequate program for the world today is the abolition of war itself."[38]

"Dr. Cadbury, is there anything in the world worse than war?" a senator asked him after he had presented his long and thorough argument and proposals.

"Yes, and war causes it," Henry Cadbury said, paraphrasing a famous French general.[39]

After the sessions at the capitol, he went to Westtown School for the 150th anniversary of its founding. His talk on the influence of Quaker teachers over the years was wise and witty. In this speech he introduced a topic that was to be a theme for many years, the danger of nominalism, of trying to find words for ideas "to the neglect of other duties regarding them." The rush to put his thoughts into suitable words often kept him from formulating them more fully, he confessed, and perhaps blocked his vision of ways of putting them into action.[40]

But if this were a fault, it was not apparent to a great many people. "He talked less about being a Christian and acted more like one than anyone I have ever known," a Friend who knew him well from that period observed. "He was probably the smartest man I ever knew, but he never let you know it."[41]

CHAPTER 11

Defending Our Liberties

With the unsettled war years behind them, the Cadbury family was beginning to grow, to everyone's delight. On November 26, 1949, the first grandchild, Dorothea Musgrave, was born. She was premature, and Betty and John Musgrave were swamped by the hospital expenses. Henry and Lydia Cadbury, who could be very frugal, could also be very generous. All the bills must be sent directly from the hospital to him, Henry Cadbury insisted.

The following June, Christopher married Mary Foster, a Rhode Island Wilburite Friend whom he had met while teaching at the Olney Friends School in Barnesville, Ohio. It was during that same summer that Winifred, the younger daughter, met Martin Beer, a teacher at Westtown School, attending the Harvard Graduate School of Education. The two were married in June of 1951.

In the spring of 1950 Henry Cadbury was busier than ever with lectures. He persuaded the Ministers' Association of Springfield, Massachusetts, to devote a Sunday in April to peace and a discussion of "Some Quaker proposals for Peace." He himself spoke at one of the churches, warning against the growing fear psychology in the United States. "Fear is a bad advisor," he said. A few weeks later he addressed a Dartmouth Peace Conference. In early June he helped the Mt. Holly, New Jersey, Friends Meeting celebrate its 175th anniversary. Afterward came the Cape May conference, where he gave a workshop on some parables in Luke and spoke on the topic "Precept and Practice." [1]

In this workshop he once more returned to the danger of "nominalism," of substituting words for the matter one wishes to express. "The great historical religions express themselves so fully in words that we get a verbal familiarity with the things of God which is idolatry," he said. Religion was "something to learn, to feel, to choose, to do, to belong to," not a set of words only, "but words made flesh." He quoted Thomas a Kempis as saying, "far rather had I feel sorrow for my sin than know the definition of it." He repeated elements of the same lecture in a course he taught that summer at Union Theological Seminary in New York. "Nominalism is a natural temptation of our profession," he told the divinity students.[2]

The fall also was full of lectures. He spoke at the 250th anniversary of Moorestown Friends Meeting in September, a ceremony attended by the governor of the state. In a speech titled "Independence as a Quaker Tradition," he emphasized the need for nonconformity as a way to social change:

> Our critics cannot understand a religion whose genius is precisely the continuity of change. There is a living Christianity which not only in the middle of the First Century but also in the middle of the Twentieth "turns the world upside down." How different a standard this is from the medieval formula—*Quod semper, quod ubique, quod ab omnibus*— "What is held always, everywhere, by everyone." True independence does not rest on past won emancipation, to settle down into smooth conformity. It must be continually on the alert lest it become the good that is "the enemy of the best."[3]

Pendle Hill asked him to speak at its twentieth anniversary in October, and later the same month, the American Philosophical Society, of which he was a member, invited him to address the gathered scholars. In this talk, "Mixed Motives in the Gospels," he discussed the contribution of form criticism after thirty years, saying that the by-products of the technique had proved more useful than the original emphasis of the study. One of these by-products was the increased attention given to motive criticism:

> The material now in the gospel was preserved because it served a purpose. It is not an accidental residue of all that Jesus began to do and to teach. It is not primarily the automatic self recording of a notable life and mind. Sheer historical interest, antiquarian curiosity, had little to do with the making of the gospels. The motives were quite other and in fact quite varied among themselves, yet their contents served one or another of the many interests which the early Christians entertained. The traditions in the gospels even before they were written down were profitable for teaching, for reproof, for correction, and for training in righteousness, like other scriptures.[4]

Since the gospel writers had worked from earlier oral and possibly written material, they had included independent segments that had been preserved for different purposes, miracles that proved the Divinity of Jesus, for example, and other miracles that sought to teach patience and faith to the recipient. Since the evangelists did not edit the results to smooth over these differences, the result was a mixture of motives within the various gospels. The New Testament could not be seriously studied without attention to the presence of these sometimes contradictory motives.[5]

He was asked to speak almost every week at this busy juncture of his life. He was in demand for commencement addresses, particularly at Quaker colleges, at religious gatherings, especially those of Unitarians, Swedenborgians, and Reform Judaism, at theological seminaries, learned societies, civil liberties chapters, at Women's International League for Peace and Freedom meetings, and of course at Quaker meetings and AFSC groups.

In April of 1951, for instance, he was asked to address the Western College Association, meeting at Whittier College, a Quaker institution in California. Whittier seized the opportunity to offer him an honorary LL.D. (Doctor of Laws). At the same time the AFSC office in Pasadena, hearing that the chairman was coming into the area, planned an extensive round of meetings for him in and about Los Angeles. What had sounded originally like a flying visit turned into an ordeal. Henry Cadbury was very ill with an ear infection before leaving for the West Coast and made some efforts to cut down his schedule. He wrote to William Jones, the president of Whittier, suggesting that the honorary degree be skipped. "I am trying to discourage such honors," he said. But William Jones and Whittier were not to be dissuaded; and the AFSC kept adding more meetings. In the end, he managed to get through a schedule of talks and appearances that would have laid another man low. The AFSC assured him that it could put him on a plane late Saturday night that would get him back to Cambridge in time for a scheduled meeting Sunday afternoon.[6]

In his talk at the Western College Association, "Science and Conscience," Henry Cadbury made the point that science, religion, and conscience all demanded a setting of freedom: "All three have a common stake in personal liberty from state interference and control. Yet all three have been repeatedly restrained and curtailed. All three have had their heroes and martyrs. Just as religion has been repressed by the state, so science has been repressed by religion, and conscience by both religion and the state."[7]

Speaking at public meetings and to the press on this trip he returned again and again to the theme of improving relations with the Soviets. The AFSC was about to publish a second set of Quaker proposals for peace: *Steps to Peace: A Quaker View of Foreign Policy.*

The *Los Angeles Times* headlined his talk "Russ Peace Possible." But the tides of public opinion were now running strongly against trusting the Russians, and both the AFSC and its chairman were sometimes accused of being naive tools of the communists.[8]

Returning to the West Coast to teach at the Pacific School of Religion that summer, Henry Cadbury had occasion to learn how the townspeople of Whittier had reacted to the AFSC proposals. The Seventeenth Annual Whittier Institute of International Relations was to be held during the first week of July, and some of the sessions had been planned for the auditorium of the public grammar school. But the school board, responding to public fear that the AFSC was "red," barred this use of public property, and an alternative site had to be found. Henry Cadbury, who was presiding over the institute, was alarmed and saddened.[9]

Lydia Cadbury had accompanied Henry Cadbury on this summer trip, and the two had taken time out to visit the Grand Canyon, Lake Tahoe, and Yosemite and to stop and see friends on the way out and back. Lydia Cadbury thought the "treelessness" of the West tiring but enjoyed the trip. They hurried back for time at Back Log Camp before they prepared to greet Henry Cadbury's British cousin Paul Cadbury on tour in the United States after having been one of seven British Quakers to visit the Soviet Union during the summer. Henry Cadbury chaired a meeting at which Paul Cadbury spoke in Cambridge, where some four hundred people had to be turned away. He also went to Philadelphia to attend a party held in Paul Cadbury's honor by the American Cadburys and to hear Paul speak at Swarthmore College. Paul Cadbury was impressed with Henry Cadbury's fearlessness at this time. "This was the period when Senator McCarthy was harassing those who were trying to build bridges and Henry himself was under suspicion for supposedly pro-communist views," he remembered.[10]

Speaking at an AFSC meeting in New York in December, Henry Cadbury referred to the growing climate of hysteria: "It is little expected today that a Samaritan will help a Jew, an American will help a Japanese, a Protestant will help a Catholic." He told of a German former Nazi who had repented and trained to become a Methodist minister: "It must have taken courage in both hands for him to do so. What could a Committee on Anti-Samaritan activities say?" But he was also concerned that Friends not respond to the climate by substituting words for deeds. "We are repeatedly asked to join in petitions and public statements. I think they have limited value compared to positive example. Much of the impulse toward public statements caters to self-righteous indignation," he said.[11]

By spring, the climate had grown still worse. In a commencement address at Guilford College, he spoke of the subtle and dangerous unseen controls the country was developing, a press that was nominally free but in fact published only a portion of the facts, and a youth that feared singularity and suffered from self-censorship. He told the story of a little boy who, when asked by his mother if he would not like to own a magic carpet, replied, "but wouldn't that be a little conspicuous?" Parents ought to encourage children to be free, independent, and adventurous: "If it had not been for rebellious sons and daughters over fifty thousand years, man would still be gnawing bones in the Mousterian caves." [12]

The year 1952 was celebrated as the three hundredth anniversary of the founding of the Religious Society of Friends. Writing in the London *Friends Quarterly,* Henry Cadbury observed that the date was only approximate; there were many other possible dates to fix for the birth of the movement. George Fox himself referred to 1644 as the beginning. He did not object to the celebration in 1952, but as usual he was cautioning Friends to be themselves a little more cautious. [13]

The AFSC was also celebrating its thirty-fifth birthday. Lewis Hoskins of Oregon had succeeded Clarence Pickett as executive secretary in 1950 and was now confronting a rising tide of McCarthyite accusations against AFSC staff members at a time when the AFSC work both domestically and overseas was expanding. The AFSC appeals for clemency in the espionage case of Julius and Ethel Rosenberg had added to the charges of communist sympathies. Henry Cadbury was his chief source of wise counsel in this trying time, and his trips to Philadelphia by "The Quaker via Hellgate" were as frequent as possible.

In the summer of 1952, the Cadburys had a brief respite from the overheated atmosphere in the United States. Henry Cadbury had been asked to speak at the Friends World Conference to be held in Oxford in August, and Lydia Cadbury was accompanying him. Writing to his sister Elizabeth Jones during the crossing, Henry Cadbury had nothing more pressing on his mind than learning to understand the British accent through his new earphone: "Maybe it needs a transformer such as I have supplied for my electric razor." [14]

At the Friends World Conference, held July 28 to August 6, Henry Cadbury was one of three speakers on "The Life and Witness of Friends," sharing the platform with Ranjit Chestsingh of India and Margarethe Lachmund of Germany, a sign of how international the Quaker movement had been growing in the past five years. His topic was the independence of Friends from the stands and popular positions of the day and the resulting distrust of them not only in political but also ecclesiastical circles: "I believe we are as much an enigma to Moscow as to Geneva, and not merely to red Moscow and red Peking but also to Whitehall and the White House." He warned Friends to be wary of the tendency to become allergic to change. He also attended a stimulating group discussion on problems of race, he wrote his sister Emma Cadbury.[15]

Following the conference, the Cadburys spent several days in London, where Henry Cadbury could treat himself to time at both the British Museum and the Friends Library. He had been asked to undertake a daunting task: the revision and reediting of the two standard volumes on early Quaker history written by William Charles Braithwaite, *The Beginnings of Quakerism,* published in 1912, and *The Second Period of Quakerism,* in 1919. They had been meticulously researched and had stood the test of time very well. Still, after forty years there was enough new information to warrant a revision. Geoffrey Nuttall, an outstanding historian of the religious enthusiasms of the seventeenth century, had been in correspondence with Henry Cadbury for the last four years and was becoming a close friend and colleague. Although he was not a Friend, his wife and many of his friends were Quakers, and he was extremely interested in and knowledgeable about Quaker history. He wrote to Henry Cadbury to encourage him to undertake the revision.

When Henry Cadbury was through in London, the Cadburys crossed the channel to Germany, their first visit since 1933. They visited Frankfurt, where Henry Cadbury looked for the sites of the Quaker Speisung he had visited with Francis Bacon in 1920, and asked himself what lasting effect that enormous effort had had. There were a few street names here and elsewhere incorporating the word Quaker, and not a few Germans remembered being fed. A few phrases from the program had even crept into the language. But how many of the children who came to the centers had grown up to be perfect little Nazis? He recalled that when he visited Essen in 1920 the Quaker child-feeding program was in progress and an American army group was supervising the dismantling of the Krupp arms factory for conversion to civilian use. Neither the Quakers nor the army had prevented the coming of Hitler. But success in the short run was not the criterion to judge the work of Quakers, he decided: "Friends work neither now nor then depends on the assurance of success, but that it is our duty so to act."[16]

The Cadburys also attended the German Yearly Meeting at Bad Prymont, where their old friend Emil Fuchs, now an East German professor of religion, was present, and then visited the AFSC centers in Darmstadt and in Kranichstein, the central office for the work in Germany. The staff here were self-governing, the cook, the cleaning woman, the maintenance man, and the manager playing an equal role in decision making along with the overseas staff and the head of mission, Barbara Graves. Henry and Lydia Cadbury stayed around several extra days because Henry Cadbury wanted to see this process actually functioning. "This is the way our Quaker method is always supposed to work," he told Barbara Graves.[17]

A trip to Berlin in search of German New Testament scholars was depressing. The city was in ruins. Henry Cadbury was also finding it very hard to understand the spoken German after so many years, and having to listen through a hearing aid did not help. But Lydia Cadbury's German was functional, and she undertook to secure Henry Cadbury and herself a hot bath and a warm bed wherever they stayed. "You can trust Aunt L to supply not just the austerities but the amenities of life," Henry Cadbury wrote to his niece, Mary Hoxie Jones.[18]

Hanging over the Cadburys' enjoyment of this holiday was worry over Elizabeth Jones. In July word had come that she was very ill and suffering a good bit. On October 26, shortly after their return to the United States, she died. Henry Cadbury had been close to this older sister since he was a small boy, had written to her faithfully and lovingly wherever he traveled, and had considered her house as a second home. He had mourned the death of his brother John in 1948. This was a second painful break in the family circle. Others were to follow throughout the 1950s.

Age was beginning to creep up. Henry Cadbury would be sixty-nine in December, and he should have retired at age seventy in June of the following year. James Conant, president of Harvard, however, urged him to return for one more year. Dean Willard Sperry was retiring that spring, and Conant himself was leaving Harvard, to be replaced by Nathan Pusey, in September of 1953. Two of Henry Cadbury's colleagues at the Divinity School were past normal retirement age. It was felt that for Henry Cadbury to leave just now would be a heavy blow.

Following the war, enrollment at the Harvard Divinity School had soared, thanks in part to returning chaplains who wished to obtain further education under the G.I. Bill of Rights. In 1946 a commission, known as the O'Brian Commission, had been appointed with John M. Moore, associate dean at Swarthmore College, as secretary. This commission recommended in 1951 increasing the size of the faculty and launching a major fund drive. Harvard Divinity School had weathered its uncertain years and was on its way to stability and unity in diversity. Henry Cadbury's crucial role as peace-maker, his habit of respecting the differences of opinion among students and faculty, during the years of anxiety and turmoil was recognized as one of the factors that had helped the school to make the transition.[19]

Already, Henry Cadbury had been invited to return to Haverford to teach Quakerism by President Gilbert White, a former AFSC staff worker. Other invitations were arriving. He would clearly be retiring to teach elsewhere. Finally he decided that he ought to stay at Harvard one more year, and furthermore he would deliver one more set of Lowell lectures in the spring of 1953.

In these lectures he returned to the subject of his most intense scrutiny, the Book of Acts. This time he concentrated less on the literary style of the unknown author than the historical setting of the book. Just as we would come to understand Jesus better if we studied his language, culture, religion, and place in society, so we could better interpret the Book of Acts if we could understand its relationship to history, Henry Cadbury believed. It should be studied in terms of "five concentric cultural environments: Oriental, Greek, Roman, Jewish and Christian." His purpose, he stated, was "to establish not so much the accuracy of the book as the realism of the scenes and customs and mentality which it reflects."

> There is too much tendency to regard Christianity as something unique and apart in its origin. Yet it did not grow up in *vacuo*. It bore close likeness to the world which surrounded it. They were typical first century minds that gave form to its thought, as they were first century cities that gave it geographical setting. Even much of its religion was in accord not merely with Jewish but even with pagan outlook. If we are to distinguish in historical Christianity either the primitive or the original elements we must recognize what is simply common in antiquity. . . . The setting of the New Testament in its contemporary environment should correct also the tendency to unduly modernize it.[20]

These lectures, and some additional talks he had given elsewhere, were combined to produce a book that was published by Harper and Brothers in 1955 as *The Book Acts in History*. Reviewing it in the *Journal of Biblical Literature*, a colleague called it another of Henry Cadbury's contributions to scholarship in the New Testament and said it was "a solid, instructive and interesting book which students and scholars alike can read with profit."[21]

In addition to preparing and delivering the Lowell lectures, Henry Cadbury published in 1953 a bibliography on the life of Jesus, wrote some additional articles on the translation of the *Re-*

vised Standard Version of the New Testament, edited *Beginnings of Quakerism,* and continued to commute to Philadelphia to attend the AFSC and Bryn Mawr board meetings. His schedule for a week in May reads: "Tuesday, Bryn Mawr Commencement [he always gave the opening prayer]; Wednesday, AFSC Board; Thursday: 50th anniversary of graduation for Haverford; Friday, Haverford commencement ceremonies."[22]

But if he wrote and traveled and spoke with his usual zest at this time, he was also deeply troubled by the ever-worsening crisis in public confidence of what we now call the McCarthy period. With several other Harvard professors, he signed a public advertisement decrying the police state methods of the various government investigating committees. When a Massachusetts legislator, Thomas Dorgan, who called himself the father of the teacher's oath, wrote to the *Harvard Crimson* to say he felt that these same professors were bound by the oath they took to testify if called upon, Henry Cadbury drafted a spirited letter in response, saying that the promise he had made to support the Constitution would be violated if he testified before one of the investigating committees, which he believed themselves violated several constitutional safeguards:

> If under these conditions I participate as a "witness" in a process which I thus regard I commit an offense—I violate the very oath which Mr. Dorgan and his associates once required me to take. To avoid this present crime and self-incrimination I do well, not to try to clear myself, as I could do, of charges of communism, violence or conspiracy but to stick conscientiously to my former promise whatever the consequences.[23]

Bryn Mawr College was worrying about the effects of the investigations on academic freedom, and Katherine McBride wrote to Henry Cadbury asking him to serve on a committee to advise the board and administration on a course of action. The AFSC already had a Civil Liberties Committee and made a number of statements in support of civil liberties. The organization opposed the witch-hunting features of the McCarran-Walters Immigration Act, continued to plead for clemency for the Rosenbergs, and was kept busy answering charges that the AFSC itself or members of its staff were actually communists or sympathetic to communism. That the AFSC had permitted Alger Hiss to participate in an international relations seminar the summer after he had been accused, but not found guilty of spying, was brought up frequently, as well as Clarence Pickett's decision to appear as a character witness for him.[24]

Charges of this nature had, however, been with the committee since its birth and were based on the inability of segments of the public to understand Quaker pacifism. They reached a height of silliness during this period, when a woman in Indiana, a member of the State Text Book Commission, suggested that all references to Robin Hood and to the Quakers be removed from the school books: Robin Hood because he robbed the rich and gave to the poor, and the Quakers because they did not believe in fighting.

Naturally Henry Cadbury was stimulated to write a "Letter from the Past" called "Robin Hood and the Quakers." He also wrote ones called "The Era of the Oath" and "Pleas for Clemency." In the latter, he told of a petition that eighty-seven Englishmen had written on behalf of James Nayler, the early Quaker enthusiast who was punished for blasphemy. Henry Cadbury declared that in the spirit of the current compilers of the "*Red Network*" he was going to track down every one of the daring signers, who had taken the step in defense of civil liberties. "I shall have a regular witch hunt, using heavily the well known technique of guilt by association," he wrote.[25]

In a more serious vein he developed several articles for the London *Friend* on civil liberties. In the first of these, he likened the situation of American Quakers suspected of being communists with that of seventeenth-century Quakers suspected of being Papists and participating in the so-called Popist plot. In the second, "Freedom from Self-Incrimination," he explained why some conscientious persons were taking the Fifth Amendment. The right to be free of self-incrimination had been won in part by two early Friends, John Lilburne, tried in 1637 as a nonconformist (he later became a Quaker); and William Bradford, a printer and American Friend, both of whom insisted on their right not to testify against themselves.[26]

In the second of these articles he mentioned that few Friends had actually been victims of public persecution. At about this time, however, a woman who had attended the Cambridge Meeting became a central figure in the investigations. Mary Knowles was a slender, modest, quiet woman who worked as branch librarian at the public library at Norwood, Massachusetts. In May of 1953 she was called to Washington to appear before the subcommittee of the Senate Judiciary Committee headed first by Senator William F. Jenner and later by Senator James O. Eastland because she had been named by an FBI underground agent, Herbert Philbrick, as having once been secretary to the head of the Samuel Adams school near Boston, which was listed on the so-called subversive list. She took the Fifth Amendment, in an effort, many thought, to protect others, including possibly her former husband. She was in consequence discharged by the public library in Massachusetts. She moved to Wayne, Pennsylvania, where she had friends, and began to attend Radnor Meeting, meanwile looking for a new job.[27]

Henry Cadbury knew that the William Jeanes Memorial Library, under the care of the Plymouth Friends Meeting, needed a temporary librarian, and he suggested Mary Knowles for the position. Mary Knowles told the committee that interviewed her about her past but assured them that she had not been a member of any "subversive" organization for many years. She was given the job and did so well that the next year she was offered it permanently.[28]

Meanwhile, however, a group of townspeople in Plymouth Meeting, learning of her so-called radical background, began to agitate to have her fired by the library committee. A major community battle developed between the liberals, who wanted to retain Mary Knowles, and the conservatives, who wanted her fired. Persons who had long been inactive in Plymouth Meeting now came forward to say that the meeting had acted undemocratically in hiring her in the first place. Charges were hurled back and forth in the public press.[29]

To try to resolve their problem, the meeting of Worship and Counsel of Plymouth Meeting invited some Philadelphia Quakers to meet with them. Among these were Lewis Hoskins and Henry Cadbury. When the group arrived they discovered that three members of the anti-Knowles faction were already present, and one of them was inebriated and loud. Lewis Hoskins said he felt a sinking of the heart. Henry Cadbury, however, proceeded to deal with the situation with perfect deftness and diplomacy. He gave as an analogy a dispute that had arisen in Upper Dublin Meeting over slavery in 1698, and he told how the problem of that disunity was carried not only to Philadelphia Yearly Meeting but to London Yearly Meeting, then considered the parent body; it took many years, but the Quaker stand against slavery was now a matter of pride. Disunity could lead in time to finding the right solution, if the light were earnestly sought, he said, knowing that some older members of the meeting wanted to get the problem settled and were tempted to give way to pressure, at whatever cost to civil liberties. His voice was quiet, urbane, and reasonable, and under his influence the meeting grew subdued and the dissidents thoughtful.[30]

Unfortunately, this was not the end of the matter. In July of 1955, the Fund for the Republic gave the Jeanes Memorial Library a grant of $5,000 for its courage in retaining its librarian in the face of public pressure. This infuriated the anti-Knowles group in the community and evidently resulted in the Eastland Committee deciding to call Mary Knowles back to Washington to testify once more. This time she did not take the Fifth Amendment, on advice of counsel, but refused to answer all questions that might incriminate others. She was in consequence cited, tried, and convicted of contempt of Congress, but she was finally cleared of this sentence when her lawyer, Henry Sawyer, pleaded her case before the Supreme Court in 1960. Henry Cadbury kept in close touch with the case and prepared memorandums and short articles for the *Friends Journal* to summarize the facts and the issues involved. He also wrote a thoughtful review, "Friends and the Law," published in the *Journal* in 1955.[31]

The FCNL celebrated its tenth anniversary with a dinner during this beleaguered period, and Henry Cadbury titled his keynote speech "The Basis of Quaker Political Concern." He mentioned that many Friends objected to Quaker involvement in politics and told of a Quaker neighbor, who, when asked if he had been to the polls, said piously, "Our citizenship is in heaven." Nevertheless, Friends had been involved in politics since the birth of the movement, when it was necessary to lobby the British Parliament to prevent further persecution of the group. George Fox spent the last ten years of his life in close touch with "parliamentmen," and his diary for the period, consisting of a line or so a day, read very much like the daily calendar of Raymond Wilson, the secretary of FCNL.

The real basis of Quaker social concern was often unconscious, Henry Cadbury said on this occasion, as he had said many times before. The reasons Friends gave in 1688 for their opposition to slavery were various and scattered:

> First, is this to do as you would be done by? Second, we Quakers (it's written Friends) made great talk about liberty of conscience, about liberty of body. Third, slaves we suspect, were captured in Africa as the spoils of war and we pacifists can have nothing to do with war spoils. Fourth, the system as practiced in America, the sale and movement and exchange of slaves, abets the practice of wholesale adultery. And finally, and fifth, if a Quaker colony practices slavery in America it will give Quakers a bad reputation in Europe. You see how unsatisfactory to one of those neat, logical minds this approach to Quaker concern is.[32]

Yet one hundred years later, when the Declaration of Independence was written with egalitarian phrases and complete logic, it ignored the question of slavery. Similarly, though the concern for the equality of women went back to the beginnings of the movement and blossomed again in 1848 under the leadership of Lucretia Mott and other Quaker women, it was not a logical deduction from a Quaker theory of democracy.

Abstractly, that sounds like wonderfully pure, theoretical democracy. Maybe it was, but they were not conscious of it. They operated in a more immediate way. The real roots of their concern were psychological rather than logical. It's only another way of saying that they were religious, rather than theological. They involve a sense of the relevance of religion to all life.[33]

He made another effort to get at the roots of Quaker social concern in a chapter he wrote in this period for a book published by Jack Kavanaugh of the AFSC staff, *The Quaker Approach*. In "Peace and War," he spoke of the inner, unconscious religious rejection of war on the part of Quakers and the gradual development of a consistent testimony as individual Friends struggled with their consciences over when and where it was wrong to use guns. This "progressive extension of conscience" occurred for Friends again and again.[34]

Henry Cadbury was spending more and more of his time in the pursuit of Quaker history, as a glance at his articles on that subject published in the *Journal of the Friends Historical Association*, attests. Pressed by both the AFSC and Harvard with constant demands, he found history a source of refreshment. He turned to it as some of his colleagues turned to reading and even writing detective and mystery stories: "Even in such a limited field as Quaker history there are unsolved mysteries, with the chance for the amateur to be his own Sherlock Holmes. . . . When one begins he never knows whether the answer will turn up at once, or never. The fun is in the search."[35]

One of his favorite subjects for research and writing was the relationship of Quakers to the Bible, drawing together two areas of his most intense interest. As far back as 1929, he had begun to write a series of articles for the various Quaker journals on Friends' use of the Bible. He was therefore pleased to find an opportunity for a major lecture on the subject when Guilford College asked him to deliver the Fourth Annual Ward lecture in November of 1953. He called it "A Quaker Approach to the Bible."

Since early Friends believed that the same Holy Spirit spoke directly to them as had spoken to the ancient writers of Scripture, they felt they ought to read the Bible in light of their own inner revelations, Henry Cadbury said, and respond when the experiences and insights of the saints of old were the same as, or "answered" to, theirs. Henry Cadbury quoted Robert Barclay, the theologian of early Quakerism, in calling the Scriptures a "looking glass," in which this comparison might be made. One might call the

Bible "Operation Mirror." Or another approach might be "Operation Dictionary":

> The dictionary is not the authority that dictates how words ought to be used. It is rather the record of how words are used and what they commonly mean. In like manner the Bible is not the dictator of our conduct and faith. It is rather the record of persons who exemplified faith and virtue. It does for religion that which the dictionary does for speech. Its value consists of its agreement with experience, or with Truth, as Friends used to use the word. What is true in the Bible is there because it is true, not true because it is there. Its experiences "answer" to ours, that is, they correspond with ours.[36]

Friends, however, needed to be thoroughly familiar with the Bible as a whole to make use of it in this fashion, Henry Cadbury felt. And though the literary translation of it, in which so much of his life had been spent, had its place, a social translation, a translation of language into life, was the business of Friends in the world.[37]

In March of 1954 Henry Cadbury's retirement was announced in the newspapers, and a round of events in his honor began. The Cambridge Meeting arranged an evening when he was asked to reminisce over fifty years of teaching. Bryn Mawr College asked him to be its Baccalaureate speaker. Swarthmore College presented him with an honorary doctor of law degree. His Harvard colleagues prepared a book in his honor, *The Harvard Divinity School: Its Place in Harvard University and the American Culture*, edited by George H. Williams and presented to him at a luncheon on September 13, 1954, its publication date. The dedication reads:

> To Henry Joel Cadbury,
> Hollis Professor of Divinity, 1934–1954,
> Incumbent of the Oldest Endowed Chair in America.
> During a half-century of instruction he has known
> how to balance the scholarly claims of the past
> with the urgent necessities of the hour.
> Unofficial Quaker Pastor to Colleagues and
> Students alike.
> He has been the very embodiment of the ideals of
> the community of memory and hope chronicled in the
> pages of our book.[38]

Henry Cadbury's career and writings were described in the text of the volume. He was at the time of his retirement the ranking member in academic seniority of the Harvard Faculty of Arts and

Sciences. He was widely regarded as the greatest living authority on Luke and Acts. He was also known as an excellent teacher. The book stated, "He did his teaching by adding observations and corrections to the comments he encouraged from his students . . . he inspired both ministers and teachers, through his genial kindliness, scrupulous fairness and outstanding scholarship."[39]

These were not just ceremonial words. Henry Cadbury had indeed been a much beloved member of the Harvard community and a source of strength to the Harvard Divinity School. Writing to Mary Hoxie Jones six years later, Nathan Pusey said, "That our Divinity School flourishes today is attributable in no small measure to Henry Cadbury." And George Williams recalled at a much later date that Henry Cadbury had been a wise and kind guide to him personally when he came to Harvard as the youngest faculty member of the Divinity School. Looking back from the vantage point of twenty years, he remembered him as a man who was interested in human nature and "could penetrate it at a glance" and whose mind and spirit were so translucent he was able to think effortlessly and avoid being drawn into the turbulence of scholastic controversy: "His faith as a Friend allowed him to get through the white waters in his sturdy canoe, less disturbed by the ravaging currents around him than any other religiously stimulated New Testament scholar, and to arrive at his destination with the calm with which he started out."[40]

Former students remember him with affection. "Among Harvard Divinity School students it was said one could earn one's Ph.D. by the wrath of A. D. Nock, and the mercy of Henry J. Cadbury," Leroy Garrett of North Texas State College in Denton, Texas, remembered. Arthur Nock sometimes growled at the students, whereas Henry Cadbury was unfailingly gentle, though sometimes sharp in his attack on ideas with which he disagreed. Leroy Garrett remembers being amazed to hear him say that if Jesus were to return to earth he would be killed again and it would be the clergy who did the deed. Another former student, Robert Grant of Chicago Divinity School, recalls that "he encouraged his students to think their own thoughts, no matter how unlike his they might seem. He was admirably honest, learned, and thorough, a thoughtful and sensible scholar." He remembers once consulting him on the problem of preaching in the faith-versus-reason context: "He quietly suggested thinking of the congregation's faith, or faiths, as a circle which my own intersected. 'Preach where they overlap,' he said. I have found the advice useful and important, for over forty years."[41]

The house on Buckingham Place was rented and the bags

packed. Cambridge Meeting held a farewell tea. Choosing between many offers, Henry Cadbury had agreed to spend the next two years living and lecturing at Pendle Hill. Throughout the first semester he would also lecture three days a week at Drew Seminary in Madison, New Jersey, an arrangement suggested by a New Testament colleague, Howard Clark Kee. During the second semester he would accept Gilbert White's invitation to return to Haverford at long last to teach an undergraduate course on the history and philosophy of Quakerism. For the average seventy-year-old it might seem a heavy schedule, but Henry Cadbury with his boundless enthusiasm, curiosity, and energy was no average man.

CHAPTER 12
An Active Retirement

At Pendle Hill, the Cadburys settled into Upmeads, a good-sized stone house near the entrance to the serene campus. Henry Cadbury had been close to Pendle Hill since its creation, and both he and Lydia Cadbury had often been on campus for a conference or a course of lectures, so the move in 1954 was in many ways a home-coming. Both Cadburys were glad to be near old friends and family. Their daughter Winifred, her husband Martin, and their new granddaughter, Michelle Beer, lived near Philadelphia. Another granddaughter, Carol, was born the following March.

Their good friends Howard and Anna Brinton, former directors, were back living on the Pendle Hill campus, having returned from a two-year AFSC assignment in Japan. The Brintons shared with the Cadburys both AFSC loyalties and scholarly interests. Anna Brinton was an outspoken woman, like Lydia Cadbury. Howard Brinton was quiet, thoughtful, and contemplative. Students at Pendle Hill during this period felt his spiritual influence, at the same time they responded to Henry Cadbury's intellectual challenges. It was the best of both worlds.

By now, Henry Cadbury was Quakerism's most popular lecturer, and to have him on campus was a delight to the Pendle Hill staff and students. Although he was very busy with his teaching, first at Drew and then at Haverford, as well as with chairing the AFSC and Bryn Mawr boards, he was able to find time to deliver a series of Monday night lectures and occasional weekend seminars. For ten years his talks were a consistent Pendle Hill feature, centering on Jesus, on John, on Paul, on the Book of Daniel, on the Apocrypha and the Book of Revelation, as well as such topics as the Resurrection, the Holy Spirit, and perfectionism, and the Quaker testimonies. He spoke as usual with a combination of simplicity and erudition, challenging his listeners to use their full intellectual capacities to understand the times from which the gospels were written or in which Quakerism was born.

People came from miles around to attend these talks. Pendle Hill staff would always count on a full house whenever Henry Cadbury spoke, and more often than not the big room in the barn would rock with happy laughter.

It is hard to pinpoint what made Henry Cadbury so funny. He told little jokes in the course of his talks, which he had culled from reading, or small incidents from his daily life that he had found amusing, but it was not the words so much as his aptness and his manner of delivery that delighted his audience. When something funny occurred to him, he would open his mouth and shut his eyes, and a delightful, mischievous look would steal over his face. Those who knew him were immediately prepared to hear something funny. Or he would deliver his little asides with a flat voice and a blank face, followed by a sudden flash of laughter. His cousin Leah Furtmuller remembers hearing his voice flattening out in a droll fashion when he was delivering a prayer at Bryn Mawr College and thinking to herself, "Henry is having his little joke with the Lord." A British Friend, Hugh Doncaster, said that when he thought of Henry Cadbury he thought first of the word "twinkle": "This applied not just to his eyes, but the whole of his face, and even more! It was a spontaneous delight in people and in life, seen in the perspective that is humor, and creating at once a positive setting and attitude, disarming and creative." [1]

Henry Cadbury liked to tell about one father who entrusted his son to his instruction with the injunction, "Now don't teach Robert anything he doesn't already know." He described a visitor to the Baltimore Yearly Meeting, in which the Thomas family was very prominent, who, not knowing this, said during testimony in the course of the meeting, "I wonder if there are any doubting Thomases present?" Commenting on a new Catholic pronouncement on the Assumption of the Virgin Mary, Henry Cadbury said that he tended to take a dim view of any unwarranted assumptions. He frequently told of seeing a woman asleep on a train with a book, *The Secret of Concentration,* open on her lap. [2]

Another favorite story was that of a young divinity student who came to him to ask if he would look at the original Greek of a line in Luke 11:5 to see if its meaning could be changed slightly. The verse is Jesus' parable about the arrival of a friend at midnight, and the line reads, "Do not bother me; the door is now shut, and my children are with me in bed." His wife did not think this sounded very seemly, the seminarian said. Henry Cadbury agreed to look at the original text and report back the next day. "Well, I do have a change to suggest," he told the student on his return, "but it may not be to your wife's taste. I have looked at the verse again and I think it could read, "My children are with me in the bed."[3]

He did not like risqué humor. The nearest he ever came to such a joke was one he told only to close friends and family. It concerned a Bible in a hotel in New York City, in which there were various texts suggested for the traveler: Worried? See verse such and such. Troubled? See verse so and so. Lonely? See verse this and that. After the suggestions for lonely someone had written in" "Still lonely? Call Mabel at 342-1800."[4]

Henry Cadbury rarely repeated himself, and the information he presented was designed to raise questions in the minds of his listeners, rather than to help them find easy answers. The question about what Henry Cadbury himself really believed came to plague his Pendle Hill audiences as it had Friends in Cambridge, and with it the effort to pin him down. Asked whether he was a mystic, he responded that he was neither a mystic nor a nonmystic. It need not be either/or, he constantly reminded his listeners. One Pendle Hill teacher, Mary Morrison, compared Henry Cadbury to the Sphinx in her journal at one time:

> Yesterday he came close to saying that Jesus could not possibly mean anything to modern minds because the two approaches to life, that of the first century and ours of the twentieth, were radically different.
>
> It all made me think, somehow of the Sphinx and its/her riddle. Perhaps the Sphinx asked no riddle after all. Perhaps the Sphinx just sat there and was a riddle, filling people with the frantic feeling that if only the right question could be formulated, the Sphinx would answer it. Somebody once defined the universe as a structure which gives answers to only the right questions. Well, I think the Sphinx personifies the universe, then. And in his own human way HJC personifies the Sphinx. Now, after years of digesting Rilke's famous saying about loving the questions themselves and living along some day into the answers, I am not so puzzled by Henry Cadbury as I was when I wrote that entry. I have come to think of that Rilke quotation as an almost exact description of him and to realize he did a most remarkable job of living his answers to the Gospels questions that he refused to answer in words.[5]

Friends meetings invited him to speak at their forums or suppers and occasionally assigned him such topics as "The Committed Life," or "What the Bible Means to Me," or "My Religious Pilgrimage." Although he complained mildly in each case that these topics were not congenial to him, he addressed them willingly enough, as he had answered his Harvard theological students. Speaking on "My Religious Pilgrimage" at the Doylestown Meeting, he stressed his reluctance to influence other people's views and his sense that much of his own religious conditioning had come to him from his Quaker home and associations: "If I am willing to share experience with others it is to assure them that what they long for may not be necessary or even vouchsafed by God . . . God leaves us to shift for ourselves." He was reaching out, as he had done long ago at Bryn Mawr, to those who had difficulty with theology or mysticism and still felt themselves to be religious. At about the same time, he delivered a similar message to the Radnor Meeting, using an analogy. One should not spend one's time endlessly consulting the seed catalog; one ought to plant one's garden and see what comes up, he said. For at least one listener it was the beginning of a life of involvement in Quaker service.[6]

He was still in demand nationwide, and he traveled that first year of retirement to Boston to lecture at Tufts, to Wilmington College in Ohio, and to Dallas, Texas, where he gave a series of lectures at the Perkins School of Theology. He took time off from his heavy schedule to spend six weeks over the Christmas holidays in Jamaica, taking Lydia Cadbury along for sun and companionship while he researched Quaker settlements on the island and spoke—of course—to the Jamaican Friends. He investigated the great earthquake at Port Royal on June 7, 1692, in which about two-thirds of the population perished. The earthquake occurred on monthly meeting day, and those who happened not to go to meeting were lost—some thirty persons in all. The London Yearly Meeting could not refrain from pointing out the obvious moral: "Since some of you were preserved in a meeting, let it engage and encourage you to frequent meeting to wait upon the Lord," its pious epistle said.[7]

In the spring of 1955 an event occurred for which Henry Cadbury had been working for more than forty years: the joining of the Hicksite and Orthodox Yearly Meetings in Philadelphia into one body. The two Central Philadelphia Meetings, Twelfth Street, to which the Cadburys belonged, and Race Street, the Hicksite branch, were also in the process of coming together. Henry and Lydia Cadbury once more became active members of this group, called Central Philadelphia Monthly Meeting, and drove into the city every First Day to attend.

They spent the month of July at Back Log Camp as usual, dealing with complications—too few guests, precarious cooks, and par-

Back Log Camp. Cadbury brothers enjoy canoing, circa 1936. Left to right, Benjamin, John, William, Henry. Private collection of Mary Hoxie Jones. Photo copied by Theodore Hetzel.

ties of hikers getting lost, as Lydia Cadbury wrote Emma. Although over seventy, Henry Cadbury was still a strong and vigorous woodsman, able to carry heavy packs and go for miles without tiring. He knew the flora and the fauna of the Adirondacks well and shared a naturalist's joy in the events of forest life. One nephew remembers an especially happy occasion hiking with Uncle Henry when a mother fox and her young approached them while they were eating supper by the trail, and the cubs were so tame that they crept close enough to take crumbs from Henry Cadbury's fingers. Although Henry Cadbury was of slighter build than Lydia Cadbury's Brown brothers, he was always able to do his share of the heavy lifting, using his intelligence and his knowledge of the fulcrum and other ancient Grecian principles to solve problems rather than muscle power alone. His intellectual and spiritual contribution to the camp remained high. He read verses from the Bible at meals, always with an appropriate and frequently amusing reference to some feature of camp life, gave talks at the Focus Tent, and conferred with individual guests. One camper of this period remembers vividly a time when a guest made an inappropriate and prejudiced remark during one of the Focus Tent gatherings. Several other guests bristled, prepared to dispute him. Instead, Henry Cadbury began a conversation by asking the guest an innocuous question, then another, and then, after a while, another, until at the end of a low-keyed exchange the offender had made a complete circle and himself offered the appropriate rejoinder to his own previous statement.[8]

Lydia Cadbury's joy in Back Log had been increased considerably by the addition of a gasoline-run washing machine. She also liked occasionally to leave camp to take a hot bath or shower. There is one famous Lydia Cadbury story of her going to town by boat and on foot, entering the one small hotel, and calling for the manager. Getting no response, she went upstairs, helped herself to clean towels, took a hot bath, put the towels in the laundry chute, returned to the entry, called again for the manager, and finding no one, went back to camp.[9]

After Back Log and one of their frequent visits to South China, Maine, the Cadburys went to Chicago to visit their son Christopher, who was doing graduate work in psychology at the University of Chicago, and daughter-in-law Mary, while Henry Cadbury spoke at an AFSC meeting. The topic was a familiar one, the relationship between action and beliefs, and Henry Cadbury told a story of a churchman who had asked him: "Why don't you Quakers preach what you practice?"[10]

Returning from these wanderings to Pendle Hill in the fall of 1955, they found a new couple in residence. Wilmer and Mildred Young had left Westtown School, where Wilmer Young taught, in the late 1930s to live in South Carolina among the sharecroppers and to help with improving farming methods and the establishment of a cooperative. For years the Youngs had lived simply and had refused to pay income taxes for war purposes. Now they were nearing retirement age and had decided to return to Philadelphia. Wilmer Young had met Henry Cadbury at Westtown years ago, but they had known each other only slightly. Now, however, a deeper friendship emerged between the two couples, which meant a great deal to them both. In the manner of a schoolgirl, Lydia Cadbury invited Mildred Young to be her best friend. Mildred Young was interested in the study of Dante, but felt constrained because she had had no scholarly training. Henry Cadbury encouraged her to not only pursue Dante but to teach a course on the subject, and he brought her books that were helpful. Henry Cadbury and Wilmer Young spent a great deal of time together, especially discussing peace issues. Wilmer Young was an activist. His influence may have had something to do with Henry Cadbury's willingness to join vigil lines in the early 1960s.

As she came to know the Cadburys more intimately, Mildred Young saw how devoted a couple they were and how skillfully Lydia Cadbury played the role of the wife of a distinguished scholar. Despite her forthright and sometimes undiplomatic manner, she managed always to give Henry Cadbury the floor when there was a chance for him to express himself to people who interested him. She never worried or fussed over him or called attention to his hearing loss, and she never tried to adapt her ideas to his. Mildred Young was interested that Lydia Cadbury taught her own Bible class, presenting a different interpretation of Jesus than her famous husband. Within the Cadbury family "yes/and" was evidently the rule. Some people occasionally still wondered if Lydia Cadbury's outspoken ways bothered the courtly Henry Cadbury, but Mildred Young noticed that when Henry Cadbury entered the dining room at Pendle Hill, it was Lydia Cadbury with whom he wanted to sit.[11]

That second year at Pendle Hill, Henry Cadbury taught a course at Bryn Mawr as well as at Haverford. In March of 1956, he was asked to become chairman of the Bryn Mawr board. Since he was still deeply committed to the AFSC, it meant taking on two major responsibilities at the same time, but Henry Cadbury agreed readily. He told a friend in a joking fashion that it paid to have two such assignments; you could always get away from one set of duties by pleading the heavy pressure of the other. Katherine McBride came to depend on Henry Cadbury for advice and counsel in many matters, and the two corresponded vigorously from then on.

After two years at Pendle Hill the Cadburys decided to return to the Haverford community. The Pendle Hill staff pressed them to stay and offered them a permanent home, but to both Cadburys the thought of being back in the Haverford community was attractive. They sold the house in Cambridge, and in June of 1956, while Henry Cadbury was spending his usual two weeks in Northfield, working on the Apocrypha, Martin Beer and Lydia Cadbury moved them back into Millbrook Lane. They spent a month resting in Back Log, where they heard the news of the birth of a new grandchild, Vivian, daughter of Christopher and Mary. Refreshed and pleased, they were ready to set sail for Europe and new adventures.

In recognition of his lasting contribution to New Testament scholarship on the world scene, Henry Cadbury had been named a member of the Studiorum Novi Testamenti Societas (SNTS) in the fall of 1955. In 1956 he became deputy president-elect and was asked to read a paper at the annual meeting in Holland that fall. Henry Cadbury's talk at the SNTS meetings, "'We' and 'I' Passages in Luke-Acts," was published in *New Testament Studies,* and he was

Henry J. Cadbury, Senator Joseph Clark, and President Katherine McBride. Bryn Mawr College Commencement, 1962. Copyright Bryn Mawr College, All rights reserved. Photo courtesy of Bryn Mawr College Archives.

named president-elect for the following year. After the meetings, the Cadburys traveled to Germany, Switzerland, and Denmark, where they attended an AFSC international seminar, then spent a few days in London before going to Woodbrooke, where Henry Cadbury was to begin the fall term on September 29. He had decided to continue his research on the unpublished papers of George Fox. As usual, he was called upon for many lectures, and in late October he traveled back to Germany to speak to a conference of AFSC workers at Darmstadt.

He had been asked to talk about the ideals and history of the AFSC and the connections between Quaker beliefs and action. He made the point he frequently liked to make that action sometimes preceded its expression in ideas: "Now a man was asked 'what do you think?' and he said: 'Let me see what I do first and then I'll tell you what I think.' . . . I have a notion that Goethe was more nearly right when he took the phrase in the Gospel and turned it upside down and said, 'In the beginning was the deed.'" [12]

The history of the AFSC, he said, had been that of a "whole series of improvisations of response to opportunities." Friends had been pioneers in a great many social movements, because they let their works and their lives speak instead of creating theological definitions. Motives are complex, and it is hard to explain them. Were a psychologist to ask members of the AFSC family to explain why they were doing what they were doing, he said he thought the answer would be, "It is because I like doing this sort of thing." "I have spent very few weeks in my life at the foreign end of the Service Committee's work, a few weeks in Germany in 1920, three weeks in England in 1941. I have never felt, I believe, that more than in those weeks I was doing exactly what I wanted to do." Skills were important, but the inner motive behind the work meant that AFSC workers were far more interested that the means should be appropriate to the end in view: "Wars are waged for nominally good purposes, it is a question of means." [13]

Returning to England and Woodbrooke, Henry Cadbury joined Lydia in celebrating an American Thanksgiving with another American Quaker family, Herbert and Ruthanna Hadley and their children, then said a series of good-byes before leaving for home and Haverford just before Christmas.

Shortly before their departure, Henry Cadbury was invited to return in May to London to give the annual Swarthmore Lecture. It was not practical for Lydia Cadbury to accompany him on this venture, so he flew over alone. His talk, "Quakerism and Early Christianity," gave him an opportunity to draw some of the parallels between the two movements he had been studying; the same burst of enthusiasm, the same conflict between rejection of old values and acceptance of new, the same tendency toward extremes and over-conversion, he stated. Today both movements suffered from the efforts of present-day modernizers to make them fit a neat pattern. Quakerism must beware of using the historical approach to create a theology out of the writings of the early Friends, just as it was currently fashionable to try to create a biblical theology from the Bible. We must instead continue to study such writings in their historical settings and accept their variety and ambiguities:

> Present-day Quakerism owes a special debt to those interpreters who do justice to more than one of its multiple strands, the mystical, the evangelical, the rational and the social. . . . It would be a pity if the natural variety in Quakerism were artificially restrained. Even unconsciously we are subject to powerful tendencies to conform to a single standard in religion as well as in other ideologies and practices. If the role of Quakerism among the denominations is precisely one of enriching their variety and challenging their standards of uniformity, we ought by the same token to welcome variety within our small body.[14]

"The lecture went o.k., I think," he wrote his niece, Mary Hoxie Jones. There were other lectures that spring. The AFSC had celebrated its fortieth birthday at the end of April, at which event Henry Cadbury had compared his role as chairman to living in the eye of a hurricane. He traced some of the history of the AFSC's development and repeated Rufus Jones's favorite quotation from Oliver Cromwell: "A man never goes so far as when he does not know where he is going." His first alma mater, Penn Charter School, gave him its Alumni Award that year, and he told stories of his days at the school, including that of the Wanamaker fire and of his failing the entrance math exam at Haverford. The New York Yearly Meeting invited him to give a keynote address in July, and in August he traveled to Indiana to talk to the Western Yearly Meeting on "The Place of Friends among the Churches."[15] Speaking of the immediacy of the Quaker worship and action in a world increasingly dominated by spectatorship, he argued that the group had a contribution to make:

> Our mere presence is often a silent reminder or corrective when solutions are proposed to which Quakerism offers an obvious challenge. Some of our special witness—the high role of the laity and especially of women—with difficulty enters the understanding of many ecclesiastical bodies. Not by preaching but by practicing we can quietly challenge

what in spite of some progress is the widespread indifference to these matters in some churchmen—and a neglect of potential manpower and womanpower in the church.[16]

In September the huge project of producing a Revised Standard Version of the Bible came to an end with the publication of the Apocrypha, on which Henry Cadbury had worked steadily. His lectures and writings throughout this period were studded with examples from the books of the Apocrypha. In one of his "Letters from the Past," he said he felt Friends should acquaint themselves with these books, approaching them as they approached the canonical sections of the Bible for the truth that answered to the light within.[17]

At this same period, Henry Cadbury helped to write and edit a statement of the AFSC on nuclear testing, "Our Only Shelter Is Peace." To carry its message to the highest level of government, the Board of Directors of the AFSC asked Henry Cadbury as chairman and Lewis Hoskins as executive secretary to seek an interview with Vice-President Richard Nixon, a birthright Friend from Whittier, California. Some of Nixon's relatives were close to the AFSC, although his views differed markedly from theirs.

The trip to the White House actually came in February of 1958. Anna Brinton joined the two men. According to Lewis Hoskins, Henry Cadbury set the tone of the interview and kept it on a dignified level, cordial and yet penetrating. Nixon seemed genuinely pleased to talk about his Quaker connections and was willing to listen to AFSC suggestions about ways to reduce tensions with the USSR and work toward disarmament. Later, when he became president, he consistently refused to meet with such Quaker delegations, but on this trip the three Quakers came away feeling that they had at least been heard.[18]

The AFSC was trying to ease European tensions by holding a series of international seminars and conferences for diplomats. During the summer of 1958, Henry and Lydia Cadbury attended a seminar in Yugoslavia, visited the Friends centers in Paris and Vienna, attended the German Yearly Meeting, and then went to Clarens, Switzerland, where an annual gathering of diplomats for off-the-record conversations was held. He wrote Lewis Hoskins from Clarens that he was much impressed with the level of the discussions and with the staff. He also said he was enjoying himself and that "I am not letting my sense of possible shirking of AFSC duties spoil what is proving an interesting and not too strenuous series of visits, conferences, and sightseeing."[19]

With Colin Bell, 1958. At the AFSC Diplomats Conference at Clarens, Switzerland, 1958. Photo courtesy of Elizabeth Musgrave.

After the sessions in Clarens were over, the Cadburys went to Strasbourg, where Henry Cadbury, as president, presided over the annual meeting of the SNTS and gave the presidential address, "The Dilemma of the Ephesians."

Amos Wilder, who succeeded Henry Cadbury as the Hollis Professor of Divinity at Harvard, recalled Henry Cadbury's diplomatic aplomb at the august gathering:

> Those present will recall another kind of dilemma he faced as our spokesman at the ceremonial dinner with our French hosts. The guests included official representatives of the city and University of Strasbourg, and also colorfully garbed and decorated members of the Alsatian hierarchy, and even of the French army of eastern France. It would have taken a master of protocol and of the Almanach de Gotha to toast each with his proper title. With Quaker simplicity our president was able to solve the problem easily by addressing each as "Mr." or "Monsieur." [20]

The paper itself, concerning the question of whether Paul was really the author of the Epistle to the Ephesians, was written in Henry Cadbury's typically cautious style. He carefully marshaled all the evidence that it was, and then that it was not, Paul but said he was content to let the question remain unanswered until more evidence was unearthed. "We continue to conjecture and are restless with the agnostic answer 'Ignoramus'. We grasp at straws where acknowledgment of ignorance would better befit us."[21]

He finished the lecture with a story about a beloved English schoolmaster, A. Neave Brayshaw, known to generations of schoolboys as "Puddles." Puddles was known for his recitation of a poem about a prehistoric animal called Eohippus. At an alumni gathering there was a contest to see which old boy could come closest to achieving the same effect. All the contestants were placed behind a curtain, and Neave Brayshaw himself entered, and came in third. Henry Cadbury was, of course, illustrating the difficulty of assigning authorship. Another New Testament scholar, George Boobyer, remembers that the occasion was made delightfully informal by Henry Cadbury's use of the nickname "Puddles" before the august body.[22]

The meetings in Strasbourg lasted four days. Afterward, the Cadburys crossed the channel to England, glad to be done with the constant changing of language and currency. Henry Cadbury was delighted to have time to work in the British Museum and the Library at Friends House as a reward for his labors. They settled in a small hotel near the British Museum, and Henry Cadbury wrote that he was having "the time of my life." He was examining the early records of the persecution of Friends, looking at the original folio manuscripts which Joseph Besse later condensed into a two-volume work on "Sufferings." Poring over such ancient and hard-to-read records might not be everyone's favorite occupation, but it suited Henry Cadbury exactly.

This respite lasted until November, when the Cadburys returned to their home in Haverford and Henry Cadbury to his teaching, writing, and lecturing. In the spring of 1959 he gave his third William Penn lecture, "The Character of a Quaker." Earlier, *Liberty Magazine* had asked him to write an article on what makes a good Quaker, one of a series with similar titles, but the publication had folded before the article was published. In this talk, he expanded on the theme he had developed in the Swarthmore Lecture, discussing the variety of belief within Quakerism, from a conservative, evangelical view to the broader definitions of the

"Inner Light." He was concerned that some Christocentric Quakers were attempting to base a theology on a precise interpretation of the writings of George Fox, and he pled for an acceptance of diversity.[23]

During this same busy spring Henry Cadbury also gave the Ingersoll lecture at Harvard, "Intimations of Immortality in the Thought of Jesus." Returning to the theme of the Jewishness of Jesus' thought and of his apocalyptic beliefs, Henry Cadbury suggested that they might not have seemed very important at the time:

> The very incidental character of the references suggests alike two almost contradictory conclusions.
>
> 1. The after life was taken for granted by Jesus and by his hearers generally. He did not need to impress it or correct it. It was not for him or them a question of hesitation and debate. It is therefore an assured ingredient in his perspective.
>
> 2. By the same token his allusions do not allow us to reconstruct any very definite or circumstantial impression of this future. They were innocently imprecise, intimations rather than descriptions, and were employed in connection with other matters of which Jesus had something emphatic and significant to say.[24]

The Wordsworthian phrase "Intimations of immortality" was a tongue twister, and each word could be confused, "intimations" for "imitations" and "immortality" for "immorality," Henry Cadbury pointed out. The word "intimations," meaning hint or obscure allusion, however, was perhaps apt for the small amount of information the gospels provided on the subject.[25]

That same spring he received an honorary doctorate in humane letters, his fifth honorary degree, from Howard University. He addressed the New England Yearly Meeting that summer and later taught a course at Union Theological Seminary in New York. A short vacation at Back Log Camp was marred by his falling and hitting his head on a rock, but he recovered rapidly for a man his age and was able to meet his fall classes at Haverford and Pendle Hill. In November, the Cadburys were asked to travel for the AFSC, visiting Friends groups in Georgia and Florida. On the way south they stopped at Fort Dietrick, Maryland, where Friends were conducting a vigil line protesting the development of instruments of chemical-biological warfare. It was Henry Cadbury's first experience in public witness, and characteristically he welcomed it as a new development in the continuing saga of Quaker service. Lydia Cadbury joined him, and he came back later in January to picket again. The older he grew, it seemed, the more he spoke of the need to be obedient to a continuing revelation, to grow and change. He frequently quoted from Tennyson's Morte d'Arthur:

> The old order changeth, yielding place to new
> And God fulfills himself in many ways,
> Lest one good custom should corrupt the world.

At the AFSC he was aware of being part of the old order, the only remaining board member whose tenure stretched back to 1917. Moreover, he was having increasing problems with deafness. With some sadness he told the Board of Directors that he intended to resign as board chairman at the corporation meeting, held in January 1960. At that meeting he was named honorary chairman, and his old friend and colleague, Harold Evans, was appointed chairman in his place.

On this occasion, Henry Cadbury was asked to reflect on his long years with the AFSC. His brief and extemporaneous remarks were taped and proved so valuable that they were later incorporated into a phonograph record published by the AFSC in 1967. He said he thought that AFSC must always listen with care to its staff and its donors, since its purpose remained serving as an outlet for the resources and spiritual energies of Friends and those who appreciated Friends' way of doing things. He himself learned a great deal by listening carefully to the staff. Though some people said that preoccupation with providing service prevented one from thinking clearly about the theory of the work, he was inclined to think not: "If preoccupation with service is a form of escape from clear thinking out of religious doctrine I wonder whether the clear thinking out of religious doctrine is a form of escape from service? It could go both ways." He said that he had always been glad when the Board of Directors undertook a project, not because they thought it might succeed but because it was the right thing to do: "And I am also happy in the board meeting when a proposal to go a little further in a more radical direction than we have gone is before us and the most conservative member of the Board gets up and says we've got to look forward, that things have to be done a little differently now from the way Friends have always done them."[26] He was never an emotional speaker, and the voice in the tape is dry and elderly, but one hears nevertheless the depth of feeling with which he ended his long years as board chairman.

In those years, the AFSC had changed in many ways. The

experience in World War II had broadened it into a recognized international agency, and the development of regional offices throughout the United States had turned it from a provincial organization with a strong Philadelphia orientation to one known and active throughout the country. Following the war, the AFSC had developed strong programs in the area of community relations, including fair housing, fair employment, and school integration. Internationally, it had begun a series of seminars for diplomats, leaders, and students, aimed at increasing international understanding and getting at the roots of war. Its peace education programs in the United States were now far more sophisticated, and the materials produced were used in schools and colleges. The development of the FCNL had been accompanied by other programs in Washington, ensuring a Quaker influence on the national scene. As Henry Cadbury would insist, these changes were not the work of any one leader but the result of a group process, but his quiet encouragement to those with new and forward-looking ideas had much to do with these changes.

In October of 1960, the AFSC moved to new headquarters at 160 North Fifteenth Street, the former site of Friends Central School. Opening ceremonies were planned for October 30. Henry and Lydia Cadbury were invited to attend, only to discover that the gathering had actually been organized to pay tribute to Henry Cadbury and his long years of AFSC service.

The highlight of the occasion was the presentation of a book in his honor. His old friend, Anna Brinton, had edited a collection of twenty-one essays by prominent Friends and entitled it *Then and Now,* a reversal of the "Now and Then" signature Henry Cadbury had used for his "Letters from the Past." In presenting it she called it a "spiritual mustard pot, to make the soul sneeze with devotion."

The book came as a complete surprise. It contained a long and charming biographical essay by his niece Mary Hoxie Jones, which she had put together without his knowing about it, and for which she had gathered tributes from many colleagues at Harvard, Bryn Mawr, and the AFSC. Deeply touched by the book, Henry Cadbury wrote individual notes of appreciation to each contributor. To author Elizabeth Gray Vining, whose essay was called "Penn and the Poets," he confided he was so intrigued by her statement that parts of Chaucer's "Plowman's Tales" had been tampered with by an editor in an early edition, and that Penn therefore was not reading a true version at his time, that he went to the library and looked up every edition of the poem he could find. She was of course correct, and he was glad for this information, he wrote her. She thought the letter revealed the courtesy and charming attention to detail that were characteristic of the man. It was also an example of his awesome curiosity.[27]

Despite the ceremonies, Henry Cadbury was by no means retiring from the AFSC. As honorary chairman, he continued to meet with the board for years and years, and he served as well as chairman of the Peace Education Committee until he was into his late eighties. He was frequently asked to give orientation to new staff members or student volunteers preparing to take part in work camps or programs abroad or to enter into exchange programs. The young volunteers loved him for his simplicity and his wry sense of humor.

Marthalyn Dickson was the director of student exchange for the School Affiliation Service of the AFSC, and she asked Henry Cadbury several times to address the students going overseas. On one such occasion, when the group was meeting in a conference center at Schwenksville on Halloween, Henry Cadbury arrived rather tired an hour or so before supper. Marthalyn Dickson suggested that he go back to her room and take a nap. She knew he knew the way, so she did not conduct him. She did not know that the students had placed a large cardboard skeleton in her bed hoping to scare her. Henry Cadbury found the figure, removed it carefully, took his nap, restored the skeleton, made up the bed, and said nothing about the event to Marthalyn until the next morning, when he innocently inquired, how she had slept. The group of young students loved him for going along with their joke.[28]

The year 1960 marked the three hundredth anniversary of the Quaker peace testimony, which members of the Society of Friends date from "the declaration from the harmless and innocent people of God called Quakers, against all plotters and fighters in the world" to Charles II: "We utterly deny all outward wars and strife and fightings with outward weapons, for any end, under any pretense whatsoever. This is our testimony to the whole world."[29]

A number of Quaker groups banded together to honor the occasion by organizing a pilgrimage of Friends to Washington to present "The Quaker Peace Testimony, 1660–1960" to the president and to stand in silent vigil in front of the Pentagon. Henry Cadbury was asked to serve as chairman of the administrative committee coordinating the event, which was also to be celebrated in other cities and in Quaker meetings across the nation. The vigil was originally set for October but later switched to November. Henry Cadbury had agreed to visit the Seattle office of the AFSC at the time and was unable to be present in Washington, but he worked vigorously to

With A. J. Muste, March 1961. Before participation in the vigil at the Boeing Vertol plant, Morton. From the collection of and by Theodore Hetzel.

make it a success and to defend public witness from the criticism of more conservative Friends who were still dubious about it as a Quaker tactic. A few months later he joined A. J. Muste in a vigil before the Boeing Vertol plant in Morton, Pennsylvania.

In a discussion on public witness, held in April 1961 at Pendle Hill, he said he felt the time had come for a more active witness against war: "I would ask whether the situation demands new, vigorous, and convincing behavior on our part to challenge the policy of mass extermination?" Perhaps the new vocabulary of public witness and civil disobedience and nonviolence were only new names for older and forgotten Quaker experience, he suggested.[30]

After a short visit to Back Log Camp in the summer of 1961, the Cadburys prepared for yet another trip abroad, with visits to Friends' groups in Paris and Amsterdam and attendance at several conferences before arriving in London in September. At that time Henry Cadbury was to represent the AFSC at an international meeting on disarmament held in London, called by pacifists from many lands to protest the resumption of nuclear testing. Eric Fromm and A. J. Muste joined Henry Cadbury in this effort.[31]

Henry and Lydia Cadbury in the March for World Order, 1962. Courtesy of Eliza-beth Musgrave.

Once the meeting was over, there was time for visits, for research, even for soccer. Henry Cadbury had always loved soccer, and when he and Lydia Cadbury had lunch with a young Quaker couple, Jim and Jean Matlack, studying that year at Oxford, and Henry Cadbury learned that Jim was planning to spend the afternoon at a major London soccer match, he asked Jim Matlack if he might go along. Jim Matlack hesitated, thinking of the crowded ride by tube and the jam-packed public arena, but Henry Cadbury clapped his battered hat on his head and appeared determined. The subway was jammed, just as Jim Matlack had feared, and in the stands at the field they had to stand shoulder to shoulder and cheek to jowl with their neighbors, the crowd leaning first one way and then the other, like some giant organism, to watch the play. It was a cold day, and Henry Cadbury at seventy-eight looked frail. Jim Matlack suggested at the half that they perhaps had had enough and might leave, but Henry Cadbury said no, he wanted to see the rest of the match. Nor would he leave a few minutes early, to avoid the crush. He wanted to stay for the final outcome. Jim Matlack gave up worrying, and they stood to the very end and battled a floodtide of people on the way home, Henry Cadbury struggling gamely alongside of his much younger friend.[32]

Returning to the United States that fall, the Cadburys found the American peace movement deeply troubled about nuclear testing. Henry Cadbury did not himself often join in lawsuits, sharing the Quaker tradition that disputes should be settled out of court, but early in 1962 he agreed to become a signatory in a case against the U.S. government for violating the civil rights of those who objected to such testing.[33]

In late April, more than one thousand Friends converged on Washington, D.C., for a Friends Witness for World Order. Henry, Lydia, and Emma Cadbury joined the group. After the vigil, President John F. Kennedy consented to see a delegation of six to discuss ideas for peace, and Henry Cadbury was one of those chosen. Kennedy remembered that Henry Cadbury was a distinguished and beloved professor at Harvard when he was himself an undergraduate. He said that he had never spent much time at the Divinity School and now it was perhaps proving regrettable that he had not. He was gracious and seemed relaxed, but Henry Cadbury came away saddened by the intuition that here was a man somehow trapped by his position.[34]

Henry Cadbury himself refused to be trapped by advancing age or other people's perceptions of him as a has-been. In 1961 a candidate for a degree of doctor of philosophy at Boston University had titled his dissertation "The Contribution of Henry Joel Cadbury to the Study of the Historical Jesus." It was a good summary of Henry Cadbury's writings on the subject to date—quoting extensively from Henry Cadbury's own formulations—but the assumptions that these contributions were in the past was implicit. Nevertheless, in the spring of 1963 a new work appeared. *The Eclipse of the Historical Jesus,* based on some Library Lectures Henry Cadbury had given at Haverford, recapitulated the history of the quest for the historical Jesus from the time of Schweitzer to the present and explained how this quest was being overshadowed by the effort to concentrate on the message or kerygma of Jesus. It was switching emphasis from the gospel of Jesus to a gospel about Jesus, Henry Cadbury felt, and the effort to build a biblical theology was overshadowing the need for continued research.[35]

As a historian of, and one might say a disciple, of Jesus, Henry Cadbury made it clear in this brief book that he regretted the new emphasis, believing that there was still much to be learned not only for the sake of scholarship but also for that of moral leadership in a painstaking quest for the historic figure. But if the historical Jesus was now in eclipse, he comforted himself that it need not be forever: "Eclipses in the sky are not permanent and are rarely total. There is usually at least what the astronomers call the penumbra or corona. And there is another analogy I may mention. An eclipse of the sun is due to a relatively small satellite like the moon temporarily shutting it out while an eclipse of the moon is due to our own planet's being in the way—getting in our own light, as we say."[36] It was a clear and forceful statement, and many of his colleagues in New Testament studies wrote to say that he had once more contributed fresh ideas to their thinking.

Henry Cadbury continued to be concerned that a study of the history of the Society of Friends in general, and the writings of George Fox in particular, not be used in an effort to impose a new orthodoxy on the rich diversity within Quaker thought. In a new edition of *The Journal of George Fox,* as edited by Rufus Jones in 1902 and republished in 1963, he wrote a chapter on the influence of the journal on the Society of Friends, putting in a nutshell the source of the varying strands within Quakerism:

> Fox's language is fundamentally Biblical, and he retains alongside of his revolutionary ideas a great deal of traditional terminology. Immediate guidance is identified with historical revelation. The Light within is not detached from Christ or the Holy Spirit. It is the same spirit as gave forth the Scriptures. He leaves the reader in no doubt—or if he does, his opponents leave none—that he put inner experience above scripture record, religion today above divine acts in the past. But he ac-

knowledged the past much as more orthodox folk did. It was the same God or spirit at work in history as today, in the life and death of Jesus as in the inspired and empowered lives of Fox and the early Quakers.

This unresolved ambivalence in Fox's message has given his Journal a strange effect among his followers. These followers, generation after generation, have divided their own emphasis. Besides the mystical— or if you prefer, the prophetic—understanding of religion like Fox's understanding, in every generation some Friends have clung to an evangelical emphasis, similar to that of Fox's own opponents. There is in the Journal enough of this common Christian theology for them to claim that their own position is identical with Fox's. Thus in a curious and unsuspected way Fox's Journal is honestly believed by quite contrasting groups of Friends to justify precisely their own understanding of Quakerism and not its opposite. They naturally claim on both sides to be in accord with the message of their founder.[37]

For many years Henry Cadbury had been corresponding with Lewis Benson, a New York Friend, a printer, who had made an extensive study of George Fox's writings and was urging that modern Quakerism adopt a more Christocentric religion in light of the centrality of the Christian message, "Christ has come to teach his people," which Benson found in Fox's journal. Though admiring Benson's mastery of Fox's works, Henry Cadbury continued to insist that the journal was open to a variety of latter-day interpretations in the light of the Living Spirit, just as was the Bible. "Must it be either/or? Why not both/and?" he frequently queried Benson.

That spring, Henry Cadbury celebrated the sixtieth anniversary of his graduation from Haverford. It was time finally to retire from active teaching at his alma mater. Edwin Bronner, a Quaker historian who had become curator of the Quaker Collection, was going to teach his classes on Quakerism. Being eighty did not seem too old to teach, however, and for the next three years Henry Cadbury taught in the graduate program of religion at Temple University.

Once more Henry and Lydia Cadbury traveled abroad that summer, this time crossing with their old friends from Haverford, Dorothy and Douglas Steere. The Steeres remember a joyous time of laughter over every meal. After a gathering at Woodbrooke, the Cadburys moved down to London, where they took a top floor suite at a hotel they had never stayed at before. The Cadburys were always trying different hotels; on one occasion they took a room in an establishment that had the reputation of being frequented by high-priced call girls. Of this they seemed blissfully ignorant. Their current choice puzzled Edward Milligan, the librarian at Friends House:

I must confess I felt it was not quite like them. Rather lush and pricey. . . . On the last day all was made plain. The space enabled Lydia to potter happily and they had been able to do virtually all their laundry, affecting a considerable saving. They had hugely enjoyed frugal meals of French bread and fruit and cheese—all bought in nearby Marchmont Street affecting (this time) a more than considerable saving. They had used the hotel, in effect, merely for bed and breakfast. "The way they looked at me when I paid the bill" HJC said to me with that slight nod of his head, "we shall never be able to go there again. But it was fun while it lasted." [38]

CHAPTER 13

A Green Old Age

At the meetings of the Society of Biblical Literature in December of 1963, a former student, Henry Clay Niles, gave a talk called "Wit and Wisdom of Henry Joel Cadbury" in honor of Henry Cadbury's eightieth birthday on the first of the month. Henry Cadbury, looking more puckish than ever as he aged, with his long, pointed ears, small body, and bandy legs, sat in the front row so he could hear the speech, which was drawn almost entirely from his own writings. Niles remembered that Henry Cadbury had often repeated to his students the New Testament adage that a disciple is not above his teacher. But if Henry Cadbury had heard all his own witticisms before, the other assembled scholars had not, and the room was filled with laughter.[1]

Among his colleagues, Henry Cadbury was known not only for his wit and scholarship but also for his forthrightness. Julius Seelye Bixler had been his colleague at Harvard for many years. Once he gave him a chapter of a forthcoming book for comment. In returning it, Henry Cadbury said, "I didn't expect to like it, but I think it is quite good." Remembering this, Bixler wrote, "Afterwards I thought: how like Henry! Honest to a fault, and yet considerate and eager to be encouraging; shunning fulsomeness like the plague itself, yet not wanting to downplay friendliness." With several other older scholars, Henry Cadbury always sat in the front row at the meetings of the Society of Biblical Literature, William Beardslee now recalls. "Frequently, after one of the younger scholars gave a paper he would ask a question that would probe the weak points of the presentation and lead to a vigorous discussion. . . . His astringent honesty and integrity were memorable."[2]

Having spent a good part of his life being the youngest person present at any gathering—in his class at school, as a teacher, as a member of the committee to produce the Revised Standard Version of the American Bible—he was now beginning to experience being the oldest. Of his brothers and sisters, only Emma Cadbury survived, living quietly in a Quaker home in Moorestown, New Jersey. He was the patriarch of the American Cadburys now, and he began to gather information with which to publish a *Sesquicentennial Memento and Cadbury Pedigree,* commemorating the arrival of Joel Cadbury, his grandfather, in the United States in 1815.

Lydia Cadbury, meanwhile, was experiencing the delights and frustrations of seeing her own first book published. Friends and relations who had received her letters over the years and noticed her vivid and expressive style had urged her to write her memoirs. She had undertaken this task some years earlier, concentrating on her life as part of the Brown clan at Westtown School and Back Log Camp. In 1964, the results of this labor, a charming book, *A Quaker Girlhood,* was published by her children and widely read and admired in Quaker circles.[3]

But neither of the Cadburys spent much time thinking exclusively about the past. Henry Cadbury took up his new teaching duties at Temple University that fall with zest and journeyed in November to Earlham College in Richmond, Indiana, to serve as visiting Quaker lecturer. He was interested in the AFSC's major effort to resettle Algerians made homeless by the war with the French. One of his "Letters from the Past" in this period told the story of some Quakers who had been captured by the Moslems in the seventeenth century and held prisoner in Algiers. Then Quakers had been busy raising money to free them. Now the effort was to help the Algerians secure their new freedom through resettlement and development. Asked by the AFSC's Information Services to appear on a CBS TV program to give the Quaker background for the Algerian program, he readily agreed. At the studio, the producer feared he looked too old for the merciless television cameras and sent him to make-up, from which he emerged coated with pancake and blush.

"Well, this is a new experience," he said cheerfully, "I never thought I would end up wearing rouge."[4]

In the spring of 1964, Henry and Lydia Cadbury went to Canada, visiting Friends in Montreal and Toronto. In the latter city Henry Cadbury gave the talk, "Vital Issues for Friends Today." He spoke of the need to express the Quaker message in the world through action, which he called incarnate Quakerism, and of the religious basis for social concern.

There is an assumption abroad that religion comes first and social action after, as shown in the title of a recent conference in Philadelphia,
"Beliefs into Action." By religion is understood something inward, perhaps mystical, perhaps theological—but not very extrovert. Now historically Quakerism has both aspects; we have been social pioneers, also
quietists. How did the first derive from the second? It seems an unlikely
origin. My answer would be that the alleged relation, "basis," is not the
whole truth. The two aspects are complementary, and I am impressed
how much inner religion is fostered by social concern. If social work
can be an escape from inner religion, as is sometimes suggested, is not
the opposite also true? Action, often incoherent and inarticulate, leads
to thought and can also lead to spiritual growth.[5]

In Toronto Henry Cadbury had a cousin, George W. Cadbury,
who had left England in the 1930s and settled in Canada, where he
had been active in socialist politics. He felt a bond with Henry and
Lydia Cadbury because the two seemed more liberal politically than
other members of the Cadbury clan. (Henry and Lydia Cadbury
had frequently voted for Norman Thomas when he was on the
ballot.) George Cadbury was an officer of International Planned
Parenthood, and Henry Cadbury had been asked in May to serve
on an AFSC Family Planning Committee, to represent the Peace
Education Division in investigating the question of whether family
planning could help alleviate the population explosion as one potential cause of modern war. Henry Cadbury was glad to have an
expert in the family to consult.

Another issue to which Henry Cadbury was giving increasing
time and thought was the payment of war taxes. As the United
States seemed to be sliding deeper and deeper into an involvement
in Indochina, more and more Quakers were feeling uncomfortable
about paying that portion of their income tax that went for war
purposes. Some refused to pay the whole amount, feeling that if
they limited themselves to the 50 percent that supposedly went for
peacetime purposes, the government would still use their 50 percent to buy armaments.

One such refuser was Maurine Parker, a member of Central
Philadelphia Monthly Meeting, employed as secretary of that meeting. One day in 1964, Maurine Parker returned from lunch to find
a subpoena on her desk, requiring her to go directly to the Internal
Revenue Service office, bringing her records. Maurine Parker decided to comply with the order by going to the office, but instead of
bringing her records she asked Henry Cadbury if she might bring
him along to be with her at the hearing.[6]

The agent directed most of his questions to Maurine Parker, evi-

dently thinking that Henry Cadbury was a lawyer, despite her introduction of him as a member of her meeting, but Maurine felt
supported by his presence and was able to explain her position. At
one point the agent began to urge her to pay her tax because it was
probably only a very small amount. Henry Cadbury explained that
"the amount was unimportant, even if it were only one dollar, it was
important not to pay it. He explained that it is the principle of not
contributing to killing and death that is important."[7]

His files from this period are full of letters from tax refusers. He
prepared a lecture on Friends and the payment of war taxes and
developed the material into articles for the *Friends Journal* and for
Fellowship. Several of his "Letters from the Past" dealt with the subject. In "Render unto Caesar," published in 1970, he made the
point that Jesus' true purpose was to be found in the second half of
the commandment, "and unto God the things that are God's."

In October of 1964, Clarence Pickett turned eighty. Several of
his colleagues who were also octogenarians or close to it, and their
spouses—Henry and Lydia Cadbury, Howard and Anna Brinton,
Hugh and Alma Moore (Hugh Moore had begun working for the
AFSC in 1929 during the strike in Marion, North Carolina, and had
been with it ever since)—appeared at an AFSC staff meeting to
celebrate the occasion, to talk about the origins of the committee, to
tell some of the memorable stories, and to joke about themselves as
being "the old toads." For AFSC staff members at that time, it was a
highlight of the decade. A few months later, on March 17, 1965, an
era ended when Clarence Pickett died while traveling in the West.
Henry Cadbury spoke to the AFSC staff meeting the following
Monday, telling of the decision to hire Clarence in 1929 and the difference he had made to the history of the AFSC. In a memorial
meeting at Race Street Meeting house several days later he spoke of
Clarence's extreme sensitivity to others and his influence on many
lives, including his own.[8]

Clarence Pickett in many ways embodied Henry Cadbury's ideals
of what a man should be. Clarence Pickett, like Henry Cadbury, did
not consider himself a mystic. He simply followed a line of duty that
seemed clear to him and that others perceived as expressing the
best in Christian ethics. But there had been less duality in his sense
of duty. He did not have to make constant choices between the life
of a scholar and of an activist as Henry Cadbury did. He had made
his choice long ago. Perhaps this is what Henry Cadbury was thinking when he told the story of a man who had written to tell how
much Clarence Pickett had influenced him twenty-five years earlier
and said, rather wistfully, "We have been exposed to this influence

and many of us don't have twenty-five years left to admit that we have not been as sensitive to it in our own lives as we might have been."[9]

Attending the services for Clarence Pickett, Henry Cadbury was grieving also for his sister Emma, who had died on March 6 shortly after her ninetieth birthday after a life given primarily to service abroad under the AFSC. Both Clarence Pickett and Emma Cadbury must have been on Henry Cadbury's mind a few months later when he joined a large Quaker vigil before the Pentagon to protest the escalating involvement in Vietnam. Lydia Cadbury as well as Wilmer and Mildred Young were both with him, but he was the oldest Friend present to bear witness as well as the oldest living member of the Cadburys.

With age and a slight letup in demands on his time, opportunity came at last to finish a project on which he had been at work for twenty years. This was a study of John Woolman's voyage to England in 1772 ending in his death from smallpox in York. Scholars were familiar with Woolman's own account of this trip in his *Journal,* but Henry Cadbury conceived the idea of searching out what records existed independently of Woolman. In other words, he wanted to find clues to his travels against the background of his times, just as he had studied Jesus, and the Book of Acts, and Paul against the background of their times. His method was to track down the names and places referred to in Woolman's *Journal* and then try to find verifying information. He carried this research into minute details, almost making a game of it, giving his intense curiosity free reign. Sarah Logan and her maid were mentioned as fellow passengers on the ship on which Woolman sailed. But who was the maid, and why was she going to England? He kept at it until 1973, when he finally solved the puzzle. The woman's name was Mary Siddens. He continued to maintain catholic interests in Quaker history, working further on the Fox papers, the Norwegian Quakers, the Caribbean Quakers, and several other lines of research, but from his correspondence of the period it appears that the Woolman project was nearest to his heart.

In May of 1966, Harvard invited him to return to speak at the 150th anniversary of the founding of the Society for the Promotion of Theological Education at the university. He worried about being too deaf to hear questions, but the affair went smoothly. His oldest grandchild, Dorothea Musgrave, was graduating from Westtown that June, and he was the commencement speaker, touching on the special bond between grandparents and grandchildren, "confused elderly Friends and crazy mixed up kids." Some of his friends felt that, having been too preoccupied to be close to his children, he was reaching out to his grandchildren.[10]

The day after graduation, the Cadbury clan celebrated Henry and Lydia Cadbury's fiftieth wedding anniversary at the Westtown cabin. All four children, their spouses, and seven grandchildren were in attendance. In 1965 Warder had married a young Canadian woman, Julia Graham, so Henry and Lydia Cadbury felt that their family was complete. They had scarcely rested up from this excitement when it was time to go to the Cape May Conference, where Henry Cadbury lectured on Paul. Later in the summer they attended the New England Yearly Meeting and Henry Cadbury gave a series of workshops on Paul. After a brief visit to Back Log Camp, Henry Cadbury flew to Oregon to give a talk. On August 2 they sailed for England aboard the *Queen Mary.*

Henry Cadbury was in great form. In a postcard to Frederick Tolles from shipboard he told of being interviewed by a British immigration officer who asked where he was staying in London. When Henry Cadbury replied Friends House, the officer asked politely, what was the name of the friends? Although the Cadburys survived this trip without seasickness, others did not, and Henry Cadbury came back with a new joke. A beginning American writer, who crossed the ocean frequently, was asked where he was published and replied that he was a frequent contributor to the "Atlantic."

On this, their last trip to England, the Cadburys visited all their favorite haunts. Henry Cadbury attended meetings of the STNS in Cambridge, and they stayed with Friends in Swanage, Jordans, Woodbrooke, and Dublin, as well as London, where Henry Cadbury spoke at the Annual Meeting of the Friends Historical Society on his discoveries about Woolman. It had been commonly believed and often repeated in history books that on Woolman's arrival at London Yearly Meeting, his undyed clothes and unkempt appearance so shocked London Friends that they urged him to feel that he had accomplished his mission and might return to the United States. Henry Cadbury, however, could trace this story only to an article written in 1865, which gave no documentation, and he suggested that the British Friends might have been more hospitable than previously thought.[11]

The library at Friends House was packed for this lecture, which Elfrida Vipont Foulds, a British Quaker author, described as "distinguished, wise, and witty." The announcement that Henry Cadbury's researches on Woolman's trip would be published as a supplement to the journal of the historical society was greeted with delight. No one could have guessed that it would take six more years to accomplish this publication.

Studying in the library of Friends House that fall was a young graduate student, J. William Frost, beginning work on what was to be his dissertation, published as *The Quaker Family in Colonial America.* Henry Cadbury befriended him, made suggestions for his research, and offered to help him find a place to stay when he and his wife returned to the United States. This was the beginning of a friendship that influenced Jerry Frost to become a Friend and ultimately to become the curator of the Friends Historical Library at Swarthmore.[12]

From their last, delightful trip abroad, the Cadburys returned to Haverford in early November. For the first time since 1910, Henry Cadbury had no college classes to meet this year, but his lectures at Pendle Hill and at various Friends meetings kept him busy. He wrote a foreword to the *Journal of William Edmondson,* published in 1968 by a friend from Earlham days, Caroline Nicholson Jacob, and he prepared a manuscript for a Pendle Hill pamphlet, *Behind the Gospels,* summarizing the contribution of form and motive criticism to the understanding of the New Testament, in language accessible to the intelligent lay person. With Frederick Tolles, he prepared a picture collection, "Quaker Reflections to Light the Future," a compilation of maps, silhouettes, pictures of meeting houses, illustrations, and pages from minute books, covering three hundred years of Quaker history. In the foreword Henry Cadbury made the point that "the ultimate purpose of a picture book like this is not to set the pattern for future Quakerism by copying the past exactly but to suggest from the past what would be appropriate for Friends today and tomorrow." And he helped several authors, including the present one, to prepare books on various aspects of Quaker history.[13]

The spring and summer of 1967 were full of events. The AFSC celebrated its fiftieth anniversary at the Haverford College Field House, and Henry Cadbury spoke of the constant rebirth and renewal that had kept the organization alive and growing through the years. The Women's International League for Peace and Freedom asked him to speak on the demise of the Massachusetts Loyalty Oath, under which he had suffered a crisis of conscience, now struck down by a state supreme court decision. In June, Earlham College presented him with an honorary Doctorate in Humane Letters, his sixth honorary degree. He and Lydia Cadbury visited the Musgrave family in Ann Arbor, then traveled to the Friends General Conference sessions, held that summer in Missouri. Here Henry Cadbury lectured on "Friends and the Bible." In August they went to Guilford College in North Carolina for the Friends World Conference. For Henry Cadbury and for a few others, its was the fourth such event in a lifetime.[14]

At the 50th Anniversary of the Founding of AFSC, 1967. Colin Bell, executive secretary, Henry Cadbury, honorary chairman of the board, and Gilbert White, chairman of the board. Photo courtesy of AFSC Archives.

He was still serving as chairman of the board of Bryn Mawr College. In the fall of 1967 he had the pleasure of welcoming a younger colleague, Howard Clark Kee, to the Rufus Jones Chair of the History of Religion, for which he had recommended him. He was delighted to have Kee nearby and frequently popped into his office with a typical Henry Cadbury query: "'Howard, tell me what I ought to know,' and would then fall into discussing the latest developments in New Testament scholarship, revealing his capacity to keep up with the field in spite of his advancing years."[15]

Although he was now in his eighties and very deaf, his health remained good, and he often walked from his home in Haverford to make his calls on President Katherine McBride, Howard Kee, and others on the Bryn Mawr campus. In 1965, he had frightened his friends by having an episode of uncontrollable hiccupping that landed him in the intensive care room at the Bryn Mawr hospital.

When it was finally diagnosed as resulting from a virus infection in the chest and treated accordingly, he recovered well.

In the summer of 1968, however, while vacationing at Back Log Camp, he developed an abscess of the colon and had to be rushed down the lake by boat and then by ambulance to a hospital in Albany, New York, where he underwent major surgery and was given a colostomy. It was thought at the time that a second operation would be necessary, but he adjusted well, and further surgery was not needed.

Far more serious than the operation itself and the temporary change of plans it caused was the blow to his spirits. The bleak depression he had suffered during the early days of World War II came back to hang like a dark cloud over his spirits for the remaining years of his life. "Mentally I was ill prepared for such a cataclysmic experience," he wrote to Katherine McBride of his operation, in a letter reflecting his dark mood.[16]

Although he sought psychiatric help once more, this time it was felt that there was no point to further attempts at psychotherapy, and his illness might be managed by mood-elevating drugs. With his lifelong habit of making heavy demands, and no concessions to himself, Henry Cadbury felt as though he ought to be able to manage without the pills, and he fought taking them. "Does thee really think I need to take one today?" he would ask Lydia Cadbury, and Lydia Cadbury would patiently remind him that the doctor had said to take one every day. At times his spirits would brighten considerably, and he would give up medication, but sooner or later the dark clouds would return and he would have to be convinced to start taking his pills again.[17]

Whatever the source of this depression, the drugs seemed to manage it, and he was not as incapacitated as he had been in 1941. Only those very close to him knew about the dark feelings; the rest of the world found him as loving, gentle, witty, and hardworking as ever. In fact, it took the exercise of considerable valor for him to keep going as he did for another six years, manifesting such an apparently bright spirit that a reporter for the *Philadelphia Evening Bulletin* entitled an article about him "The Green Old Age of Henry Cadbury."[18]

He resigned from the chairmanship of the Bryn Mawr board that fall but continued to serve on the board until 1970. As a member of the AFSC's Peace Education Committee, as well as honorary chairman of the board, he stayed close to the heart of the service committee he loved as it met the challenges of the late 1960s and early 1970s.

One difficult task was taking part in the working party that produced a study, *Who Shall Live? Man's Control over Birth and Death,* a survey of opinion on worldwide population problems and on the termination of life at conception or at brain death. The working party took no formal position on euthenasia, but it did agree that the right of a woman to make a conscientious decision about abortion in consultation with her physician should be upheld. Henry Cadbury took responsibility for the chapter "Religious and Ethical Questions" and circulated many drafts in an effort to reach a consensus of views among concerned Friends.

In 1968 the AFSC decided to couple its medical work in Quang Ngai, South Vietnam, with a shipment of medical supplies to civilians in areas held by the National Liberation Front, giving witness to its testimony that the humanity of persons on both sides of a struggle deserve equal respect. Since the U.S. government would not grant it a license to do so, it was a case of civil disobedience, the first in AFSC's fifty-year history. Henry Cadbury approved the decision and wrote an article, "Conscientious Disobedience," for the *Friends Journal.* He said he did not agree with those who felt that precedents from the past were needed to validate present action. Nevertheless, there had been a long history of civil disobedience by Quakers when the commands of God and the commands of government were in conflict. Dissent and disobedience could be alternatives to violent ways of solving conflicts as the lives and teachings of Mahatma Gandhi and of Martin Luther King, Jr., had demonstrated.[19]

The rise of black power brought fresh challenges to the AFSC and to the Philadelphia Yearly Meeting. At a session of the latter, some black Friends arranged a sit-in, bringing other blacks for support, to demand reparations. The old order was now changing very quickly indeed, it seemed, but Henry Cadbury was there to reassure Friends once more that change was not bad. In a "Letter from the Past" in 1969 he gave examples of Quaker experiences with reparations. The colony of Massachusetts had offered payment to the grandson of Mary Dyer for her sufferings, but he felt he could not accept payment for the price of her blood. Many Quakers, when they freed their slaves, made them cash payments in lieu of the wages they ought to have received as free men and women after the age of twenty-one, then regarded as the end of apprenticeship. After a descendant of William Penn had tricked the Indians into selling land at too low a price in the Walking Purchase, a Quaker committee had raised a large sum to make up the difference, another form of reparations.[20]

The rapidly changing times did not seem to frighten him at all. In fact, he took an almost mischievous delight in pointing out that George Fox with his long hair had been viewed very much as the current world was viewing hippies, that the practice of "streaking" might be likened to those Quakers who felt called upon to "go naked as a sign," and that women's liberation was deeply rooted in the Quaker past. The *Friends Quarterly* devoted an issue in the fall of 1974 to articles commemorating the 350th anniversary of George Fox's birth. Henry Cadbury's contribution was "George Fox and Women's Liberation," covering Fox's support for women's spirituality and their right to preach and prophesy, as well as his defense of the separate women's meetings for business. Careful not to modernize Fox, he nevertheless pointed out that there was good reason why the small Society of Friends had produced such women as Lucretia Mott, Susan B. Anthony, and Alice Paul.[21]

Nor did his acute powers of observation become dampened. Betty Taylor, an Irish Friend working for the Philadelphia Yearly Meeting, lived from 1969 on in an apartment on the third floor of the house on Millbrook Lane. In due course she became a good friend of both the Cadburys. Henry Cadbury was always a courtly and attentive landlord, wanting to be sure that she had enough heat and hot water. Even in his late eighties he was able to attend to the furnace and fix things around the house. He had no thought of going to live in a retirement community as many in his generation were doing, preferring to live within walking distance of the Haverford library.

Betty Taylor commuted by train to and from Philadelphia. One evening, on her way home, she was walking along the road near the Haverford campus, when a man came along and snatched her handbag. When she reached the Cadbury house and told them about her loss, they called the police. Like most people, Betty Taylor cared less about the small amount of money she was carrying than about the papers and other personal items in the bag. The police produced a possible robber, but he was the wrong man.

Afterward, Henry Cadbury asked her to repeat to him the exact story of the robbery, listening very carefully. The next day he retraced the steps of the robber, trying to reason which way he might have taken after seizing the purse. Coming to a big tree, Henry Cadbury decided the man might at this point feel safe enough to stop behind it and examine the bag. Henry Cadbury searched the ground. Sure enough, there was Betty's pocketbook, minus the cash but with other items intact. Henry Cadbury would have made a great detective, Betty concluded.[22]

A former Bryn Mawr student of his, Margaret Evans, was cleaning out some family papers at about this time, when she came across a little notebook with a blue cover and a text inside in a clear, old-fashioned hand. Thinking it might be of some importance, she took it along with some other family papers to Henry Cadbury, who discovered to his great excitement and joy that the notebook was a copy of "A Plea for the Poor," one of John Woolman's most important essays, here entitled "A Word of Remembrance and Caution to the Rich etc." It was a once in a lifetime experience to find such an important document, and Henry Cadbury's spirits were raised considerably. "I couldn't sleep all night," he confided to a friend.[23]

Only one other handwritten copy of the Woolman essay was known to be extant, and that was in the Historical Society of Pennsylvania. Henry Cadbury deposited the newly found copy at Haverford. There proved to be some important differences between the two, including the name. The first copy was known as "A Plea for the Poor, or A Word of Remembrance and Caution to the Rich," while the second copy was called, "A Word for Remembrance and Caution to the Rich etc." The difference of title is significant, for in this essay Woolman is pointing out the danger of riches and suggesting that "we look to our treasures, the furniture of our houses, and our garments and try and see whether the seeds of war have nourishment in these our possessions." He also says in this essay that "to turn the treasures we possess into the channel of universal love is the business of our lives."[24]

He was continuing to lecture, and he was becoming, if possible, funnier. "The times are so out of joint I scarcely know where to begin," he said solemnly, opening a talk at Pendle Hill, "In fact, I feel like a mosquito in a nudist colony." At an intense AFSC gathering, developed to produce goals for the AFSC in the 1970s, he pointed out that AFSC had rarely known where it was going and that had been an asset, not a deficit, he believed. He told the story of a small boy leading a large dog. When asked where he was going he said, "First I want to see where the dog wants to go." He was delighted to quote an author friend of his who once said, "I don't know what I think until I hear what I say."[25]

After 1968, Back Log Camp was no longer run as a commercial venture, but the Brown family kept it for summer vacations. Henry and Lydia Cadbury liked to go whenever one or more of their children were present for company and to give some aid in coping with the rigors of camp life. Starting in 1969, they traveled to Florida in the coldest winter months. There was a small Quaker meeting in St. Petersburg, augmented in the winter by elderly Friends from the

North, and Henry Cadbury spoke to discussion meetings of this group as often as once a week. Many wives might have objected to this as an interruption of a shared vacation, but Lydia Cadbury saw that the reading and preparation helped Henry Cadbury through some low moments and wisely encouraged him to participate.

He still intensely disliked speaking autobiographically, but when he was asked in June of 1972 to tell about his life, as part of a series of such talks given by different members of the Central Philadelphia Monthly Meeting, he complied, saying, "I ought to be willing to do my share, as we have enjoyed what other people have told about their past."[26]

His talk, witty and informative, covered the major events of his life. He told of going to school and college at an early age: "As a matter of fact, all my early years I was precocious and all my later years I am the oldest person in the room. . . . My wife often asks me when I come home now, 'was there anybody older than thee there?' And I remember and I say, 'Well, I don't think so.' That's the way it has mostly been."[27]

The talk came at an auspicious moment. A week earlier a collection of his "Letters from the Past," *A Friendly Heritage*, had been published by the *Friends Journal*, and the week before he had received his first copy of *John Woolman in England in 1772*, published as a supplement to the *Journal of the Friends Historical Society*. This had taken so long to produce that Henry Cadbury had come to call it his posthumous work. A third book, *Narrative Papers of George Fox*, the final fruit of his work in Woodbrooke in 1933, was being published by Friends United Press. Three books in the same year was quite an achievement for a man of almost ninety, or of any age for that matter. Characteristically, he did not mention this achievement in his talk, but only in response to a pointed and leading question.[28]

The next day he conducted his final class at Pendle Hill and was given a huge suitcase as a parting gift. The following week he traveled to Cambridge with his daughter Winifred to be honored at a special luncheon at the alumni meeting of the Divinity School. Winifred reported to her mother that he had not felt well but had given a great talk, as usual. It was around this time that, speaking at the Germantown Meeting forum, he was asked how long he wanted to live. "Well, I don't want to stay too long, and I don't want to go too soon," was the answer.

Henry Cadbury had been a featured speaker at the Friends General Conference held in Ocean Grove, New Jersey, in 1970, and in 1972 all the Cadburys gathered at a new conference site in Ithaca, New York, to hear him speak on a topic of his choosing, "Where

Would I Be Pioneering Now if I Were Seventeen?" He spoke of early Quaker pioneering in the antislavery and womens' rights movements and urged more attention to peace and economic justice. He was never more amusing or more future-oriented as he advised the young people, "Pioneer! Pioneer with Abandon!"[29]

The Cadbury children were somewhat concerned about their parents living independently in the house on Millbrook Road. Lydia Cadbury was becoming crippled with arthritis and needed a cane to get around. She had a chronic bladder problem that required frequent operations. They were consequently grateful when Maurine Parker of the Central Philadelphia Monthly Meeting offered to live with them and help take care of them, out of affection for both of them and gratitude for Henry Cadbury's continued assistance with her tax refusal. She made breakfast in the morning, since Lydia Cadbury had formed the habit of staying in bed late and eating her breakfast from a tray to conserve energy.

The new arrangement worked to everyone's satisfaction. The following spring the three of them were asked to participate in a special Pendle Hill panel on new living arrangements. Their topic was "Integrating a Third Person into a Couple." Another threesome, a young woman and two young men who were living in a three-way marriage, also took part.

"Lydia was asked how she was able to make this adjustment so easily," Maurine wrote to describe the discussion. "She said that earlier she had observed other women who could no longer do their own work and who were very disagreeable and hard to please to a person who was trying to help. She had decided long ago that if this ever happened to her she would not be like that, that she would not only accept, but would enjoy the arrangement."[30]

Lydia Cadbury may have been thinking about her mother-in-law in Moorestown, New Jersey, who had sometimes found her caretakers difficult. Whatever the reason, there were strong bonds of affection between Maurine Parker and Lydia and Henry Cadbury and a youthful attitude on the part of the elderly Cadburys which people found both endearing and inspiring.

The year of 1973 was Henry Cadbury's ninetieth. There were outpourings of love and respect for him all year long. Bryn Mawr College began it by announcing at graduation in June the establishment of the Henry Joel Cadbury Fellowships, to which contributions were invited. In short order, $220,000 rolled in.

It was during the summer of 1973 that Henry Cadbury appeared for the AFSC in the U.S. District Court to challenge the right of government to force the committee to be its agent in collecting income taxes from those conscientiously opposed and spoke of bearing witness by preaching only what one practiced. And in the fall he agreed to give one more lecture series at the Haverford Meeting House, choosing as his subject the Epistles of St. Paul. Though he was so deaf that he could not hear his own voice to determine whether he was speaking in a normal range, he yet managed to entrance his audience with his usual mixture of humor, scholarly knowledge of the ancient world, and apt illustrations. He insisted once more that his listeners understand that Paul's way of thinking was quite different, and even foreign to modern thought, but that it was worthy of respect and understanding in its own terms.[31]

In October of that year, the *Friends Quarterly* devoted eight pages to tributes to Henry Cadbury on the occasion of his ninetieth birthday. Contributors included old friends and fellow scholars: Alfred Braithwaite; Edward Milligan, the librarian at Friends House; Edwin Bronner, the curator of the Quaker Collection at Haverford College and professor of Quaker history; and Geoffrey Nuttall, the scholar of Puritanism. Nuttall wrote:

> Henry Cadbury is one of the most remarkable persons I have ever known or am likely to know. About this I am in no doubt at all. Not that I think him to be perfect! He can even be annoying.
> At this he will smile. "Is not-annoying necessary for perfection?" I hear him ask, with his quizzical smile. This capacity for conversation at a distance, conversation one forgets is really made-up, so lively is his part in it, is one of the most remarkable things about him.[32]

His friend Alfred Braithwaite added a touch of Cadbury humor: "'We had a precious meeting,' Henry will read out in the course of a lecture on some eighteenth century Friend and diary of his travels. Then he will add, without any change of emphasis, 'That means, I think, that he spoke.' A few minutes later, having turned a page or two: 'we had a precious and blessed meeting.' That means he spoke at some length."[33] Issues of the *Friends Journal* and of the *Quaker Monthly* for December 1, 1973, also carried articles about Henry Cadbury. On November 28 there was a birthday celebration at the Haverford College Library with Edwin Bronner, President John Coleman of Haverford College, and President Harris Wofford of Bryn Mawr College sharing the podium. Henry Cadbury himself spoke at some length, recalling his associations with Haverford, which went back at least seventy-five years. He described how he walked from his home to the library almost every day, stopping

Henry Cadbury's 90th birthday. Celebrated in the Quaker Collection at the Haverford College Library. November 28, 1973. Photo from the collection of and by Theodore Hetzel.

for short rests, and how recently on one of these trips a freshman had come up to him when he was pausing and asked if he might help, evidently thinking the old man to be lost. Henry Cadbury started to tell him how many years he had known the Haverford campus, and then, realizing that he had visited it before he became a student, when his brothers were attending, he gave up: "I decided it took more time for me to remember than I wanted to wait, and I told him that I felt at home."[34]

He regaled the audience with many funny stories of early Haverford days, including the tale of his failure to pass the math exam, of M. Carey Thomas's efforts to keep the Haverford boys away from the Bryn Mawr campus, and the not so funny account of his suspension during World War I. But he told also of the honorary degree Haverford had awarded him in 1933 and of the warmth and affection with which he now felt himself to be surrounded: "I can hardly put into words the feeling I have of gratitude for the love and affection which I feel as I move about this community and no-

With Mary Hoxie Jones at the birthday celebration. Photo from the collection of and by Theodore Hetzel.

where more than in this building, this library, so different from the earlier hall I remember as the library, but where all the staff are particularly friendly to the old man who walks across and stops as he walks and looks around and thinks of those days going back at least to the first two decades of this century." [35]

CHAPTER 14

An Appropriate Farewell

Following his ninetieth birthday, Henry Cadbury became noticeably more frail, people thought. His hearing was worse, if possible. He could understand only if people shouted directly into his ear, and then only certain voices. He began to carry around a small school-boy's slate and pencil and to ask his friends to write their messages on it.

As the world of silence in which he lived became more total, he felt increasingly cut off from life. After the publication of three books in 1972, he had undertaken no more major projects. Although he kept up his "Letters from the Past" and wrote book reviews and articles for *Quaker History*, he felt that his life work was accomplished. Stephen G. Cary remembers seeing him watching a soccer game at the Haverford field about this time. It was cold, and he was bundled up and looked miserable. "Steve, never grow old," he said. In the early fall of 1974, his colleague Howard Kee visited with him on his porch one evening after dinner and found him feeling low and out of touch with the scholarly world he so loved. The dark cloud over his spirits which he had fought so valiantly and hidden so well from the world was beginning to show through.[1]

In mid September, Maurine Parker, who had been a member of the household for the past two years, left and a young couple came to take her place in the house and give aid to the Cadburys. Henry had come to depend on Maurine and to feel toward her as though she were a daughter. He mourned her departure, although he liked Abigail and John Fust.

He was busy during the last week of September preparing a speech he was to give Saturday, September 29, 1974, at George School in Bucks County. The Twelfth Street Meeting House, to which he had belonged from birth, had been closed, its site sold to the Redevelopment Authority, and the building itself moved to the George School campus, where it arose again like the phoenix. Henry and Lydia had been intensely interested in the process of removal and reconstruction and had been taken by a meeting member, Richard Moses, to see the work in progress. Now he was to speak at its opening and rededication.[2]

When he was first introduced that Saturday and rose to speak, he seemed to many in the audience too frail and weak to deliver a lecture. But as he warmed to his subject, his voice regained its old vigor and his eyes their twinkle. Several of his deadpan asides soon had the audience laughing with joy. Besides tracing the history of the meeting house since its construction in 1812, using materials from an earlier meeting house, he spoke of his own family connections with it and its use by the AFSC during the first years of the committee's life: "The whole property came to symbolize much more than before a more immediate expression of religion—social service, racial justice, international understanding. . . . Where we stand today in the evolution of the Society of Friends and of society

Henry and Lydia. Photo from Friends Journal *December 1, 1974.*

in general one hesitates to predict. Let us hope that what this building symbolized in the past may be the kind of association it will find in the future of George School."[3]

He was very tired after the lecture, but he recovered enough energy to spend a good part of the next week at the Quaker Collection at Haverford College Library. His current interest was learning more about what had become of the elm tree at Shackamaxon, where William Penn is supposed to have signed his famous treaty with the Indians, and he was ruthless about separating fact from fiction. He chatted with Edwin Bronner, the curator, about the project.

Warder and Julia Cadbury, with their children Joel and Adrianne, drove down from Albany that next weekend for an early celebration of Lydia Cadbury's eighty-fifth birthday, October 8. On Saturday the family drove to Kendal at Longwood, a Quaker retirement home, to celebrate another October birthday, that of Alice Walker, the wife of the former headmaster of Westtown and an old friend. On the way home Henry Cadbury quipped that it was a nice place to visit, but he wouldn't want to live there and reiterated his desire to remain near the Haverford College Library.[4]

That Sunday morning Lydia had her breakfast in bed, as usual. When it was time for someone to go up and fetch her empty tray, Julia, Warder, and Abigail Fust were ready to make the trip, but Henry said no, he would prefer to go himself. He never put it into words, but others saw that this small daily act of service was one of his ways of expressing his enduring love for his wife.

Starting back down the stairs with the tray, Henry lost his footing at the very top and fell the entire flight. Warder rushed to him, the others following, but Henry did not seem to have any broken bones and appeared only very dazed and semiconscious. After consultation, it was decided to take him to Bryn Mawr Hospital for x-ray and observation, and he was allowed to walk to the police car. His own doctor was away, and those who examined him immediately did not know how sharp his mind had remained and may have thought him simply a very confused old man. Winifred and Martin Beer were called and came over from their home in New Jersey to be with the family in this hour of crisis. Toward evening the hospital called to report that he was apparently, miraculously, all right, but they would keep him overnight for observation. Warder Cadbury decided to fly back to Albany to meet his Monday classes, and Winifred and Martin Beer returned to New Jersey. Julia Cadbury stayed to keep Lydia Cadbury company. Monday October 7 there was no change. Lydia Cadbury spent most of the day at Henry

Cadbury's bedside, but he never regained consciousness. Winifred Beer stopped in on her way to a Westtown School Committee meeting and noticed that her father's breathing was labored. Lydia went home for supper but returned for an hour or so. She was very tired, and she shortly went home and went to bed. She had just gotten settled for sleep when the hospital called to report that at 10:45 P.M. Henry Cadbury had breathed his last. Post-mortem examination revealed he had suffered a massive cerebral hemorrhage in the fall. It was a miracle that he had survived for thirty-six hours.

Henry Cadbury had been such a modest, humble, quiet man that few realized how much he was loved or how many lives he had touched and changed. This lack of information was quickly rectified in the days after his death, as an obituary appeared in the *New York Times* and was carried by the Associated Press and the United Press International and published in virtually every major paper in the United States and abroad. Letters of condolence began also to pour in. There was a large memorial gathering at Haverford Friends Meeting House and another at the Race Street Meeting House, under the auspices of the AFSC. The editor of the *Friends Journal,* James Lenhart, began to receive such an outpouring of unsolicited manuscripts and poetry in memory of Henry that it was necessary to devote an entire issue of the magazine to their publication. The London *Friend, Friends Quarterly,* and other magazines carried memories and tributes. Amos Wilder wrote about him for the *Harvard Magazine* and *New Testament Studies;* Edwin Bronner for the *Yearbook of the American Philosophical Society.* The Society of Biblical Literature named a New Testament Fellowship in his honor.[5]

Twenty years earlier a newspaper columnist had pondered the meaning of greatness after meeting Henry Cadbury:

> He is a rather slight man, balding, and of an indeterminate age, like all men who are immersed in what they are doing. He lives in a modest yellow house at the end of a small deadend lane in Cambridge. Indeed, it was difficult for me to visualize the lines of communication running from that small house to practically every civilized country on earth. . . . As I left him I thought to myself that he confirms the pattern that has been growing in my mind for many years concerning the real qualities of greatness—first of which is a kind of unaffected modesty.[6]

It was this modesty or simplicity, coupled with an unusual independence of mind and an endless enthusiasm for digging knowledge out of the invisible crannies of life, along with his twinkling humor and his kindness, that people chiefly had remembered.

Elfrida Vipont Foulds put it well: "Most of all when I realized how vulnerable his tender spirit was, and how even if wounded himself, his constant preoccupation was never to inflict the slightest wound upon the bruised feelings of others. Only a great spirit could show such caring. . . . When thanking God for every remembrance of Henry Cadbury we thanked Him for one who never ceased to learn and whose daily discoveries have enriched our lives."[7] And a younger colleague and friend, Kenneth Carroll, summarized many of the messages when he wrote, "To give the message you must be the message."[8]

The subsequent years have not diminished the impact that this remarkable man had on the many lives he touched, or revised the assessment of his colleagues. Robert Stevens, the president of Haverford College, has recently called him "one of few truly great scholars the Religious Society of Friends has produced." Amos Wilder, now emeritus professor of divinity at Harvard, continues to feel that his contribution to New Testament scholarship will remain important to scholars for many years to come. His caution in accepting unexamined evidence and making generalizations has had an effect on a generation of scholars. Some feel that he was too cautious and that he might have made a larger contribution if he had been willing to give his remarkable mind a little more free range. But the caution was part of the nature of the man. And as Amos Wilder has said, "Thanks to scholars like Cadbury we move from fact to interpretation with more circumspection." In the field of social action, and especially in the American Friends Service Committee, his years of democratic leadership are remembered, and his wise counsel still missed.[9]

Coming of age at the beginning of the twentieth century, when the optimistic view that the advance of knowledge would help humankind solve all its problems was still strong, Henry Cadbury invested his life in the proposition that incremental gains in our knowledge of the life of Jesus, the origin of the gospels, and the later social translation of the gospel message in the lives of a Fox, a Woolman, a Mott, could shed light on that religious impulse which he recognized as the finest attribute of humankind. He was unimpressed by latter-day arguments that the truth was unknowable because we distort it in the very act of searching for it. It might be more difficult than we had once thought, but it was still our task to search, he believed. For all the sophistication of his mind, his approach to the truth was very like that of his Quaker ancestors. It was there and available to all men and women. And if in our search for truth we are forced to set aside the comforts of an unexamined faith and live our lives with certain ultimate questions held in abeyance, unanswered, he still saw no reason why we should not live these lives in a spirit of complete dedication to those impulses toward nonviolence, love, and justice which well up in men and women, generation after generation, as the deepest affirmation of their being.

Henry Cadbury himself, with his open, probing mind and his committed heart, served as a bridge for many men and women who longed to make a religious commitment that did not challenge their intellectual honesty. In a time when many people either silenced that longing, or silenced their intellectual integrity in order to become true believers in religious or political cults, his life itself was the message that neither sacrifice need be made. And through the instrument of service he helped to fashion and guide through many turbulent years, the AFSC, he provided a means through which many such men and women learned that a commitment to service could lead to a deepening of spiritual growth, just as he so often said. Many came into the Society of Friends through their associations with the AFSC, an important source of renewal and rebirth in the life of the Religious Society of Friends today.

On Firbank Fell, in England, where George Fox first spoke to the multitudes, there is a bronze tablet set on a stone, engraved with Fox's message, "Let Your Lives Speak." It was a message that Henry Cadbury often repeated in words and always in action. He never said it was simple, and he never backed away from the dilemmas that confront those who base their actions on conscience, or accepted sentimental shortcuts to their solutions. To all who knew him his message was, it may be hard, but thee can do it. It became easier to believe in yourself when he believed in you, and you learned to recognize the iron core of courage and integrity within this apparently simple, friendly man. Having known him is to have renewed hope for the future of the human race.

Notes

INTRODUCTION

1. Transcript, Proceedings, U.S. District Court for Eastern District Pennsylvania, August 1, 1973, Civil Action, American Friends Service Committee, Lorraine Cleveland and Leonard Cadwallader, Plaintiffs, v. the United States of America, Defendant. American Friends Service Committee (AFSC) Archives, Philadelphia, Pa.

2. Report of address given on April 24 at Toronto Meeting House and on April 25 at the formal opening of Montreal Meeting House, *Canadian Friend* 60, no. 3 (June–July 1964): 3–9.

3. *The Basis of Quaker Political Action,* speech given by Henry J. Cadbury at the Tenth Anniversary of the Friends Committee on National Legislation. Washington, D.C.: Published FCNL. 10-1-54.

CHAPTER 1

1. Nobel Lecture, December 12, 1947, in Frederick W. Haberman, ed., *Nobel Lectures, 1926–1950,* vol. 2, *Quakers and Peace,* pp. 391–98 (Amsterdam, Elsevier, 1972).

2. Henry J. Cadbury, "The Contribution of Negroes to the Education of Friends," Address at the Centennial of the Cheyney Training School for Teachers, Cheyney, Pa., October 16, 1937, *Friend* 3 (12-16-1937): 220.

3. Talk by Henry J. Cadbury at Philadelphia Monthly Meeting Forum, June 4, 1972, Fifteenth and Cherry Street Meeting House, Henry Joel Cadbury Papers, Quaker Collection, Haverford College Library, Haverford, Pa. (hereafter referred to as Cadbury Papers).

4. Mary Hoxie Jones, "Henry Joel Cadbury: A Biographical Sketch," in Anna Brinton, ed., *Then and Now,* Quaker Essays: Historical and Contemporary (Philadelphia: University of Pennsylvania Press, 1960), p. 14.

5. Henry J. Cadbury to John W. Cadbury, 8-2-94, Cadbury Papers.

6. Talk by Henry J. Cadbury at the Philadelphia Monthly Meeting Forum.

7. "The Heritage of the Meeting House," speech by H. J. Cadbury, 9-29-1974, Cadbury Papers.

8. Notes from the 1913–1914 Study Circle on Separation, Cadbury Papers.

9. Lecture notes, Harvard Divinity School, March 1944, Cadbury Papers.

10. *Reminiscences of Penn Charter,* brochure published by Penn Charter School. Circa 1970.

11. Transcript, Henry Cadbury's Birthday Celebration, 11-28-73, Cadbury Papers.

12. Rufus M. Jones, *Haverford College: A History and an Interpretation* (New York: Macmillan, 1933); Robert Stevens, *Philadelphia Friends and Higher Education: The Case of Haverford College,* speech to the Newcomen Society, 11-16-1983. Haverford, Pa.: Haverford College, 1984.

13. Cadbury course transcripts, 1899–1903; Haverford College Catalogs, 1899–1903, Haverfordiana Collection, Quaker Collection, Haverford College Library.

14. Elizabeth Gray Vining, *Friend of Life: A Biography of Rufus M. Jones* (Philadelphia: Lippincott, 1958); Melvin B. Endy, "The Interpretation of Quakerism: Rufus Jones and His Critics," *Quaker History* 70, no. 1 (Spring 1981): 3–15.

15. Haverford Library Lectures, 1899–1903, Haverfordiana Collection, Quaker Collection, Haverford College Library.

16. *Haverfordian* 23 (November 1902): 105–6, Haverfordiana Collection Treasure Room, Haverford College Library.

17. Transcript, Henry J. Cadbury's Birthday Celebration.

18. Talk by Henry J. Cadbury at Philadelphia Monthly Meeting Forum.

19. Henry Cadbury to Rufus Jones, 4-5-1905, Rufus M. Jones Papers, Quaker Collection, Haverford College Library.

20. Anna K. Cadbury to Henry J. Cadbury, 4-28-1905, Cadbury Papers.

CHAPTER 2

1. Talk by Henry J. Cadbury at Philadelphia Monthly Meeting Forum, 6-4-1972, Cadbury Papers.

2. Lydia C. Cadbury, *A Quaker Girlhood* (Haverford, Pa. Privately published, 1964), p. 38.

3. Lecture notes, Harvard Divinity School, March 1944, Cadbury Papers.

4. Talk by Henry J. Cadbury at the Philadelphia Monthly Meeting Forum.

5. Mary Hoxie Jones, "Henry Joel Cadbury: A Biographical Sketch," in Anna Brinton, ed., *Then and Now* (Philadelphia: University of Pennsylvania Press, 1960), p. 18.

6. Harvard University Records, Office of the Registrar, letter to the author, 6-21-1983.

7. Levering Reynolds, Jr., "The Later Years, 1880–1953," in George H. Williams, ed., *The Harvard Divinity School: Its Place in Harvard University and American Culture* (Boston: Beacon Press, 1954), p. 166.

8. Ibid., p. 188.

9. Ibid., pp. 194–96.

10. James Ropes to Henry Cadbury, 12-29-1910, Harvard University Archives (hereafter referred to as Harvard).

11. Jones, "Henry Joel Cadbury," p. 18.

12. Interview with Leah Cadbury Furtmuller, 6-7-1983.

13. Reynolds, "The Later Years, 1880–1953," p. 181; Henry J. Cadbury, *The Eclipse of the Historical Jesus,* Haverford Library Lectures, Pendle Hill pamphlet 133 (Wallingford, Pa., Pendle Hill Publications, 1964), p. 14.

14. Cadbury, *Eclipse of the Historical Jesus,* p. 5.

15. James Leuba, *A Psychological Study of Religion* (New York: Macmillan, 1912).
16. Lecture, Harvard Divinity School, March 1940, Cadbury Papers.
17. Ibid.
18. Ibid.
19. Henry J. Cadbury to "Dear Mother," 9-19-1912, Paris, Harvard.
20. Notes from the 1914 Study Group, Cadbury Papers.
21. Henry Cadbury, ed., *Differences in Quaker Belief in 1827 and Today* (Philadelphia: Biddle Press, 1914).
22. "The Development of the Young Friends Movement in America," *Friends Intelligencer* (6-13-1914): 370.
23. Henry Cadbury, *The Style and Literary Method of Luke* (Cambridge, Mass.: Harvard University Press, 1920), Preface, p. vi; Amos Wilder, "A Grammarian with a Difference," *Harvard Magazine* 78 (May 1975): 46–52.
24. "Quakerism as an Experiment Station," *Friends Intelligencer* (9-18-1915): 593–94.
25. Wilbur Kamp to the author, 11-28-1983.
26. "Social Servis [sic]: Spirit and Method of a Great Movement in the Christian Church," Cadbury Papers.
27. Henry Cadbury to Rachel Knight. See *All Friends Conference Report.* London: Friends Bookshop 1920, p. 133.
28. "Fried Chicken," Earlham College Library Archives, Richmond, Indiana.

CHAPTER 3

1. Henry J. Cadbury to Lydia Cadbury, 4-28-1916, letters in private possession of the Cadbury family.
2. Sarah Cadbury to unknown, 6-17-1917, letters in private possession of the Cadbury family.
3. Interview with Dorothy and Douglas Steere, 3-10-1983.
4. Ibid.
5. Henry Cadbury, "Christ and War," unpublished MS, Henry J. Cadbury Papers, Peace Collection, Friends Historical Library, Swarthmore College, Swarthmore, Pa. (hereafter, Peace Collection, FHL).
6. Ibid.
7. Shailee Matthews to Henry J. Cadbury, 3-26-1917, Cadbury Papers.
8. *St. Louis Post Dispatch,* 3-30-1917, clipping in Peace Collection, FHL.
9. *Philadelphia Public Ledger,* 4-9-1917.
10. AFSC Minutes, 4-30-1917. From the Philadelphia Yearly Meeting (Arch Street) came Alfred Scattergood, Charles J. Rhoads, Stanley Yarnell, Henry W. Comfort, and Anna G. Walton; the Friends General Conference of Hicksites sent Jesse H. Holmes, Lucy Biddle Lewis, Arabella Carter, and William Cocks; and the Five Years Meeting sent L. Hollingsworth Wood, Homer L. Morris, and Vincent D. Nicholson (AFSC Archives).
11. Ibid.
12. Lydia Cadbury to Anna K. Cadbury, 6-17-1917, letter in the private possession of the Cadbury family.
13. Ibid.
14. Rufus M. Jones, *Service of Love in Wartime* (New York: Macmillan, 1920), p. 92.
15. *Philadelphia Press,* 9-18-1917.

16. Ibid.

17. Editor of the *Biblical World,* to Henry Cadbury, 1-10-1918, Peace Collection, FHL.

18. Henry J. Cadbury, "Freedom of Thought and the Colleges," *Haverfordian* 39, no. 8 (March 1918): 257–60.

19. "Are We Honest?" *Friends Intelligencer* 75 (8-3-1918): 486–87.

20. Ernest W. Saunders, *Searching the Scriptures* (Chico, Calif.: Scholars Press, 1982), p. 31.

21. William W. Comfort to Rufus M. Jones, 7-12-1918, Jones Papers.

22. Haverford College, 1903 Class Letter for 1919, AFSC Archives, Cadbury File.

23. *Philadelphia Public Ledger,* 10-12-1918.

24. Henry J. Cadbury to William Wistar Comfort, 10-16-1918, Cadbury Papers.

25. Henry J. Cadbury to faculty, 10-24-1918, Cadbury Papers.

26. Haverford College Board of Managers Minutes, 10-22-1918, Quaker Collection, Haverford College Library; *Philadelphia Evening Bulletin,* 10-23-1918.

27. Haverford College Board of Managers Minutes, 11-1-1918, Quaker Collection, Haverford College Library.

28. Henry Cadbury to Clarence Pickett, 11-9-1918, AFSC Archives.

29. Henry Cadbury, "The Basis of Early Christian Anti-Militarism," *Journal of Biblical Literature* 37 (1918): 94.

30. George Robinson to Henry J. Cadbury, 12-16-1918, Harvard.

CHAPTER 4

1. Rufus M. Jones, *Service of Love in Wartime* (New York: Macmillan, 1920), p. 122.

2. Henry J. Cadbury to Rufus Jones, 1-1-1919, Jones Papers.

3. James Ropes to Henry J. Cadbury, 1-7-1919, Harvard.

4. Henry J. Cadbury, *National Ideals in the Old Testament* (New York: Scribners, 1920), p. vi.

5. Ibid., pp. 98–99.

6. Ibid., p. 169. Also published as "The Unpopular Patriot," in the *World Tomorrow,* Vol. I No. 10 (October, 1918), pp. 258–61.

7. Ibid., p. 110. Also published as "Ruthlessness Abroad and at Home," the *New World,* (Changed June, 1918 to the *World Tomorrow,*) 1: No. 3 (March, 1918), pp. 55–57.

8. Ibid., pp. 110–111.

9. Ibid., p. 217.

10. Karl Budde to Henry Cadbury, 5-10-1920, Harvard.

11. H. N. Gardiner to Rufus Jones, 2-2-1919, Jones Papers.

12. Haverford College, 1903 Class Letter, November 1919, AFSC Archives.

13. Haverford College Board of Managers Minutes, 3-2-1919, Quaker Collection, Haverford College Library.

14. Ray H. Abrams, *Preachers Present Arms,* University of Pennsylvania, Philadelphia: Round Table Press, Inc. 1933, pp. 230–31. (Also Scottsdale, PA: Herald Press 1969).

15. William Henry Chamberlain, *Confessions of an Individualist* (New York: Macmillan, 1940), pp. 34–35.

16. Levering Reynolds, Jr., "The Latter Years, 1880–1953," in George Williams, ed., *Harvard Divinity School, Its Place in Harvard University and the American Culture* (Boston, Beacon Press, 1954), pp. 185–229.

17. Adolf von Harnack to Henry Cadbury, 11-17-1920, Harvard.

18. Henry J. Cadbury, "The Strike as an Unethical Means of Conversion," *World of Tomorrow*, 3, No. 5 (May, 1920), p. 132.

19. Anna K. Cadbury to Lydia Cadbury, 2-20-1919. Letter in the private possession of the Cadbury family.

20. Henry Cadbury to Lydia Cadbury, 6-19-1920, AFSC Archives; Henry Cadbury to Lydia Cadbury, 6-16-1920, uncataloged Cadbury Papers.

21. Henry Cadbury to Lydia Cadbury, 6-19-1920, AFSC Archives.

22. Henry Cadbury to Lydia Cadbury, 6-26-1920, AFSC Archives.

23. Ibid.

24. Henry Cadbury to Lydia Cadbury, 7-1-1920, AFSC Archives.

25. Ibid.

26. Henry Cadbury to Lydia Cadbury, 7-8-1920, AFSC Archives.

27. Henry J. Cadbury to Rufus Jones, 7-4-1920, Jones Papers.

28. Henry Cadbury to Lydia Cadbury, 7-26-1920, letter in the private possession of the Cadbury family.

29. Henry Cadbury, "Letter to the editors of the Quaker; Dear Friends," 7-15-1920, AFSC Archives.

30. Henry Cadbury to Lydia Cadbury, 8-4-1920, AFSC Archives.

31. Henry Cadbury to Lydia Cadbury, 8-8-1920, AFSC Archives.

32. *All Friends Conference Report*, Official Report, London: The Friends Bookshop, 1920, pp. 128–30.

33. Henry Cadbury to Lydia Cadbury, 8-20-1920, letter in private possession of Cadbury famiy.

34. Henry Cadbury to Lydia Cadbury, 8-24-1920, letter in private possession of the Cadbury family.

CHAPTER 5

1. Henry Cadbury, "A Nationwide Adventure in Friendship," *Survey* 23, no. 2 (11-27-1920): 309–13.

2. Henry Cadbury to Wilbur Thomas, 10-28-1920, AFSC Archives.

3. Adolf Julicher to Henry J. Cadbury, 6-29-1922, Harvard.

4. Henry Cadbury, "The Social Translation of the Gospel," *Harvard Theological Review,* 15 (1922): 1–13.

5. Ibid., p. 8.

6. Ibid., pp. 11–12.

7. Henry Cadbury, "The Christian Verdict on War," *World Tomorrow* 5, no. 1 (January 1922): 15–17.

8. Henry Cadbury, "The Conscientious Objector of Patmos: The Revelation of John," *Christian Century* 39, no. 23 (6-8-1922): 719–22.

9. Henry Cadbury, "An Inadequate Pacifism," *Christian Century* 41, no. 1 (January 1924): 9–11.

10. Henry Cadbury, "Between Jesus and the Gospels," *Harvard Theological Review* 16 (1923): 81–92.

11. William Beardsley to the author, 7-20-1983; Amos Wilder to the author, 8-12-83.

12. Henry Cadbury to Rufus Jones, 12-3-1922, Jones Papers.

13. Daniel Evans to Rufus M. Jones, 4-20-1921, Jones Papers.

14. Lydia Cadbury to Anna K. Cadbury, 3-11-1922, letter in the private possession of the Cadbury family.

15. Lydia Cadbury to Elizabeth Jones, 2-20-1923, uncataloged Cadbury Papers, Quaker Collection, Haverford College Library.

16. Henry Cadbury, "Faith of Our Fathers Living Still," *Friends Intelligencer* 81 (5-31-1924): 356–58.

17. Henry Cadbury, "A Disputed Paper of George Fox," *Bulletin of the Friends Historical Association* 13 (1924): 78–82.

18. Lydia Cadbury to Elizabeth Jones, 11-29-1924, uncataloged Cadbury Papers.

19. Amos Wilder, "A Grammarian with a Difference," *Harvard Magazine* 78 (May 1975): 46–52.

20. E. F. Scott, "The Genesis of Luke-Acts," *Journal of Religion* 8 (1928): 285–87.

21. George Moore to Henry Cadbury, 10-23-1927, Harvard.

22. Henry Cadbury to Elizabeth Jones, Autum 1926, letter in private possession of Cadbury family.

23. Benjamin Bacon to Henry Cadbury, 4-10-1926, Harvard.

CHAPTER 6

1. Telephone interview with Rebecca Hetzel, 6-7-1983.

2. Notes for a Cambridge Bible Class, 4-21-1929, Cadbury Papers.

3. Notes for a talk, Bryn Mawr Chapel, 5-16-1927, Cadbury Papers.

4. Henry J. Cadbury to Emma Cadbury, uncataloged Cadbury Papers.

5. Pendle Hill lecture notes, Summer 1931, Cadbury Papers.

6. Mary Hoxie Jones, *Swords into Plowshares* (New York: Macmillan, 1925), p. 131.

7. Interview with former AFSC staff member wishing to remain anonymous, June 1983.

8. Henry Cadbury to Emma Cadbury, 2-7-1929, uncataloged Cadbury Papers.

9. Wilbur Thomas to Henry Cadbury, Chairman, AFSC, 12-27-1928; Henry Cadbury to Clarence Pickett, Western Union, February 22, 1929; Henry Cadbury to members of executive board of AFSC, 3-8-1929, AFSC Archives.

10. Henry Cadbury, "Individual Faithfulness," Letter 212, *Friendly Heritage: Letters from the Quaker Past* (Norwalk, Conn: Silvermine Publishers, 1972), pp. 290–91.

11. Notes on a speech, AFSC Fifteenth Anniversary, 1932, Cadbury Papers.

12. Abstract of an address by Henry J. Cadbury, *Friends Intelligencer* 89 (2-6-1932): 107.

13. Willard Sperry to Henry J. Cadbury, 2-21-30, Harvard.

14. W. Russell Bowie, "The New Testament: A New Translation," *Atlantic* 179 (August 1946): 122–27.

15. Lydia Cadbury to Emma Cadbury, 5-15-1932, uncataloged Cadbury Papers.

16. Henry Cadbury to Rufus Jones, 8-11-1932, Cadbury Papers.

CHAPTER 7

1. Henry Cadbury to "Dear Ben," The Hague, 9-10-1932, uncataloged Cadbury Papers.

2. Henry Cadbury, "Quaker Site Seeking in Amsterdam," *Friend* 166, no. 27 (1-1-1933): 315–16.

3. Lecture Notes, talk, Cotteridge, November 1932, Cadbury Papers.

4. Henry Cadbury, "George Fox's Library," *Friend* (London) 90 (3-25-1932): 255.

5. John L. Nickalls to Henry Cadbury, 12-23-1932, Cadbury Papers.

6. Geoffrey Nuttall, "Tributes to Henry J. Cadbury," *Friends Quarterly* 18, no. 4 (October 1973): 147–50.

7. Willard Sperry to Henry Cadbury, 1-10-1933, Cadbury Papers.

8. Henry Cadbury to Rufus M. Jones, 1-13-1933, Jones Papers.

9. Kirsopp Lake to Henry Cadbury, 2-20-1933, Cadbury Papers.

10. Clarence Pickett to Henry Cadbury, 2-28-1932, AFSC Archives.

11. Henry Cadbury, "Colonial Quaker Antecedents to British Abolition of Slavery," *Friends Quarterly Examiner* 67 (Spring 1933): 268–75.

12. Henry Cadbury to Clarence Pickett, ca. 3-29-1933, AFSC Archives.

13. Willard Sperry to Henry Cadbury, 2-23-1933; Marion Park to Henry Cadbury, 3-8-1933, Cadbury Papers; Henry Cadbury to Clarence Pickett, 4-23-1933, AFSC Archives.

14. Henry Cadbury, "The Oldest Philadelphia," *Friend* 107, no. 4 (8-17-1933): 51–52; *Friends Intelligencer* 90, no. 33 (8-19-1933): 603–4.

15. Henry Cadbury, "Roman Milestones on the Beth Horon Road," MS, Cadbury Papers; Lydia Cadbury to Ben Cadbury, 8-2-1933, uncataloged Cadbury Papers.

16. Lydia Cadbury to "Dear Ben," 8-2-1933, uncataloged Cadbury Papers.

17. Henry Cadbury to Elizabeth Jones, 9-6-1933, uncataloged Cadbury Papers.

18. Ibid.

19. Ibid.

20. Lecture notes, Race Relations Conference, 1-7-1934, Cadbury Papers; Clarence Pickett to Henry Cadbury, 10-4-1934, AFSC Archives.

21. Lecture notes, Westtown Assembly, February 1934; interview with Spencer Coxe, 6-24-1983.

22. Emma Cadbury to AFSC, March 1934; Henry Cadbury, "To Whom It May Concern," April 22, 1934, AFSC Archives.

23. Henry Cadbury, "The Responsibility of the Christian Church for Jewish Persecution, to Protest Against It," Lecture notes, Conference of American Rabbis, June 1934, Cadbury Papers.

24. *New York Times,* June 15, 1934.

25. *New York Times,* June 16, 1934.

CHAPTER 8

1. Interview with Mrs. Rupert Emerson, 5-3-1983.

2. Sharmen E. Johnson to the author, 8-6-1983 (the story was told me many times by others, as well).

3. Interview with Mrs. Emerson.

4. Interview with Harry Meserve, 9-23-1985.

5. Henry Cadbury, "My Professor's Closet," *Harvard Alumni Bulletin* 39 (1936): 297–301; "What Happened to John Harvard's Books?" *Harvard Alumni Bulletin* 41 (1938): 241–48.

6. George Williams, ed., *The Harvard Divinity School: Its Place in Harvard University and American Culture* (Boston: Beacon Press, 1954), dedication.

7. "Richardson Mss. Further unpublished writings by George Fox," Henry J. Cadbury, *Journal of the Friends Historical Society* 32 (1935): 34–37.

8. Thomas Drake, "HJC, Quaker Scholar," *Friends Journal* 20 (12-1-1974): 624–25.

9. Drake, "HJC, Quaker Scholar."

10. Lecture notes, October 1935, Cambridge Meeting; November 1936, Richmond, Indiana, Cadbury Papers.

11. Henry Cadbury, "Hebraica and the Jews in Early Quaker Interest," in Howard Brinton, ed., *Children of the Light* (New York: Macmillan, 1938), pp. 133–63.

12. John Knox, book review, *Journal of Biblical Literature* 57 (1938): 351–52.

13. Henry Cadbury, *The Perils of Modernizing Jesus* (New York: Macmillan, 1937), p. 190.

14. Ibid., pp. 118–19.

15. Willard Sperry to Henry Cadbury, ca. May 1937, letter in the private possession of the Cadbury family.

16. Henry Cadbury, "Friends and Their Social Testimonies," *Friend* (London) 93, no. 24 (6-14-35): 557–58.

17. Ibid.

18. Joshua Cope to Henry Cadbury, 9-25-1935; Harold Evans to Henry Cadbury, 10-17-1935; Otto Reinemann to Henry Cadbury, 12-30-1935, Peace Collection, FHL.

19. Robert Yarnall to Henry Cadbury, 11-12-1935; Clarence Pickett to Henry Cadbury, 12-18-1935; Yearly Meeting Peace Committee to Henry Cadbury, 12-13-1935, Peace Collection, FHL.

20. Henry Cadbury to Benjamin Cadbury, 12-5-1935, uncataloged Cadbury Papers.

21. "The Teachers' Oath and Religious Reservations," mimeographed statement marked "Not for publication at present," Peace Collection, FHL.

22. Henry Cadbury, "The Quaker Concern for Academic Freedom," *Friends Intelligencer* 93, no. 31 (8-1-1936): 499–501.

23. "My Personal Religion," Harvard Divinity School, February 1936, Cadbury Papers.

24. Ibid.

25. Stanza from "The Kingdom of God," *The Works of Francis Thompson, Poems;* Vol. 2 (New York: Scribner's, 1913).

26. "My Personal Religion."

27. Ibid.

28. Ibid.

29. Harold B. Kuhn to the author, 3-24-1986.

30. Interview with Harry Meserve.

31. Leroy Garrett, "The Resurrection Faith," *Restoration Review* (April 1985): 62–64.

32. Interview with Harry Meserve; LeRoy Garrett to the author, 3-29-1983.

33. Notes for a talk at the Wellesley Hills Unitarian Church, 1935, Cadbury Papers.

34. Henry Cadbury, "Negro Membership in the Society of Friends," *Journal of Negro History* 21 (April 1936): 151–213.

35. "The Contribution of Negroes to the Education of Friends," *Friend* 111, no. 13 (12-16-1937): 217–20.

36. Henry Cadbury, "Motives of Biblical Scholarship," *Journal of Biblical Literature* 56 (1937): 1–16.

37. Henry Cadbury to American Consul in Belgium, 4-26-1939, Cadbury Papers.

38. Clarence Pickett, *For More Than Bread* (Boston: Little, Brown, 1953), p. 141.

39. Lydia Cadbury to Emma Cadbury, October 1939, uncataloged Cadbury Papers.

CHAPTER 9

1. Notes for Civil Liberties Committee of American Bar Association, 1940, Peace Collection, FHL.
2. Howard Brinton, *Byways in Quaker History* (Wallingford, Pa.: Pendle Hill Publications, 1944), pp. 41–66; Rufus Jones to Henry Cadbury, 2-8-1940, Jones Papers.
3. Henry Cadbury, ed., *The Swarthmore Documents in America,* Supplement 20 to the *Journal of the Friends Historical Society* (London, 1940).
4. Rufus Jones to Henry Cadbury, 10-23-1940, Jones Papers.
5. "The Informality of Early Christianity," *Crozer Quarterly* 21 (1944): 246–50.
6. *Boston Herald,* 4-22-1940, Peace Collection, FHL.
7. Henry J. Cadbury to Rufus M. Jones, 5-8-1940, Jones Papers.
8. "A Quakerism Adequate for Today," Pendle Hill, 1940, Cadbury Papers.
9. Mary Hoxie Jones, "Henry Joel Cadbury: A Biographical Sketch," in Anne Brinton, ed., *Then and Now* (Philadelphia: University of Pennsylvania Press, 1960), pp. 45–46.
10. Ibid., p. 46.
11. Henry Cadbury, "Quaker Memories in Days of Blitzkreig," in *Friendly Heritage: Letters from the Quaker Past* (Norwalk: Conn., Silvermine Publishers, 1972), pp. 1–2.
12. Ibid.
13. "New Column," *Friends Intelligencer* 98, no. 13 (3-29-1941): 196–97.
14. Moses Bailey to the author, 5-12-1983.
15. Lydia Cadbury to Elizabeth Jones, 12-4-1941 and 12-15-1941, uncataloged Cadbury Papers; interviews with Warder Cadbury, 5-1-1983, and Christopher Cadbury, 11-7-1983.
16. Lydia Cadbury to Elizabeth Jones, 1-12-42; Lydia Cadbury to Emma Cadbury, 10-30-1942, uncataloged Cadbury Papers; interview with Jean Fairfax, November 1983.
17. "My Personal Religion," talk to Harvard Theology Students, 1944, Cadbury Papers.
18. HJC notes on illness, material in private possession of the Cadbury family.
19. Willard Sperry to Henry J. Cadbury, 2-4-1942, Harvard.
20. Lydia Cadbury to Emma Cadbury, 10-30-1942, uncataloged Cadbury Papers.
21. Interview with Christopher Cadbury, 11-7-1983.
22. Henry Cadbury to Elizabeth Jones, 8-11-1943, Jones Papers.
23. Elizabeth Gray Vining, *Friend of Life* (Philadelphia: Lippincott, 1948), p. 153.
24. "Alternatives to Frustration," in Cadbury, *Friendly Heritage,* p. 50.
25. Interview with Wilmer Tjossem, May 1983.
26. Henry Cadbury, "The Validity of Religious Pacifism," *Christian Century* 60, no. 52 (1943): 1534–35.
27. Henry Cadbury, "War as God's Judgment and War as Man's Sin," unpublished MS, Peace Collection, FHL.
28. *Two Worlds,* William Penn Lecture, Philadelphia: Philadelphia Yearly Meeting, 1945.
29. Anna Brinton to Henry Cadbury, 2-23-1944, Cadbury Papers.
30. Rough notes for Earlham Conference, November 1944, Cadbury Papers.

CHAPTER 10

1. Interview with Lewis Hoskins, June 1983.
2. Phone interview with Eleanor Townsend Taylor, 6-1-1983.
3. Daisy Newman, *Procession of Friends* (New York: Doubleday, 1972), p. 186.
4. Interview with Merilee and Andre Towl, 6-1-1983.
5. Interview with Spencer Coxe, 6-24-1983.
6. Interview with member of Cambridge Meeting, 5-1-1983.
7. Interviews with Jean Fairfax, Hugh Barbour, Eric Johnson, Douglas Steere, Mrs. Rupert Emerson, and Mary Hoxie Jones.
8. Henry Cadbury, *Jesus: What Manner of Man* (New York: Macmillan, 1947), p. 30.
9. Ibid., p. 45.
10. Ibid., p. 119.
11. One such review was by T. M. Taylor, in *Religion in Life* 17, nos. 1–4 (Autumn 1948): 155–56.
12. Henry Cadbury, "Revision after Revision," *American Scholar* 15 (1946): 298–305.
13. Interview with James Laird, May 1984.
14. Henry Cadbury, talk, Central Philadelphia Monthly Meeting, 6-4-1972, Cadbury Papers.
15. *After Thirty Years, 1917–1947,* AFSC pamphlet, AFSC Archives.
16. Henry Cadbury, "Have Mercy upon Me!" *Christian Century* 64, pt. I (4-16-1947): 493.
17. Henry Cadbury, "Answering That of God," *Journal of Friends Historical Society* 39 (1947): 3–14.
18. Ibid., p. 6.
19. Ibid., pp. 12–13.
20. Frederick C. Grant, Clarence T. Craig, and Henry Cadbury, eds., *Gospel Parallels* (New York: Nelson, 1949); "Report of the Commission to Study and Make Recommendations with Respect to the Harvard Divinity School," July 1947, as cited in Levering Reynolds, Jr., "The Later Years, 1880–1953," George Williams, ed., *The Harvard Divinity School: Its Place in Harvard University and American Culture* (Boston, Beacon Press, 1954), pp. 221–22.
21. Henry Cadbury, "Report to AFSC on Nobel Peace Prize," AFSC Archives; interview with Mary Hoxie Jones, 9-9-1985.
22. Cadbury, "Report to AFSC."
23. Speech by Gunnar Jahn, as reported in Clarence Pickett, *For More Than Bread* (Boston: Little, Brown, 1953), p. 306.
24. Cadbury Acceptance Speech, Nobel Peace Prize, AFSC Archives.
25. Henry Cadbury, "Quakers and Peace," in Frederick W. Haberman, ed., *Nobel Peace Prize Lectures, 1926–1950* (Amsterdam: Elsevier, 1972), 2: 389–98.
26. Henry Cadbury to Emma Cadbury, December 1947, uncataloged Cadbury Papers.
27. Clarence Pickett, *For More Than Bread*, pp. 262–66.
28. Mary Hoxie Jones, "Henry Joel Cadbury: A Biographical Sketch," in Anna Brinton, ed., *Then and Now* (Philadelphia: University of Pennsylvania Press, 1960), *Quaker Life*, Series IV, no. 1 (formerly *American Friend*) (January 1963): 10–11.
29. *The Church in the Wilderness: North Carolina Quakerism as Seen by Visitors* (North Carolina Friends Historical Society, 1948). Guilford College: Greensboro, N.C.
30. *AFSC Annual Report,* Philadelphia, Pa.: AFSC 1948.

31. Statement by Henry Cadbury, Senate Armed Services Committee, 3-30-1948.

32. Excerpt, Reporter's Transcript of *U.S.* v. *Robert McInnis*, pp. 1–13, Peace Collection, FHL.

33. AFSC staff memos, January 1949, AFSC Archives.

34. Greg Votaw to Henry Cadbury, 12-18-1948, 12-28-1948, 3-2-1949, 3-27-1949, Harrop Freeman to Henry Cadbury, 2-13-49, 2-27-49; Sarah and Hiram Norton to Henry Cadbury, 5-12-49; Robert Wixom to Henry Cadbury, 5-27-49, Peace Collection, FHL.

35. Ernest and Marion Bromley to Henry Cadbury, 3-23-1949, Peace Collection, FHL.

36. Interviews with Mildred Young, 3-18-1983, and Lillian Willoughby, 10-13-1985.

37. Henry Cadbury, notes on interview, 6-28-1949, Russian Embassy, Washington, D.C., Peace Collection, FHL.

38. Statement of Henry J. Cadbury, 5-11-1949, AFSC Archives.

39. Interview with Stephen G. Cary, June 1983.

40. Henry Cadbury, "Teachers' Influence in Theory and Practice," *Westonian* 55, no. 2 (June 1949): 24–29.

41. Interview with Henry Scattergood, March 1983.

CHAPTER 11

1. Newpaper Clippings, April 1950, Peace Collection, FHL; Lecture notes, Cadbury Papers.

2. Lecture notes, Cape May Conference, June 1950, Union Theological Seminary, August 1950, Cadbury Papers.

3. "Independence as a Quaker Tradition," *Address by Henry Cadbury 250th Anniversary of the First Friends Meeting* [Moorestown, New Jersey: Friends Meeting, 1950].

4. Henry J. Cadbury, "Mixed Motives in the Gospels," *Proceedings of the American Philosophical Society* 95, no. 2 (1951), p. 117.

5. Ibid., p. 120.

6. Correspondence in regard to "Science and Conscience," April 1951, lecture notes, Cadbury Papers.

7. "Science and Conscience," address at Western College Association *Proceedings at the Meetings*, Whittier, Ca., 1951, pp. 26–33.

8. *Steps to Peace: A Quaker View of Foreign Policy* (Philadelphia, Pa.: American Friends Service Committee, 1951); *Los Angeles Times*, 4-6-1951, AFSC Archives.

9. Henry Cadbury to Lewis Hoskins, 6-2, 6-30, 7-7-1951, AFSC Archives.

10. Lydia Cadbury to Elizabeth Jones, June 1951; Paul Cadbury to the author, 8-3-1983.

11. AFSC Annual Meeting, 12-1-1951; "Operation Neighbor," lecture notes, Cadbury Papers.

12. "Singularity," *Guilford College Bulletin* (July 1952): 3–7.

13. "The Antiquity of the Quakers," *Friends Quarterly* 7, no. 2 (April 1953): 112–17.

14. Henry J. Cadbury to Elizabeth Jones, 7-25-1952, uncataloged Cadbury Papers.

15. Friends World Conference Proceedings, 1952; Henry J. Cadbury to Emma Cadbury, 8-2-1952, uncataloged Cadbury Papers.

16. "Bread upon the Waters," in Henry Cadbury, *Friendly Heritage: Letters from the Quaker Past* (Norwalk, Conn., Silvermine Publishers, 1972), p. 184.

17. Lydia Cadbury to Emma Cadbury, 10-7-1952, uncataloged Cadbury Papers; interview with Barbara Graves, June 1983.

18. Henry J. Cadbury to Mary Hoxie Jones, 9-2-1952, uncataloged Cadbury Papers.

19. Levering Reynolds, Jr., "The Later Years, 1880–1953," in George H. Williams, ed., *The Harvard Divinity School: Its Place in Harvard University and American Culture* (Boston: Beacon Press, 1954), pp. 221–22; Nathan Pusey to Mary Hoxie Jones, 2-25-1960, in Anna Brinton, ed., *Then and Now* (Philadelphia: University of Pennsylvania Press, 1960), pp. 59–60.

20. Henry J. Cadbury, *The Book of Acts in History* (New York: Harper and Brothers, 1955, pp. v–vi, 7.

21. Floyd V. Filson, review, *Journal of Biblical Literature* 75 (1956): 74–75.

22. "Life and Character of Jesus," Special Reading List, *Bulletin of the General Theological Society* 45, no. 3 (1953): 4–6; "The Danger of Overtranslation," *Expository Times* 64 (1953): 381; "Translation Principles of the R.S.V.," *Christian Century* 70 (1953): 1388–90; Henry J. Cadbury to "Dear Ben and Anna," 5-28-1953, uncataloged Cadbury Papers.

23. Draft of a letter to the editor of the *Harvard Crimson*, May 1953, Peace Collection, FHL. This letter was apparently never published.

24. Katherine McBride to Henry J. Cadbury, Katherine McBride Papers, Archives of Bryn Mawr College, 3-26-1953; Civil Liberties Committee, AFSC ca. 1953, AFSC Archives.

25. Henry J. Cadbury, "Pleas for Clemency," in *Friendly Heritage*, p. 187.

26. "Friends and the Threats to Civil Liberties," *Friend* (London) 111 (10-16-1953): 955–56; "Freedom from Self-Incrimination," ibid., 112 (3-12-1954): 207–9.

27. Henry J. Cadbury, "The Case of the Plymouth Meeting Library," *Friends Journal* 2 (1956): 36–37.

28. "Henry J. Cadbury and His Endorsement of Mrs. Mary Knowles, Librarian," memo by Mrs. Philip Corson; Memorandum: Plymouth Monthly Meeting, both in files of AFSC Rights of Conscience Committee, AFSC Archives.

29. Memorandum, Plymouth Monthly Meeting.

30. Interview with Lewis Hoskins, May 1983.

31. "Rights of Conscience Committee," AFSC, 1956–60, AFSC Archives; Henry Cadbury, "Friends and the Law," *Friends Intelligencer* 112, no. 23 (June 1955): 320–23; and Friends Quarterly 10 (January 1956): 9–14.

32. *The Basis of Quaker Political Concern*, speech at FCNL tenth anniversary. [FCNL, 1954.] Published by FCNL: Washington, 1954.

33. Ibid.

34. Henry J. Cadbury, "Peace and War," in Jack Kavanaugh, ed., *The Quaker Approach* (New York: Putnam's, 1953).

35. Henry J. Cadbury, "The Letter in Lincoln's Pocket," in *Friendly Heritage*, p. 64.

36. *A Quaker Approach to the Bible*, Greensboro, N.C.: Guilford College, 1953. See also Henry J. Cadbury, "A Liberal Approach to the Bible," *Journal of Religious Thought* 14, no. 2 (Spring–Summer 1957): 126.

37. Ibid., p. 128.

38. George Williams, ed., *Harvard Divinity School*, dedication [p. v].

39. Ibid., Levering Reynolds, Jr., "The Latter Years, 1880–1953," p. 226. Ralph Lazzaro Theological Scholarship at Harvard from 1880–1953, p. 259.

40. Interview with George Williams, 5-2-1983.

41. Leroy Garrett to the author, 3-29-1983; Robert Grant to the author, 5-17-1983.

CHAPTER 12

1. Interview with Leah Furtmuller, 6-7-1983; Hugh Doncaster to the author, 7-13-1983.

2. Lecture notes, Cadbury Papers.

3. Interview with Betsy Balderston, May 1984.

4. Interview with Martin Beer, April 1983.

5. Mary Morrison, *The Journal and the Journey*, Pendle Hill pamphlet 242 (Wallingford, Pa.: Pendle Hill Publications, 1983), pp. 25–26.

6. Doylestown Monthly Meeting, 4-1-62; Radnor Meeting, May 1962; lecture notes, Cadbury Papers.

7. "Quakers and the Earthquake," in Henry J. Cadbury, *Friendly Heritage: Letters from the Quaker Past* (Norwalk, Conn.: Silvermine Publishers, 1972), p. 322.

8. Interview with Bartram Cadbury, 8-23-83; interview with Jan Long, 9-28-85.

9. Interview with Warder Cadbury, Visit to Back Log Camp, July 1983.

10. Lecture notes, 1955, Cadbury Papers.

11. Interview with Mildred Young, 3-18-1983.

12. Henry J. Cadbury, speech at Darmstadt, Tape, October 1956, AFSC Archives.

13. Ibid.

14. *Quakerism and Early Christianity*, Swarthmore Lecture (London: Allen & Unwin, 1957), pp. 46–47.

15. Henry J. Cadbury to Mary Hoxie Jones, 5-27-1957; uncataloged Cadbury Papers, AFSC fortieth anniversary; Penn Charter Award; New York Yearly Meeting, AFSC; Lecture notes, Cadbury Papers.

16. Quaker Lecture, *The Place of Friends Among the Churches*, given at Western Yearly Meeting of Friends, 8-20-1957 [Western Yearly Meeting, 1957].

17. "The Quaker Approach to the Apocrypha," in Cadbury, *Friendly Heritage*, p. 227.

18. Lewis Hoskins to Oscar and Olive Washburn, 3-17-1958, AFSC Archives; interview with Lewis Hoskins, May 1983.

19. Henry J. Cadbury to "Dear Lewis," 8-28-1958, AFSC Archives.

20. Amos Wilder, "In Memoriam," *New Testament Studies* 21 (1974–1975): 313–17.

21. Henry J. Cadbury, "The Dilemma of the Ephesians," *New Testament Studies* 5 (1958): 91–102.

22. George Boobyer to author, 7-19-1983.

23. *The Character of a Quaker*, William Penn Lecture, Pendle Hill Pamphlet 103, Wallingford, Pa.: Pendle Hill Publications, 1959.

24. "Intimations of Immortality in the Thought of Jesus" *Harvard Theological Review* 53, no. 1 (1960): 19.

25. Ibid., p. 25.

26. AFSC, Fiftieth Anniversary Record, voice of Henry Cadbury from January 1960.

27. Interview with Elizabeth Gray Vining, 6-7-1983.

28. Interview with Marthalyn Dickson, 9-19-1985.

29. *A Declaration from the Harmless and Innocent People of God, Called Quakers, against all plotters and fighters in the World* (London, January 1661).

30. "Peace Churches and Public Witness," 4-21-1961, lecture notes, Cadbury Papers.

31. Peace Education Minutes, 9-27-1961, AFSC Archives.

32. Interview with James Matlack, October 1983.

33. "Case Against the U.S. Government for Nuclear Test Explosions," 1962, Cadbury Papers, Peace Collection, FHL.

34. "Friends with Kennedy in the White House," in Cadbury, *Friendly Heritage*, 277; interview with George Willoughby, May 1983.

35. Henry J. Cadbury, *The Eclipse of the Historical Jesus*, Pendle Hill pamphlet 133 (Wallingford, Pa.: Pendle Hill Publications, 1963), p. 20.

36. Ibid., p. 6.

37. Henry J. Cadbury, Introduction to *Journal of George Fox*, ed. Rufus M. Jones (London: Religious Society of Friends, 1963), pp. 7–18.

38. Edward H. Milligan, "Henry J. Cadbury," *Quaker Monthly*, January 1975, p. 2.

CHAPTER 13

1. Henry Clay Niles, "The Wit and Wisdom of Henry Cadbury," *Harvard Divinity Bulletin* 29 (1965): 2.

2. Julius Bixler to the author, 7-27-1983; William Beardslee to the author, 7-20-1983.

3. Lydia C. Cadbury, *A Quaker Girlhood* (Haverford, Pa.: Privately Published, 1964).

4. "Covenant of Peace," aired as part of the "Lamp unto My Feet" series, CBS-TV, 11-11-1962, CBS-TV Files.

5. Henry J. Cadbury, "Vital Issues for Friends Today," *Canadian Friend* 60, no. 3 (June–July 1964): 3–4.

6. Maurine Parker to the author, 3-12-1983.

7. Ibid.

8. Clarence Pickett Memorial Minutes, Race Street Meeting House, 3-24-1965, AFSC Archives.

9. Ibid.

10. Westtown Graduation, lecture notes, 6-11-1966, Cadbury Papers.

11. *Friend* (London) 124 (10-14-1966): 1196.

12. J. William Frost to Lydia Cadbury, 10-14-1974, Cadbury Papers.

13. Caroline N. Jacob, ed., *Journal of William Edmondson* (Philadelphia Yearly Meeting, Philadelphia, 1968). Henry J. Cadbury, *Behind the Gospels*, Pendle Hill pamphlet 160 (Wallingford, Pa.: Pendle Hill Publications, 1968); Henry J. Cadbury, Foreword in Frederick Tolles, ed., *Quaker Reflections to Light the Future* (Philadelphia: Religious Education Committee, Friends General Conference, 1967).

14. Notes compiled by Elizabeth Musgrave from letters from Lydia Cadbury; "Friends and the Bible," lecture notes, 6-30-1967, Cadbury Papers.

15. Howard Kee to the author, 6-13-1983.

16. Interview with Warder Cadbury, April 1983; Henry Cadbury to Katherine McBride, 7-30-1968, Katherine McBride Papers, Bryn Mawr College Archives.

17. Interview with Warder Cadbury.

18. *Philadelphia Evening Bulletin*, 3-10-1974.

19. Henry J. Cadbury, "Conscientious Disobedience," *Friends Journal* 15 (1-15-1969): 41–42.

20. Henry J. Cadbury, "Reparations," *Friends Journal* 15 (12-15-1969): 713–14.

21. Henry J. Cadbury, "George Fox and Women's Liberation," *Friends Quarterly* 18, no. 4 (Autumn 1974): 370–76.

22. Interview with Betty Taylor, March 1983.

23. Interview with Margaret Evans, May 1983; Henry Cadbury, "A Woolman Manuscript Comes to Light," *Friends Journal* 17 (8-15-1971): 394; interview with Daisy Newman, 5-2-1983.

24. Henry J. Cadbury, "A Woolman Manuscript Comes to Light."

25. Pendle Hill Lectures, 1970, FHL, Swarthmore; interview with Daisy Newman, 5-1-1983.

26. Talk, Central Philadelphia Monthly Meeting, 6-4-1972, Cadbury Papers.

27. Ibid.

28. Ibid.

29. "Pioneering," Friends General Conference, 1972, tape recording, FHL.

30. Maurine Parker to the author, 3-12-1983.

31. Transcript, Proceedings, U.S. District Court for Eastern District, Pennsylvania, August 1, 1973, Civil Action, American Friends Service Committee, Lorraine Cleveland and Leonard Cadwallader, Plaintiffs, v. the United States of America, Defendant; tape recording, Henry J. Cadbury's Lectures on St. Paul, 1972, Pendle Hill.

32. "Tributes to Henry J. Cadbury," *Friends Quarterly* 8 (October 1973): 145–55.

33. Ibid.

34. Transcript, Henry Cadbury's Birthday Celebration, 11-28-1973, Cadbury Papers.

35. Ibid.

CHAPTER 14

1. Interview with Stephen G. Cary, March 1983; Howard Kee to the author, 6-13-1983.

2. Interview with Richard Moses, March 1983.

3. "The Heritage of the Meeting House," speech by Henry J. Cadbury, 9-29-1974, copied for distribution by the George School.

4. Interview with Warder and Judy Cadbury, April 1983.

5. *New York Times*, 10-9-1974; Associated Press and United Press International, 10-9-1974; *Friends Journal* 20 (12-1-1974): 610–625. *Harvard Magazine* 78 (May 1975): 46–52; *Yearbook of the American Philosophical Society, 1975*, pp. 123–29; *Friend* (London) 132 (10-18-1974): 1237–38; *Friends Quarterly* 19 (January 1975): 2–3.

6. Thomas E. Murphy, "Greatness," *Hartford Courant*, 3-25-1954.

7. Elfrida Vipont Foulds, "A Truly Great Spirit," *Friends Journal* 20 (12-1-1974): 612.

8. Kenneth L. Carroll, "He Was the Message," *Friends Journal* 20 (12-1-1974): 613.

9. Robert Stevens, *Philadelphia Friends and Higher Education: The Case of Haverford College*, speech to the Newcomen Society, 11-16-1983; interview with Amos Wilder, 5-1-1983; Amos Wilder, "A Grammarian with a Difference," *Harvard Magazine* 78 (May 1975): 46–52.

Bibliography

MANUSCRIPT COLLECTIONS

American Friends Service Committee Archives, Philadelphia, Pa.
    AFSC Board Minutes.
    Executive Peace Committee Minutes.
    Executive Secretary's Correspondence (1917–74).
    German Program Publicity, 1920.
    Taped speeches.
Andover-Harvard Theological Library, Cambridge, Mass.
    Willard Sperry to Henry Joel Cadbury, November 10, 1939.
Bryn Mawr College Library, Bryn Mawr, Pa.
    Henry J. Cadbury Committee on Family Planning and Population Education. Papers.
    McBride, Katherine. Papers. Cadbury correspondence.
    Park, Marion. Papers. Cadbury correspondence.
Cadbury Family, Michigan. New York, New Jersey.
    Letters and papers in private possession of members of the family.
Lilly Library, Earlham College Archives, Richmond, Indiana.
    Unpublished Cadbury documents.
Friends Historical Collection, Guilford College, Greensboro, North Carolina.
    Cadbury, Hery J. and Lydia. Papers.
Friends Historical Library, Swarthmore College, Swarthmore, Pa.
    Cadbury, Henry Joel. Papers. Swarthmore College Peace Collection.
    Friends General Conference. Taped speeches.
    Friends Historical Library. Correspondence, 1930–74.
    Friends World Committee, taped speeches.
    Taylor, C. Marshall. Papers. By permission of the director.
Harvard University Archives, Cambridge, Mass.
    Cadbury, Henry Joel. Papers.

Pendle Hill, Philadelphia, Pa.
  Taped lecture series.
Haverford College Library, Quaker Collection, Haverford, Pa.
  Haverfordiana Collection.
  Cadbury Family. Papers. Uncataloged
  Cadbury, Henry Joel. Papers.
  Jones, Rufus M. Papers.
  Board of Managers, Haverford College, Minutes.

INTERVIEWS

American Friends Service Committee (present and former staff and board members): Colin Bell, Stephen G. Cary, Bronson Clark, Lorraine Cleveland, Spencer Coxe, Doris Darnell, Marthalyn Dixon, Jean Fairfax, Barbara Graves, Lewis Hoskins, Elmore Jackson, James Lenhart, James Matlack, George Willoughby.
Back Log Camp: Lady Borton, Terry Borton, Mark Emerson, James Matlack, Jan Long.
Bryn Mawr College: Margaret Evans, Rebecca Hetzel, Elizabeth Gray Vining, Henry Scattergood.
Cadbury Family members: Winifred and Martin Beer, Bartram Cadbury, Christopher and Mary Cadbury, Jack and Elizabeth Cadbury, Warder and Julia Cadbury, Leah Cadbury Furtmuller, Mary Hoxie Jones, Elizabeth Musgrave.
Cambridge Meeting and community: Louisa Alger, Mrs. Rupert Emerson, Eleanor Townsend Taylor, Merilee and Andrew Towl, Virginia Townsend.
Central Philadelphia Monthly Meeting: Cynthia Adcock, Mary Cuthbertson, Richard Moses, Maurine Parker, Stephen Stalonas.
Earlham College: Hugh Barbour, Caroline Nicholson Jacob, Wilbur Kamp.
Friends General Conference: Lawrence McC. Miller, Lloyd Lee Wilson.
Friends World Committee: Herbert Hadley, Barrett Hollister, Charlotte Tinker.
Harvard College: Maria Grossman, Eric Johnson, David McClelland, Harry Meserve, Amos Wilder, George Williams.
Haverford College: Edwin Bronner, Stephen Cary, Douglas Heath, Dorothy and Douglas Steere, Gilbert White.
Others: Donald Baker, Daisy Newman, Betty Taylor.
Pendle Hill: Betsy Balderston, Yuki Brinton, Steven Stalonas, Mildred Young.
Swarthmore College: J. William Frost.
Yale University: Roland Bainton.

CORRESPONDENCE

Biblical scholars: Moses Bailey, William Beardslee, Julius S. Bixler, George
    Boobyer, Leroy Garrett, Robert Grant, Sherman Johnson, Howard
    Kee, John Knox, Paul Minear.
Scholars of Quakerism: Hugh Barbour, Maurice Creasy, Hugh Doncaster,
    Geoffrey Nuttall.
English family members: George W. Cadbury, Paul S. Cadbury, Christo-
    pher and Hannah Taylor.

BOOKS AND PAMPHLETS BY HENRY J. CADBURY*

National Ideals in the Old Testament. New York: Scribner's, 1920.
Style and Literary Method of Luke (Harvard Theological Studies 6) Cam-
    bridge, Mass.: Harvard University Press, 1920.
The Making of Luke-Acts. New York: Macmillan, 1927.
The Beginnings of Christianity: The Acts of the Apostles. With Kirsopp Lake.
    Vol. 4. English translation and commentary. Vol. 5. Additional notes.
    London: Macmillan, 1933.
"Negro Membership in the Society of Friends." *Journal of Negro History* vol.
    21 (1936): 151–213. Also published as a pamphlet. Wallingford, Pa.:
    Pendle Hill Publications, 1936.
The Perils of Modernizing Jesus. New York: Macmillan, 1937.
Annual Catalogue of George Fox's Papers, Compiled in 1694–1697. Editor. Lon-
    don and Philadelphia: Religious Society of Friends, 1939.
The Swarthmore Documents in America. Editor. Supplement 20 to the *Journal
    of the Friends Historical Society.* London, 1940.
A Quakerism Adequate for Today. Pendle Hill Tenth Anniversary Lecture.
    Pamphlet. Wallingford, Pa.: Pendle Hill Publications, 1940.
"Quaker Relief during the Siege of Boston." *Transactions of the Colonial So-
    ciety of Massachusetts,* vol. 34. Pendle Hill Historical Study, no. 4. Wal-
    lingford, Pa.: Pendle Hill Publications, 1943.
Two Worlds. William Penn Lecture. Philadelphia: Philadelphia Yearly Meet-
    ing, 1945.
Jesus: What Manner of Man. New York: Macmillan, 1947.
Letters to William Dewsbury and Others. Transcriber and editor. London: The
    Bannisdale Press, 1948. (Supplement No. 22 to the *Journal of the Friends
    Historical Society.*)
George Fox's Book of Miracles. Cambridge: Cambridge University Press, 1948.
The Church in the Wilderness, North Carolina Quakerism as Seen by Visitors.
    North Carolina Friends Historical Society. Guilford College, N.C., 1948.
Gospel Parallels. Edited with Frederick C. Grant and Clarence T. Craig.
    New York: Nelson, 1949.
Independence as a Quaker Tradition. Speech delivered at the 250th anni-

*All works by Henry S. Cadbury are given in chronological order.

versary of the First Friends Meeting in Moorestown, New Jersey, September 16, 1950. Pamphlet. Moorestown, N.J. Religious Society of Friends, 1950.

A Quaker Approach to the Bible. Ward Lecture, Guilford, N.C.: Guilford College, 1953.

The Book of Acts in History. Lowell Lectures, 1953. New York: Harper and Brothers, 1955.

Quakerism and Early Christianity. Swarthmore Lecture. London: Allen & Unwin, 1957.

The Place of Friends among the Churches. Plainfield, Indiana: Western Yearly Meeting of Friends, 1957.

The Character of a Quaker. Pendle Hill pamphlet 103. Wallingford, Pa.: Pendle Hill Publications, 1959.

Jesus and Judaism. Shrewsbury Lecture. Indianapolis: Woolman Press, 1961.

The Civil War Diary of Cyrus Pringle. Foreword. Pendle Hill pamphlet 122. Wallingford, Pa.: Pendle Hill Publications, 1962.

The Eclipse of the Historical Jesus. Haverford Library Lectures. Pendle Hill pamphlet 133. Wallingford, Pa.: Pendle Hill Publications, 1964.

Behind the Gospels. Pendle Hill pamphlet 160. Wallingford, Pa.: Pendle Hill Publications, 1968.

John Woolman in England in 1772. London: Friends Historical Society, 1971.

Narrative Papers of George Fox. Richmond: Friends United Press, 1972.

Friendly Heritage: Letters from the Quaker Past. Norwalk, Conn.: Silvermine Publishers, 1972.

INTRODUCTIONS AND CHAPTERS IN BOOKS

Differences in Quaker Belief in 1827 and Today. Editor. Philadelphia: Biddle Press, 1914.

"Commentary on Luke's Preface," "Medical Language," "The Tradition," In *Beginnings of Christianity.* Vol. 2, F. J. Jackson and Kirsopp Lake, 1922; vol. 3, edited by James R. Ropes, "Collation of the Peshitto Texts of Acts" and "Collation of the Vulgate Text of Acts." London: Macmillan, 1926.

"Divine Inspiration in the New Testament," "Questions of Authorship in the New Testament," and "Results of New Testament Research." In *An Outline of Christianity: The Story of Our Civilization.* Vol. 4, ed. Francis J. McConnell. New York: Bethlehem Publishers, 1926.

"Hebraica and Early Quaker Interest." In Howard Brinton, ed., *Children of Light.* Macmillan, New York, 1938.

"Whittier as Historian of Quakerism." In Howard Brinton, ed., *Byways in Quaker History.* Wallingford: Pendle Hill Publications, 1944.

Epilogue. In *Journal of George Fox,* edited by John L. Nickalls. London: London Yearly Meeting, 1952.

"Peace and War." In Jack Kavanaugh, ed., *The Quaker Approach.* New York: Putnams, 1953.

William Charles Braithwaite, ed. *Beginnings of Quakerism*. Editor and with notes. Cambridge: Cambridge University Press, 1955.

William Charles Braithwaite, ed., *The Second Period of Quakerism*. Editor and with notes. Cambridge: Cambridge University Press, 1961.

Introduction. In *Journal of George Fox*, edited by Rufus M. Jones. London: Religious Society of Friends, 1963.

Introduction. In Beatrice Saxon Snell, *A Joint and Visible Fellowship*. Pendle Hill pamphlet 140, Wallingford, Pa.: Pendle Hill Publications, 1965.

Foreword. In *Quaker Reflections to Light the Future*, edited by Frederick Tolles. Philadelphia: Religious Education Committee, Friends General Conference, 1967.

Foreword. In *Journal of William Edmondson*, edited by Caroline M. Jacob. Philadelphia: Philadelphia Yearly Meeting, 1968.

Introduction. In Margaret Hope Bacon, *The Quiet Rebels: The Story of Quakers in America*. New York: Basic Books, 1969.

"Quakers and Peace," Nobel Peace Prize Lecture, December 12, 1947. In Frederick W. Haberman, ed., *Nobel Lectures, 1926–1950*. Vol. 2, Amsterdam: Elsevier, 1972.

CONTRIBUTIONS TO PERIODICALS

"The Development of the Young Friends Movement in America." *Friends Intelligencer* (6-13-1914): 370.

"Quakerism as an Experiment Station." *Friends Intelligencer* 72, no. 38 (9-18-1915): 449–50.

"A Possible Case of Lukan Authorship." *Harvard Theological Review* 10 (1917): 237–44.

"Freedom of Thought and the Colleges." *Haverfordian* 39, no. 8 (March 1918): 257–60.

"Ideals and Procrastination." *War?* (February–March 1918): 28–29.

"Ruthlessness Abroad and at Home." The *New World*, 1, no. 3 (March 1918): 55–57.

"Are We Honest?" *Friends Intelligencer* 75, no. 31 (8-3-1918): 486–87.

"The Unpopular Patriot." *World Tomorrow*, vol. I, no. 10 (October 1918): 258–61.

"The Basis of Early Christian Anti-Militarism." *Journal of Biblical Literature* 37 (1918): 66–94.

"Conscientious Objection in Europe." *Young Democracy* 1, no. 8 (5-15-1919): 4.

"Luke—Translator or Author?" *American Journal of Theology* 24 (1920): 436–55.

"A New Evil and an Ancient Conscience." *Messenger of Peace* 45, no. 4 (April 1920): 49–53.

"The Strike as an Unethical Means of Conversion." *World Tomorrow* 3, no. 5 (May 1920): 131–33.

"Pioneering the Christian Faith." *American Friend* 8, no. 25 (6-17-1920): 555–56.

"Camp Supper a la Karte." *Westonian* 26, no. 7 (October 1920): 154–55.

"A Nationwide Adventure in Friendship," *The Survey* 23, no. 2 (11-27-1920): 309–311.

"Feeding Your Enemy in Peacetime." *La Follette's Magazine* (April 1921): 54–55.

"The Christian Verdict on War." *World Tomorrow* 5, no. 1 (January 1922): 15–17.

"The Conscientious Objector of Patmos: The Revelation of John." *Christian Century* 39, no. 23 (6-8-1922): 719–22.

"The Social Translation of the Gospel." *Harvard Theological Review* 15 (1922): 1–13.

"Between Jesus and the Gospels." *Harvard Theological Review* 16 (1923): 81–92.

"Creeds and Truth." *World Tomorrow* 6, no. 8 (August 1923): 233.

"An Inadequate Pacifism." *Christian Century* 41, no. 1 (January 1924): 9–11.

"Faith of Our Fathers Living Still." *Friends Intelligencer* 81 (5-31-1924): 356–58.

"David's Defense Test." Christian Century 41 (October 1924): 1302–4.

"George Fox and Sixteenth Century Bibles." *Journal of Friends Historical Society* 21 (1924): 1–8.

"A Disputed Paper of George Fox." *Bulletin of the Friends Historical Association* 13 (1924): 78–82.

"Jesus and the Prophets." *Journal of Religion* 5 (1925): 607–22.

"The Apocalypse, an Appreciation." *Crozer Quarterly* 2 (1925): 259–64.

"The Odor of the Spirit at Pentecost." *Journal of Biblical Literature* 47 (1928): 237–56.

"Our Christian Week." *Friend* (London) 68, no. 6 (2-10-1928): 102.

"Heathen Names for the Days of the Week and Months." *Bulletin of the Friends Historical Assoiation* 17, no. 2 (1928): 54–58.

"The Historic Jesus." Review of S. J. Case, *Jesus: A New Biography*, in *Journal of Religion* 8 (1928): 130–36.

"Impressions of a Norwegian Quaker in 1838." *Bulletin of the Friends Historical Association* 18, no. 1 (1929): 33–37.

"Egyptian Influence in the Book of Proverbs." *Journal of Religion* 9 (1929): 99–108.

"Friends' Use of the Bible." *Friend* 102 (1929): 373–75.

"George Fox's Library." *Friend* (London) 90 (3-25-1932): 253.

"Penn as a Political Idealist." *Friend* (London) 90, no. 43 (10-21-32): 904–6.

"Quaker Site Seeking in Amsterdam." *Friend* 106, no. 27 (1-1-1933): 315–16.

"Colonial Quaker Antecedents to British Aboliton of Slavery." *Friends Quarterly Examiner* 67 (Spring 1933): 268–75.

"The Oldest Philadelphia." *Friend* 107, no. 4 (8-17-1933): 51–52; also *Friends Intelligencer* 90, no. 33 (8-19-1933): 603–4.

"The Quaker Who Converted Clarkson." *Friend* (London) 92, no. 18 (5-4-1934): 380–81.

"Richardson Mss. Further unpublished writings of George Fox." Journal of the Friends Historical Society 32 (1935): 34–35.

"Friends and Their Social Testimonies." *Friend* (London) 93, no. 24 (6-14-1935): 557–58.

"The Quaker Concern for Academic Freedom." *Friends Intelligencer* 93, no. 31 (8-1-1936): 499–501.

"Expectancy." *Westonian* 42, no. 2 (Spring 1936): 16–19.

"The Teachers' Oath in U.S.A." *Friend* (London) 94, no. 9 (2-28-1936): 185–86.

"My Professor's Closet." *Harvard Alumni Bulletin* 39 (1936): 297–301.

"Motives of Biblical Scholarship." *Journal of Biblical Literature* 56 (1937): 1–16.

"The Quaker Way and Modern Problems." *Friends Intelligencer* 94 (6-5-1937): 383–84.

"The Individual Christian and the State." *Friends Intelligencer* 94 (9-25-1937): 654.

"The Contribution of Negroes to the Education of Friends." *Friend* 111, no. 13 (12-16-1937): 217–20.

"Quakers and Their Abettors, Middlesex County, Mass., 1663." *Bulletin of the Friends Historical Association* 27 (1938): 9–16.

"What Happened to John Harvard's Books?" *Harvard Alumni Magazine*, 41 (1938): 241–48.

"Quakers, Jews and Freedom of Teaching in Barbadoes, 1686." *Bulletin of the Friends Historical Association* 29 (1940): 97–106.

"War and Religion." Special Reading List. *Bulletin of the General Theological Library* 33, no. 2 (1941): 5–11.

"Christopher Meidel and the First Norwegian Contacts with Quakers." *Harvard Review* 34, no. 1 (January 1941): 7–23.

"America's Reaction to the War." *Friend* (London) 100, no. 8 (2-20-1942): 39–60.

"Another Early Quaker Anti-Slavery Document." *Journal of Negro History* 26, no. 2 (November 1942): 210–15.

"The Validity of Religious Pacifism." *Christian Century* 60, no. 52 (12-29-1943): 1534–35.

"The Informality of Early Christianity." *Crozer Quarterly* 21 (1944): 246–50.

"What Is Disturbing the Quakers?" *Christian Century* 61, no. 33 (8-16-1944): 945–47.

"Penn as a Pacifist." *Friends Intelligencer* 101, no. 43 (10-21-1944): 692–93.

"Persecution and Religious Liberty, Then and Now." *Pennsylvania Magazine of History and Biography* 68, no. 4 (October 1944): 359–71.

"John Farmer's First American Journey, 1711–1717." *Proceedings of the American Antiquarian Society* 53 (April 1944): 79–95.

"Peacetime Conscription and Peace." *American Friend* 33, no. 1 (1-11-1945): 6–7.

"Revision after Revision." *American Scholar* 15 (1946): 298–305.

"From One Culture to Another." *New Christianity* 12 (1946): 93–99.

"George Rofe in These American Parts." *Bulletin of the Friends Historical Association* 35, no. 1 (1946): 17–26.

"The New Translation's First Year." *Christian Century* 64 (1947): 170–71.

"Answering That of God." *Journal of the Friends Historical Society* 39 (1947): 3–14.

"Have Mercy upon Me!" *Christian Century* 64, pt. I (4-16-1947): 493.

"Fellowship Is Not Enough." Ware Lecture. *Christian Register* 147 (1948): 16–17.

"The First Faculty Courtship." *Westonian* 54, no. 2 (1948): 5–6.

The Church in the Wilderness, North Carolina Quakerism as Seen by Visitors. North Carolina Friends Historical Society, Guilford College, Greensboro, N.C., 1948.

"The Perils of Archaizing Ourselves." *Interpretation* 3 (1949): 331–38.

"Teachers' Influence in Theory and Practice," *Westonian* 55, no. 2 (June, 1949): 24–29.

"Friends' Use of the Bible." *Friend* 123 (1950): 275–77.

"The Kingdom of God and Ourselves." *Christian Century* 67 (1950): 172–73.

"Innocence by Association." *Christian Century* 67 (1950): 818–19.

"Science and Conscience," in *Proceedings of Meetings* Western College Association, Ca., 1951.

"Mixed Motives in the Gospels." *Proceedings of the American Philosophical Society* 95, no. 2 (1951): 117–24.

"Religious Books at Harvard." *Harvard Library Bulletin* 5, no. 2 (1951): 159–80.

"Singularity." *Guilford College Bulletin* (July 1952): 3–7.

"The Antiquity of the Quakers." *Friends Quarterly* 7, no. 2 (April 1953): 112–17.

"Life and Character of Jesus." Special Reading List. *Bulletin of the General Theological Library* 45, no. 3 (1953): 4–6.

The Basis of Quaker Political Concern. Friends Committee on National Legislation, Tenth Anniversary, 1953. Washington D.C.: FCNL 1954.

"Translation Principles of the R.S.V." *Christian Century* 64 (1953): 1388–90.

"The Danger of Overtranslation." *Expository Times* (1953): 381.

"Friends and the Threats to Civil Liberties." *Friend* (London) 111 (10-16-1953): 955–57.

"Freedom from Self-Incrimination." *Friend* (London) 112 (3-12-1954): 207–9.

"Friends and the Law." *Friends Intelligencer* 112, no. 23 (June 1955): 320–23; *Friends Quarterly* 10 (January 1956): 9–14.

"Our Theological Illiteracy." *Friends Journal* 1 (1-2-1955): 6–7.

"The Case of the Plymouth Meeting Library." *Friends Journal* 2, no. 31 (1956): 36–37.

"New Light on Old Scrolls." *Unitarian Christian* 11 (9-12-1955): 9–12.

"A Liberal Approach to the Bible." *Journal of Religious Thought* 14 (1957): 119–28.

"In God We Trust." *Christian Century* 71, pt. 2 (7-7-1957): 822.
"The Horizons of Fox's Early Visions." *Bulletin of the Friends Historical Association* 47, no. 1 (Spring 1958): 30–34.
"The Dilemma of the Ephesians." *New Testament Studies* 5 (1958): 91–102.
"The Exegetical Conscience." *Nexus* 11 (1958): 3–6; reprinted *Friends Quarterly* 7-1963.
"Intimations of Immortality in the Thought of Jesus." Ingersoll Lecture. *Harvard Theological Review* 53, no. 1 (1960): 1–26.
"A Quaker before the Privy Council, 1663." *Bulletin of the Friends Historical Association* 49, no. 1 (Spring 1960): 36–42.
"Varieties of Religion in the New Testament." *Friends Journal* 8, no. 6 (3-15-1962): 120–22.
"The Unappreciated Paul." *Friends Journal* 8, no. 19 (10-1-1962): 408–11.
"With All Thy Mind." *Friends Journal* 10, no. 1 (1-1-1964): 4–5.
"Vital Issues for Friends Today." *Canadian Friend* 60, no. 3 (June–July 1964): 3–9.
"The Influence of Fox's Journal." *Friends Quarterly* 15, nos. 6 and 7 (1966): 276–81, 295–304.
"Sailing to England with John Woolman." *Quaker History* 55 (Autumn 1966): 88–103.
"A Woolman Manuscript." *Quaker History* 57 (Spring 1968): 35–41.
"Conscientious Disobedience." *Friends Journal* 15 (1-15-1969): 41–42.
"George Fox and Women's Liberation." *Friends Quarterly* 18, no. 4 (Autumn 1974): 370–76.

ABOUT HENRY J. CADBURY

Brinton, Anna, ed. *Then and Now*, Quaker Essays: Historical and Contemporary. Philadelphia: University of Pennsylvania Press, 1960. Including a sixty-page memoir, "Henry Joel Cadbury: A Biographical Sketch," by Mary Hoxie Jones.
Bronner, Edwin. "Henry Joel Cadbury." *Yearbook of the American Philosophical Society*, 1975.
Friends Journal, 12-1-1974, 12-1-1983, 12-15-1983.
"Tributes to Henry Cadbury." *Friends Quarterly* 8 (October 1973): 145–55.
Hall, S. Garlin. "The Contribution of Henry J. Cadbury to the Study of the Historical Jesus." Ph.D. dissertation, Boston University, 1961.
Harvard Divinity School. "Toward a Bibliography of Henry Joel Cadbury." *Harvard Divinity School Bulletin, 1953–54*, pp. 65–70.
Niles, Henry C. "The Wit and Wisdom of Henry Cadbury." Harvard Divinity Bulletin 29, no. 2 (1965): 35–48.
Quaker Collection, Haverford College Library. "Expanded Bibliography of Henry H. Cadbury, to 1974 and including Quaker History." Haverford 1986.
Saunders, Ernest. *Searching the Scriptures: A History of the Society of Biblical Literature, 1880–1980*. Chico, Calif.: Scholars Press, 1980.

Wilder, Amos. "A Grammarian with a Difference." *Harvard Magazine* 78 (May 1975): 46–52.

Wilder, Amos. "In Memoriam." *New Testament Studies* 21 (1974–1975): 313–17.

Williams, George H., ed., *The Harvard Divinity School: Its Place in Harvard University and the American Culture* (Boston: Beacon Press, 1954).

Index